Please remember that this is a library book,
and that it belongs only temporarily to each
person who uses it. Be considerate. Do
not write in this, or any, library book.

Fifty Years Later
The New Deal
Evaluated

Fifty Years Later
The New Deal Evaluated

Edited by Harvard Sitkoff
University of New Hampshire

McGraw-Hill, Inc.
New York St. Louis San Francisco Auckland Bogota
Caracas Lisbon London Madrid Mexico City Milan
Montreal New Delhi San Juan Singapore
Sydney Tokyo Toronto

For Alexandra and Adam

FIFTY YEARS LATER
First Edition

9876

Library of Congress Cataloging in Publication Data

Main entry under title:
Fifty years later.

   Revised and expanded papers originally presented at a symposium sponsored by the Dept. of History of the University of New Hampshire and held Mar. 17–18, 1983.
   Includes bibliographies and index.
   1. New Deal, 1933–1939—Congresses. 2. United States—Politics and government—1933–1945—Congresses. 3. United States—Economic policy–1933–1945—Congresses. 4. United States—Social policy—1933–1945—Congresses. 5. Roosevelt, Franklin D. (Franklin Delano), 1882–1945—Congresses. I. Sitkoff, Harvard. II. University of New Hampshire. Dept. of History. III Title: 50 years later.
E806.F47   1985   973.917   84-17143
ISBN 0-07-554460-1

Preface

This book had its origin in the decision of the Department of History of the University of New Hampshire to commemorate the golden anniversary of President Franklin D. Roosevelt's first inauguration by hosting a historical symposium specifically for undergraduates. The overall goal was a contemporary evaluation of the significance and legacy of the New Deal. Experts in the aspects of the New Deal of greatest relevance to the concerns of students today were chosen for their abilities to explain clearly and to assess cogently that crucial era in American history. No effort was made to seek uniformity of viewpoint. The invited scholars differed markedly in their age, background, education, and interpretations of the New Deal. The symposium was held at the University of New Hampshire March 17–18, 1983, and proved immensely successful in conveying a historical overview of the 1930s, stimulating critical thinking about the meanings of the New Deal, and raising provocative questions for future research. The surprising consensus of the scholars involved, moreover, hinted at the emergence of an updated interpretation of the New Deal for our age. Accordingly, the participating historians agreed to revise and expand their papers for publication, to provide students throughout the nation with a summary of the current thinking of the historical profession about the New Deal's most important consequences. This book is the result.

Organizing a conference and editing an anthology can often be unpleasant and thankless tasks. But in this case there are more than enough thanks to go around to all those who made my work from planning to publication so enjoyable. It is a pleasure to acknowledge my appreciation to my colleagues in the Department of History for all their advice, assistance, and encouragement: to Dean Stuart Palmer, Dean Dwight R. Ladd, Vice-President Gordan A. Haaland, and, especially, President Evelyn E. Handler, for their generous and enthusiastic support; to the many members of the publishing staff for their help in turning an idea into a book, particularly David Follmer, Naomi Schneider, and Jennifer E. Sutherland; to my eight co-authors and co-conferees for exemplifying a common commitment to excellence in scholarship and teaching; and to, as always, my partner in all endeavors, Evelyn, for her laughter and love.

Contents

Fifty Years Later
The New Deal
Evaluated

Introduction

The United States in 1982 commemorated the centennial birthday of Franklin Delano Roosevelt, and the following year observed the fiftieth anniversary of the beginning of the New Deal. The events occasioned joint sessions of Congress, assorted television specials, a spate of new articles and books, and numerous special exhibits and academic conferences. They reminded Americans old enough to forget, and informed those too young to remember, of the tumultuous temper of 1930s, particularly of the intense flurry of efforts by the Roosevelt Administration to promote economic recovery, relieve distress, and prevent another depression that we call the New Deal. The celebrations also made clear that the fervid conflict over the meaning of the New Deal that raged in the thirties, and has been ardently disputed by historians since, remains a passionate controversy for many in the 1980s.

Roosevelt first used the term "New Deal" in the speech in which he accepted the presidential nomination of the Democratic Convention meeting in Chicago in 1932. As FDR addressed the delegates, a bewildered and demoralized nation staggered on the brink of chaos. In the three years since the stock market crash of 1929, national income had shrunk from $87.4 billion to $41.7 billion. The boom on Wall Street had turned to gloom and doom as AT&T dropped from $304 a share to $72, U.S. Steel plummetted from $262 to $22, General Motors plunged from $73 to $8, and Montgomery Ward fell from $138 all the way to $4 a share. Nearly 70,000 business firms had gone bankrupt since Herbert Hoover had become president; and some 5,000 banks had failed, more than the number of bank failures in the previous half-century. Unemployment, which had soared to 4 million in 1930, and doubled in 1931, topped 12 million in 1932. One out of every four regularly employed men and women was jobless. *Fortune* estimated that about 28 million Americans had no income at all in 1932. Hundreds of thousands lost their homes or farms to the forecloser's hammer. Bread lines formed. Penniless, shivering men peddled apples on street corners. More than a million jobless Americans roamed the country as hobos. There were hunger riots in factory towns and Hoovervilles, makeshift settlements of the homeless living in tar-paper and tin-can shanties, sprouted on urban garbage dumps. Americans stopped singing "My God, How the Money Rolls In" in 1932 and learned the words to "Brother, Can You Spare a Dime?" Yet, Roosevelt spoke to the Democrats in Chicago with an air of easy confidence, concluding with the assurance that "Those millions cannot and shall not hope in vain." As the pipe organ struck up "Happy Days Are Here Again," FDR brought the delegates to their feet with the intonation: "I pledge you, I pledge myself, to a new deal for the American people."

If Roosevelt had any idea of the programmatic content of the phrase, he certainly kept it a secret during the presidential campaign of 1932. He offered the American people hope rather than specific remedies. Roosevelt pledged himself to the Democratic platform promising a balanced budget and a 25 percent cut in government expenditures, and accused Hoover of "reckless and extravagant" spending and of thinking "that we ought to center control of everything in Washington as rapidly as possible." Similarly, in the four months between his election and his inauguration, Roosevelt shrouded his convention vow in silence, maintaining the mystery of the meaning of a New Deal.

In the first one hundred days after entering the White House, however, Roosevelt dramatically revealed the shape and nature of the New Deal. Pushing fifteen major bills through Congress between March 9 and June 16, 1933, the Roosevelt Administration established the Civilian Conservation Corps, the Home Owners Loan Corporation, the Farm Credit Administration, the Federal Emergency Relief Administration, the Tennessee Valley Authority, and the United States Employment Service; it took the nation off the gold standard, closed all the banks and gradually reopened most of them, and provided a federal guarantee of all deposits under $5,000; and it set up the Agricultural Adjustment Administration and the National Recovery Administration. Within a year, it also created the Civil Works Administration, the Federal Communications Commission, the National Housing Administration, and the Securities and Exchange Commission. Adding to this collection of relief and recovery programs, reform and regulatory agencies, Roosevelt later signed into law the National Labor Relations Act, the Social Security Act, the Farm Tenancy Act, the Public Utilities Holding Company Act and the Fair Labor Standards Act, as well as legislation bringing into being the Federal Crop Insurance Corporation, the Rural Electrification Administration, the United States Housing Authority, and the Works Progress Administration.

Whatever else this flood of laws and government action, spending and social planning, may have accomplished, it produced immediate political dividends for the Roosevelt Administration. The Democrats added nine seats to their majorities in both the House and the Senate in 1934; and in the greatest landslide in more than a century Roosevelt crushed Governor Alfred Landon of Kansas in 1936 and, unprecedently, won reelection again in 1940 and 1944, maintaining a Democratic Congress throughout his tenure in office. Nevertheless, Americans remained angrily divided in their judgment of the New Deal, and in their assessments of its sources, purposes, accomplishments, and consequences.

President Roosevelt, eschewing ideology, deemed the New Deal to be simply experimental and humane. He loathed theory and preferred that the New Deal "play it by ear" to restore national prosperity and provide a modicum of security to those ravaged by destitution or disease, old age or bankruptcy. "Take a method and try it," he said. "If it fails admit it frankly and try another. But above all, try something." Despite the incongruity of ingredients in the "alphabet soup" of newly created government programs referred to by their initials, Roosevelt believed the New Deal had "a consistency and continuity of broad purpose." Neither a radical nor standpatter, he pictured himself as an heir of the progressive tradition and described the New Deal as "a satisfactory combination of the Square Deal and the New Freedom," the reform agendas of Presidents Theodore Roosevelt and Woodrow Wilson. To the President, this meant "the middle way," using government as an active instrument of democratic change to meet the needs of the day without violence or upheaval. This meant government intervention for "the greatest good for the greatest number." And, this meant concern and compassion for those most in need. "The test of our progress," Roosevelt proclaimed in his second inaugural address, "is not whether we add to the abundance of those who have much. It is whether we provide enough for those who have too little."

Many on the Left, however, thought Roosevelt's actions belied his rhetoric. They characterized the President as a confidence man who sold the public a bill of goods while leaving the evils of society intact. They criticized the New Deal as incoherent, inadequate, inequitable, and ineffectual. To communists and socialists alike, the New Deal was a flawed attempt to prolong the life of an archaic and defunct economic system. In their eyes, the New Deal interceded in the economy to preserve and buttress capitalism. They considered the "state capitalism," exemplified by the National Recovery Administration, incipient fascism; they decried the New Deal's indifference to the plight of blacks; they lamented the woeful deficiencies of the social security and unemployment relief programs; they depicted the Agricultural Adjustment Administration as worsening an already desperate situation for farm tenants and sharecroppers; and they believed the humanitarian gestures of the New Deal were a deceitful effort to divert the wellspring of radicalism inherent in the suffering masses into votes for the Democratic party. Summing up the leftist condemnation in their *Economic Consequences of the New Deal* (1935), Benjamin Stolberg and Warren Jay Vinton likened the New Deal to a hurricane that blustered but caused no fundamental alterations in the land: the wealthy maintained their power and privileges, while the "forgotten men" remained unemployed, poor, and weak.

Those to the right of the New Deal similarly lambasted Roosevelt's contradictions and failure to restore employment or bring economic recovery. But, to such conservatives as Herbert Hoover and Al Smith, the New Deal's shortcomings stemmed from its attempt to "collectivize" the American system, to foster revolutionary changes in class relations and in the nature of the governmental system. The Right castigated the New Deal for creating a welfare state that turned millions of Americans into dependent wards of the government. It considered FDR "a traitor to his class," a proponent of mass unionism, and an improvident spendthrift who doubled federal expenditures and the national debt. Many on the Right, moreover, blamed the New Deal for instituting a regulatory state that stifled private enterprise and individual initiative with burdensome rules and taxes. They feared the centralization of unprecedented power in the hands of "that man," and its consequent undermining of the division of authority in the federal government and of the rights and responsibilities of state and local governments. Some saw Roosevelt as a dictator harboring authoritarian tendencies akin to Hitler. Others thought him "a Red," and depicted the New Dealers as a conspiratorial pack of radical zealots. "Mr. Republican," Senator Robert A. Taft of Ohio, charged that the "whole Roosevelt Administration was penetrated by Communists from top to bottom."

Although such accusations went out of style after the demise of McCarthyism in the mid 1950s, the welter of conflicting interpretations of the New Deal in the 1930s has continued in the historical debate over its meaning. Most historians writing in the two decades after Roosevelt's death in 1945 viewed the New Deal as essentially successful and beneficial. They lauded it for reforming capitalism, for minimizing economic insecurity, for rekindling the American faith in a time of distress, and for uplifting the basic standard of living for most Americans. But they differed vociferously on such matters as the New Deal's roots, innovative quality, development, and extent of basic change. Controversies abounded over the connection of the New Deal to earlier progressive impulses; whether the New Deal was a new departure, a novel tack in its spirit and techniques, or a culmination of a half-century of evolving reform; whether the New Deal moderately altered or fundamentally changed the American system; whether there were two distinct New Deals or an underlying uniformity of purpose; and whether the New Deal should be termed a watershed, a turning point, in American history. These disagreements aside, few historians initially dissented from positive overall assessment of the New Deal's intent and accomplishments.

Then came the mid-1960s and a torrent of dissent. The United States suddenly was embroiled in racial conflict and urban disorder, in wars against poverty at home and national liberation abroad, in campaigns against environmental pollution and corporate hegemony. Some saw all the contemporary ills of American society as the legacy of the New Deal's failures. A new generation of historians documented the flaws of the so-called "Roosevelt Revolution." They denied that the New Deal had changed and improved America significantly. Their publications logged the many New Deal shortcomings in ensuring economic security for all, eliminating poverty, redistributing wealth and income, achieving racial equality and justice, restraining corporate power, reducing the exploitation of the environment, and aiding the unorganized to develop political power. They detailed the regressive aspects of the Social Security Act; the racial discrimination in the recovery program; the capture of the regulatory apparatus by business interests; the diffident quality of banking and tax legislation; the harm done to small businessmen and consumers by the National Recovery Administration and to marginal farmers by the Agricultural Adjustment Act; the inability of the New Deal to end unemployment; and the pitiful failure to aid adequately those most in need of relief while lavishly showering subsidies on the industrial and agricultural corporations least dependent on government assistance. Questioning the whole concept of the New Deal as a reform movement to benefit the mass of Americans, these historians tended to view the New Deal basically as an effort to preserve and strengthen capitalism. In this light, the New Deal's vaunted humanitarianism was merely a means of stabilizing the corporate economy by co-opting potentially revolutionary groups. Rather than forwarding industrial democracy, the National Labor Relations Act thus institutionalized collective bargaining in the manner best calculated to sap labor militancy and dampen the conflict between unions and industry.

Only a minority of historians accepted the explanation for the New Deal's failings as inherent in Roosevelt's counterrevolutionary intent or in the impossibility of meaningful reform within a capitalistic context. But most acknowledged the persuasiveness of the bill of particulars documenting the New Deal's lack of truly substantial economic, political, or social reform. Indeed, most of the literature on the New Deal published in the last decade is based on this premise. The causes for such negligible change, however, are seen in the many external forces constraining and limiting what the New Deal could accomplish, such as the power of anti-New Dealers in Congress and the courts, as well as in state and local governments; the conservatism of the American culture; the paucity of pressure for fundamental change and the strength of commitment to traditional values and institutions; the political impotence of that one-third of the nation "ill-housed, ill-clad, ill-nourished"; and the continuing strength of vested moneyed interests. Because the barriers to reform were so formidable, they conclude, the New Deal could achieve little.

In the 1970s, moreover, the resurgence of conservatism further dimmed the luster of the New Deal. Publicists of the Right blamed the New Deal for inciting the expectations of the masses that the federal government can and will care for all their employment, health, retirement, and welfare needs. They attributed the elephantine expansion of entitlement programs, and the corresponding increase in taxes to fund them, to FDR's start of the welfare state. Many middle-class Americans, buffeted by inflation and resentful of the unavailing poverty programs, agreed with the conservative diagnosis. The Right also saw in Roosevelt's broker state the origins of the incessant clamor of organized interest groups to feed at the federal trough. Similarly, they saddled the New Deal with responsibility for the "imperial presidency." All the abuses of presidential power revealed in the Vietnam War and Watergate—the secrecy, the domestic spying, the excesses of executive privilege and impoundment, the contempt in the White House for the other branches of government—were traced to Roosevelt. The New Deal appeared to be passing from favor. And, in 1980, Ronald Reagan proved that running against the New Deal could be good politics.

The nine topical essays that follow present a brief yet comprehensive overview of the history of the New Deal and offer a guide through the maze of shifting and contrary interpretations of that significant era in American history. They emphasize what the New Deal did achieve, usually in the face of fierce opposition. They also stress the extent to which the New Deal helped to lay the foundation for the past half-century of American history. However profound and enduring the changes in American attitudes and institutions set in motion by the New Deal, the New Dealers themselves well understood how much remained to be done. "We are the children of the transition," wrote Henry Wallace at the end of the 1930s, "we have left Egypt but we have not yet arrived at the Promised Land." In that spirit, the contributors to this volume hope to enrich the continuing debate on the meaning of the New Deal with their individual insights while also encouraging each student to understand the New Deal in his or her own most relevant terms. The basics of the New Deal are still very much in place in American society, and to comprehend what is occurring today we must fathom the significance of what happened in the thirties. To know where we ought to be going, we need to know where we have been.

The New Deal and American Politics

Richard Kirkendall

Looking back on the impact of the New Deal on American politics in the 1930s, I am struck both by the actual changes that took place and the conceivable ones that did not. The New Deal did not revolutionize American politics, but it changed them significantly. It helped to safeguard the two-party system against threats to it from advocates of one-party states, as well as from champions of third parties who hoped to displace one of the two major parties. It also altered in a large way the relationship between the two long-dominant parties. If the New Deal had not changed the economy and the society, the story of American politics in the 1930s surely would have been very different. It seems certain that the forces of discontent would have grown. Revolutionaries would have stepped up their struggle to give direction to these forces, and it seems likely that a form of authoritarianism would have triumphed as people of property, anxious about their holdings, turned to a strong man who was willing and able to use military and police power to stabilize American politics. But the New Deal, continuing an American tradition of pragmatic reform, promoted social and economic changes, which helped to avoid revolution. I can imagine more desirable developments than the ones that took place during the 1930s, but I can as easily conceive of less desirable ones.

FIRST RESPONSES TO THE DEPRESSION

The story began just before the thirties got under way. Late in 1929, the American economy, which had seemed so strong to its many admirers, collapsed disastrously, producing widespread and intense suffering. In a short period of time, the economic system experienced a far-reaching change from prosperity to depression. The resulting crisis was severe. All groups in American society felt the tremendous impact of the Great Depression, and most Americans suffered from it. Caught in a crisis of serious proportions, the American people could not avoid change. The question of the early 1930s was not "Would change take place?" but, rather, "How much change would there be?" and "What kinds of changes would be made?"

President Herbert Hoover had the initial responsibility for dealing with the crisis. He did not endorse either a do-nothing philosophy for government or reliance on the military and the police to suppress the agitation and violence provoked by the Depression. Instead, Hoover enlarged the government's role in economic affairs in an effort to protect the system and promote its recovery. Hoover's philosophy, which emphasized voluntary cooperation, was further moderated by his fear of opening the door to political forces that alarmed him. Consequently, he enlarged the operations of government, while trying to rely chiefly on leaders and institutions in the private sector to restore prosperity. Hoover tried but failed to control the business cycle. As a result, in spite of Hoover's intentions, people were led to the conclusion that they should not rely as heavily on the private sector as the President had and that they should accept an even greater role for government in dealing with the economic crisis.

By 1932, pressures for change were still rising, which pointed most clearly to the removal of Hoover from power, but beyond that step the direction was unclear. While the Depression deeply discouraged some people, the sudden collapse of American capitalism stimulated others. It seemed to provide opportunities for fundamental, large-scale changes. As the economy spiraled downward and the prestige of business and established political leaders declined, the Left took on new life and hope. The day of victory seemed to be fast approaching. Radicals had long predicted that, since capitalism was unworkable, a major crisis would result and the suffering masses would overthrow the system and introduce a new one.

The Communist party participated actively in the politics of the time. It worked to gain support from the unemployed, blacks, students, unorganized and unskilled workers, farmers, and intellectuals. In search of followers, Communists moved into trouble spots, like Harlan County, Kentucky, a place with a tradition of violence, and where the earnings of miners had been slashed. When the miners struck, the coal mine operators and their guards combined with county officials to defeat the Communist National Miners Union. Communists also worked throughout the South in a quest for black support, protesting against disenfranchisement, lynching, and discrimination, and demanding self-determination for blacks. Communists joined in protests in the rural Middle West as well. And, throughout the nation, the party worked to organize the unemployed for revolution. In many cities, party members provided leadership in demonstrations by the jobless.

The largest organization on the left was the Socialist party. Nominating Norman Thomas for the presidency for the second time in 1932, the party offered the nation a platform that contained a large-scale program to deal with the emergency and numerous reforms, which linked the Socialists with progressives or liberals. The Socialist platform also included a major plank that set the party apart from those who hoped only to reform capitalism: a call for nonviolent revolution. The party proposed the public ownership and democratic control of basic industries to be ushered in by the people in the polling places.

Loud, and at times violent, protests erupted in rural America. Many corn-hog farmers in the Middle West, who had known prosperity but now faced falling income and the likely loss of property, joined the Farmers' Holiday Association (FHA) and participated in what its historian called "the most aggressive agrarian upheaval of the twentieth century." The FHA organized a farm strike that began in August and lasted until November, 1932. The participants, while usually peaceful, did employ force on several occasions in their efforts to keep farm products off the market. In addition, many protest marches and meetings during the fall and winter of 1932–33 demanded immediate action to halt debt payments, evictions, and property seizures, raise prices, distribute food to the needy, and cut the profits of the middlemen. Farmers also took direct action to halt the great wave of foreclosures and sales for tax delinquency that transformed landowners into tenants, farm laborers, or migrants.

As discontent grew and radicals tried to give it direction, farm leaders, business people, and others often prophesied revolution. American conservatives had long feared that the masses, when provoked by economic problems, would behave irrationally, follow wild leaders, and overturn capitalism. A system of repression had developed that involved the cooperation of industrialists, private police forces, politicians, and state and local law enforcement officials, often backed up by federal agencies. Now, as the time of troubles seemed to be at hand, alarmed conservatives frequently called for suppression of agitation and disorder. Since many of these people believed that radicals were responsible for protest and violence, the House of Representatives established a special committee to investigate "un-American activities." Officials provided special antiriot training for military and police units so that they would be able to defend the American system. These forces were used to disrupt meetings, to break strikes, and to suppress demonstrations of the unemployed and depressed farmers. Leaders were jailed, blood was shed. In Atlanta, for example, a young black Communist, Angelo Herndon, was arrested and prosecuted after leading a peaceful march of jobless whites and blacks in the summer of 1932. (The Supreme Court overturned his conviction five years later.) Unlike police and military forces in many nations where revolutions succeeded, the forces in the United States remained loyal to established institutions.

The most dramatic episode in suppression occurred in Washington in the summer of 1932. An "army" of more than 20,000 unemployed veterans of World War I had moved into the capital to press for full and immediate payment of the bonus that Congress in 1924 had approved for payment in 1945. The veterans assumed that the nation owed this to them and that payment now would stimulate recovery. Hoover opposed payment for budgetary reasons and because he doubted that most veterans needed help from their government. The House voted yes but the Senate defeated the proposal. Most of the veterans remained in Washington, hoping the government would reconsider. The administration urged the petitioners to leave, but they stayed put. Several small skirmishes took place and then the President sent the United States Army, under the command of the Chief of Staff, General Douglas MacArthur, into operation against the Bonus Army. MacArthur, going beyond his orders, drove the veterans out of the capital. Although dubious at first, the President had been persuaded by MacArthur and other advisers that the group was filled with revolutionary spirit and led by Communists. "Subversive influences," he explained, "obtained control. . . ." MacArthur regarded the group as "a mob . . . animated by the essence of revolution." Actually, Communists had tried but failed to gain control of the movement.

ROOSEVELT'S "MIDDLE WAY"

Although some people hoped, and others feared, that a revolution would take place in America, the main political developments of 1932 were not quite so spectacular. The most significant moves were a big swing to the Democratic party and the election to the presidency of a progressive Democrat. The American voters chose Roosevelt, not revolution.

By November, 1932, although his campaign had lacked clarity, Roosevelt had developed a proposed New Deal, which amounted essentially to an extension of the progressives' assumption concerning the importance of government action. Roosevelt had less confidence in the business system than Hoover and less confidence in government than Thomas. He accepted capitalism but called for changes in the relations between government and business in order to change business behavior and to promote the general welfare.

Roosevelt's philosophy exemplified a belief in the conservative function of reform. He believed that capitalism and democracy were seriously threatened in the world of the early 1930s. Determined to preserve capitalism and democracy, Roosevelt was convinced that the way to achieve this goal was to come to grips with the social and economic problems that threatened them. Opposed to revolution, he believed that democratic leaders must reform capitalism in ways that would convince Americans that they had no need to turn to other economic and political systems.

Most voters chose Roosevelt's "middle way." He received 57.4 percent of the popular vote and Hoover received 39.7 percent. The other candidates, including Thomas and William Z. Foster, the choice of the Communist party, divided the remainder.

Winning 472 of the electoral votes, Roosevelt had the support of every region in the nation. The race was closest in the East, the only region in which Roosevelt lost states. His victory margin was larger in the Middle and Far West, and especially large in the traditionally Democratic South.

To grasp the significance of the election, it must be compared with earlier ones. The third-party vote had increased, but by only a small amount since 1928—from 1 percent of the total to 3 percent. A much larger change had taken place in the relationship between the two major parties. The Republican presidential vote had dropped from 58 percent in 1928, while the Democratic vote had moved up from 41 percent. Never before in American history had such a large swing from one party to another taken place in four years. Obviously, many voters had given thought to politics in 1932. They had not merely relied upon their party traditions to make their voting decisions. Had they done so, Hoover would have won, for his had been the majority party since the 1890s. Many people rejected those traditions and switched from the GOP to the Democrats; many others chose a party for the first time, some because they had recently reached voting age or become citizens, and others because politics now seemed significant to them. In addition, many of the new young voters rejected the party tradition of their families.

The vote of the urban working classes was especially significant. This was the group upon whom the Left had counted most heavily for the support needed to usher in the new order. But urban workers voted for Roosevelt, giving him even more support than they had given Al Smith in 1928. And they voted for FDR even though he had displaced Smith as the Democratic leader and had devoted most of his campaign to efforts to capture the West and the South, not the working-class neighborhoods. And, the workers voted for Roosevelt even though most labor leaders did not endorse him. Many workers who voted for Roosevelt had voted for Smith in 1928, others had voted for Hoover, and some had not voted for anyone. The workers were unhappy with joblessness and Hoover's policies, which supplied almost no help for the unemployed, and they were willing to give the American system of economics and politics another chance.

Some critics have blamed Thomas and other leaders of the Left for the Left's failure, but the competition that Roosevelt supplied may have been too tough for any leader to overcome. He seems to have understood the American people better and known how to communicate with them more effectively than any actual or potential leader of the Left. Roosevelt agreed that there was revolutionary potential in the United States, but he did not see it as a force with as much strength as the radicals assumed it had.

Several factors restrained the groups the radicals regarded as potential revolutionaries. Many members had not lost confidence in the American system and its ability to supply them with satisfactory incomes. The dream of success was difficult to sustain during the Depression, but, though modified and scaled down, it persisted, kept alive in part by the mass media. Also, most of the people upon whom the Left relied were influenced by religious and nationalistic faiths that made them hostile to the revolutionary philosophies. And, many were fearful, apathetic, and demoralized by the severity of their suffering and could not be aroused and organized for revolutionary activity—or political activity of any sort.

Nonvoting was a major political characteristic of the American poor. Voter turnout had fallen sharply after the 1890s, dropping from nearly 80 percent in 1896 to less than 50 percent in the early 1920s after two large groups—immigrants from southern and eastern Europe and women—had been added to the potential electorate and most southern blacks had been disenfranchised. The Communists and Socialists—as well as other parties—were not able to draw large numbers of nonvoters into politics in the early 1930s. Thus, more than 40 percent of the adults did not vote in 1932. Many of the nonvoters, perhaps 20 percent of them, could not vote because they were black and lived in the South. Most blacks still lived there, and effective restrictions on the franchise kept all but a few off the polling lists. Many of the other nonvoters were white and poor, and apparently they were not convinced that voting was worthwhile. It seems reasonable to suggest that many of these people were alienated, not contented. The Left professed to speak for such people but failed to mobilize them for political action. Voter turnout, which had jumped above 57 percent in 1928, partly because of Smith's appeal to recent immigrants, increased by less than 1 percent in 1932 and actually dropped in at least one large city, Philadelphia. The few people who did move from nonvoter to voter status tended to vote for Roosevelt.

The others upon whom the Left was counting moved in the same direction. Midwestern farmers, most of whom had voted Republican in the past, now gave most of their votes to Roosevelt. They wanted higher prices, just as workers wanted relief and jobs. Some northern blacks deserted the Republican party in 1932 but moved to the Democrats, not one of the parties of the Left. This gave the Democrats more votes from blacks than they had received in the past. For many years, Republicans, eager to get more support from white southerners, had refused to use their power to raise the status of black Americans. Some black leaders, such as Robert L. Vann, the publisher of the *Pittsburgh Courier*, now argued that Republicans no longer served black interests and that Hoover's record in race relations was especially bad. Most black voters, however, maintained their allegiance to Hoover's party, the party of emancipation, and their distrust of the Democrats, the party of white supremacy. Few showed any interest in the Communist or Socialist parties.

THE ROOSEVELT COALITION

The Left and the Right failed while the center succeeded. Roosevelt's strong support in both urban and rural America was impressive, given the history of his party in the 1920s. During that decade, the Democratic party had been torn apart and rendered quite ineffective by a clash between the well-established rural wing and the growing urban wing—a clash that prevented the party from taking full advantage of Republican indifference and hostility to immigrants and urban workers, as well as Republican vetoes of farm relief legislation. The urban wing gained new strength in 1928 when Smith broke the hold the Republicans had had on the big cities since the 1890s and demonstrated especially strong appeal to immigrants and their children, converting some Republicans, at least for the moment, and bringing many people to the polls who had not voted earlier. The Depression submerged Prohibition and other divisive noneconomic issues and brought the urban and rural groups together in opposition to Hoover's economic policies. Roosevelt's ability to work fairly well with representatives of both groups also helped to unite them. He both benefited from—or held on to—the gains that Smith had made for his party in the cities and overcame the problems that Smith's Catholicism, urbanism, and hostility to Prohibition had produced in the South.

The Democrats under Roosevelt did not merely put together two blocs that had entered the party earlier. The two blocs also grew in size under the impact of the Depression and the promise of the New Deal. The South became solid once again. Farmers in the Far West and Middle West shifted to the Democrats. The party regained and added to its strength in the cities. Recent immigrants and their children in the cities voted Democratic once again and did so in larger numbers than before. Urban workers supplied more Democratic votes than they had in 1928. Carrying nearly all of the thirty-six largest cities, Roosevelt received 17 percent more votes in them than Smith had in 1928. Smith had generated interest in national politics and the Democratic party among certain groups but had not actually attached them to the party. They could have drifted back to their old ways after 1928. In fact, some groups, such as the Italian and Irish Catholics in Philadelphia, did not give Roosevelt as much support as they had given Smith. But Hoover's unsatisfactory response to the Depression and Roosevelt's more encouraging response persuaded most of the people who had broken with their Republican commitments or their nonvoting habits to vote for Smith to stay with the Democrats for another election. For similar reasons, other people for the first time changed their voting practices to vote for the Democratic candidate, while for these reasons and others, still other people returned to the Democratic column in the presidential race.

A new party balance was taking shape. Many American voters were eager for change in 1932, but few wanted revolutionary change. Many wanted more change than Herbert Hoover could give them but not as much as Norman Thomas proposed. Rather than switch from a Republican to a Socialist or Communist, they switched only to a Democrat. Many who voted for Roosevelt did so because they could not conceive of voting for anyone other than a Democrat. Millions of other people maintained their ties with the Republican party. The two-party tradition revealed that it still had strength, and the American people revealed that they were not as flexible as revolutionaries expected. Many people, however, voted for Roosevelt because they had confidence in the reform tradition that he represented—or at least a willingness to give it a new opportunity. They believed that the political system could rescue the economic system and make it function successfully. They saw no need to turn to a new system such as the Socialists and Communists proposed.

In power, Roosevelt established a New Deal. Its most obvious feature was a greater role for the national government in American economic life. The American economy remained capitalistic. The New Deal deliberately and actively promoted the survival and recovery of the capitalistic system. The change from Hoover to Roosevelt was significant, however, because the New Deal did not merely prop up the system that had collapsed after 1929. Alterations were made in hope that capitalism would function successfully, and efforts were made to serve the interests of many groups. Throughout, the New Deal rested on the assumption—an assumption that was not new in America in the 1930s—that the powers of government could and should be used to attack social and economic problems. At first, the administration tried hard to cooperate with business leaders, but in 1935, Roosevelt and his aides became more critical of these leaders and more actively concerned with the welfare of lower-income groups. The administration made the federal government more powerful in economic affairs, and converted it into an active promoter of the labor movement.

THE 1936 ELECTION – ROOSEVELT'S STRATEGY FOR VICTORY

In 1936, the New Deal enjoyed a spectacular victory. Most voters endorsed the man who had preserved and changed the capitalistic system, and their behavior once again suggests strong support for change but almost none for revolution. Anti-New Dealers proposed both the return to business dominance and the abolition of the business system, but the voters rejected these alternatives. Traditions explained some of their behavior but not all of the important dimensions of it, including the outcome of the election. Roosevelt received a much bigger victory than any of his Democratic predecessors and a bigger victory than his own in 1932. Millions of voters changed their political behavior. Had the New Deal not conformed to their desires to some degree, the voters would not have behaved as they did. They had other options available to them.

In his campaign, Roosevelt pursued a strategy designed to win reelection by a substantial majority to obtain overwhelming ratification of the New Deal. To accomplish this goal, he played down party affiliations. He rarely spoke of his own party; he took the Democrats for granted and went out of his way to thank such non-Democrats as Senator George Norris of Nebraska and other progressive Republicans, for their support and to draw them to him.

Sensitivity to the feeble character of the Democratic party from the 1890s to the 1930s influenced the strategy. The President knew that the old party scarcely existed outside of the South and a few big city machines in the North. The President knew that he must not tie himself too closely to his party and that he could not count on a sense of party loyalty to accomplish a ratification of the New Deal.

His party, as historian Arthur Schlesinger observed, "could stay in power only by attracting to itself traditionally non-Democratic groups."

The strategy contained still other elements. In 1936 FDR ran against Hoover, rather than the actual Republican nominee, Governor Alfred M. Landon of Kansas. Roosevelt repeatedly reminded people of the conditions that had existed four years earlier and of the improvements that had been made since then. Fortunately for him, the economy had improved somewhat.

Roosevelt also made a strong class appeal. He denounced "economic royalists" and "organized money," and presented himself as the champion of the "forgotten man." "I should like to have it said of my first Administration that in it the forces of selfishness and of lust for power met their match," he boasted. "I should like to have it said of my second Administration that in it these forces met their master."

With his rhetoric and his policies, Roosevelt was building a new party. It was not the well-organized type, united by ideology, that some desired and that Roosevelt himself sometimes talked about as desirable. Professor James MacGregor Burns, a prominent analyst of the presidency, has been especially critical of FDR for failing to build a liberal political coalition and party organization capable of sustaining and enlarging the reform movement and has argued that he failed as a party leader because of "his unwillingness to commit himself to the full implications of party leadership, . . . his eternal desire to keep open alternative tactical lines of action, including a line of retreat." According to Burns, Roosevelt could not make the needed "continuing intellectual and political commitment to a set strategy. . . . " But Roosevelt had committed himself to the construction of a much larger and much more vigorous party than the old Democratic party had been. The one coming into being was competing actively throughout the country, was more closely tied to lower-income groups and their organizations than before, and was less dependent upon the South. It was supported not only by traditional Democrats but also by people who had been hostile or indifferent to them.

The result was a landslide victory for Roosevelt and the new Democratic party. While he received nearly 28 million votes, Landon received less than 17 million. Landon carried only Maine and Vermont, good for 8 electoral votes, while Roosevelt picked up 523.

State after state that had been strongly Republican, such as Pennsylvania, Michigan, and California, had become Democratic. In contrast with Roosevelt's performance, no Democratic nominee for the presidency between the 1840s and the 1930s had received more than 50 percent of the popular vote, and between 1892 and 1932, only Wilson had received close to that amount. FDR received nearly 61 percent.

Roosevelt's support contained a number of new voters. The total vote was nearly 6 million above that in 1932, and Roosevelt's total was nearly 5 million higher than it had been in 1932. Many of these new voters had become eligible since 1932, and tended to prefer him by a wide margin. Many others, however, had been eligible earlier but had not been interested in voting. Now, Roosevelt and his programs drew them to the polls.

Urban Voters

Almost all of the substantial increase in turnout took place outside the South, outside the rural areas, and inside the urban, working-class neighborhoods. Overall turnout increased by more than 4 percent, moving from less than 58 percent in 1932 to nearly 62 percent of the nation's adults in 1936. Two important industrial states, Michigan and Pennsylvania, enjoyed especially large increases, in part because two-party competition had been restored in those states after a generation of Republican dominance and Democratic weakness. (In Philadelphia, voter participation was 32 percent above that in 1932.) New voters constituted about 20 percent of the electorate, and most of them were members of the urban working classes.

Most of those who switched from one party to another were also members of the urban working classes, and the latter made up the largest bloc in the "Roosevelt Coalition." Most workers, "old stock" as well as new, Protestants as well as Catholics and Jews, white as well as black, white collar as well as blue collar, voted for Roosevelt. Class consciousness, at least among these people, was very strong that year. As a group, the urban workers gave Roosevelt even more support than they had in 1932.

The voting behavior of these people enabled Roosevelt to carry the cities by even larger margins than before. Samuel Lubell, a pioneer political analyst of the 1930s, pointed out that Roosevelt's plurality in the twelve largest cities "leaped 80 percent, the biggest change in any single election." Twelve cities with more than 100,000 people, including Philadelphia, had not voted for him in 1932, but now all but two of them did, including all of the twelve largest. Those cities had supported the Republican party most of the time since the 1890s, but now Roosevelt won even in the big cities—Los Angeles, San Francisco, Seattle, Philadelphia, Pittsburgh, Baltimore, Chicago, and Detroit—that Smith had failed to carry in 1928. In Philadelphia, where Smith had received 40 percent of the vote and Roosevelt had received only 42 percent in 1932, FDR now picked up 60 percent, defeating a Republican machine that had been fighting for self-preservation since 1928. A man with anti-urban feelings who often spoke of decentralizing the population, Roosevelt had become the great beneficiary of big city votes. He had earned them by breaking with a national policy of neglect of the cities and giving them relief and public works.

Immigrants

Many of the urban voters who voted for Roosevelt were immigrants from southern and eastern Europe and the children of those immigrants. They had strongly opposed the adoption of Prohibition in 1920; they had long had an interest in social welfare programs as a consequence of their experiences in slums and factories; and they had become increasingly interested in government help as a result of the heavy impact of the Depression on them. Thus, they liked many features of the New Deal, including the repeal of the Eighteenth Amendment (Prohibition) in 1933, Social Security, and the various programs of relief for the unemployed. They also applauded Roosevelt's appointment policy, which recognized that people other than Anglo-Saxon Protestants could make important contributions to national life, and they appreciated the egalitarian rhetoric of those New Dealers who challenged the racist and anti-immigrant assumptions involved in immigration policy and other features of American life by defining ethnic diversity as a valuable and essential feature of the culture. Such ethnic groups as the Irish-Americans and the Jews, which often clashed in other areas, joined together in the Roosevelt Coalition.

Class was not the only factor in the support of new immigrants for Roosevelt. Most recent immigrants and their children were members of the working classes, but some were not, and those who were not also preferred him.

FDR had much more support from the new-stock Americans than from the nation as a whole, and more than his Democratic predecessors had received. Most of these people were Catholics, and Roosevelt enlarged a tendency of Catholics to vote Democratic. Many Roosevelt voters were Jews, and here the support for a Democrat constituted a large change from strong Republicanism in the 1920s.

Blacks

Most black voters also chose Roosevelt. More than 20 percent of the nation's blacks now lived outside the South and, for the first time, blacks gave a majority of their votes to a Democratic presidential candidate. They voted nearly three to one for him.

Several influences changed black voting behavior. In part, the change resulted from disgust with Republicans, who had long taken the black vote for granted. "Abraham Lincoln is not a candidate in the present campaign," one black newspaper reminded its readers. Landon's appeals to them could not compensate for the party's record in recent years.

The New Deal exerted even more influence on black voters. While signs of black discontent with Republican rule had been apparent in some places in 1932 and even earlier, the decisive change took place after the establishment of Roosevelt's policies. The Roosevelt Administration, faced with only weak and divided pressures on behalf of blacks from such groups as the National Association for the Advancement of Colored People, the Communist party, and the Urban League and from such individuals as Ralph Bunche, A. Philip Randolph, and W. E. B. DuBois, did not develop programs designed to deal with the special problems of blacks, such as lynching, disenfranchisement, segregation, and job discrimination. In fact, New Deal programs often discriminated against and segregated blacks. Nevertheless, blacks did benefit from parts of the New Deal, especially the relief programs, for most were members of the working classes and many were unemployed. The blacks who benefited most from the New Deal lived in the cities and were able to vote. Although the benefits fell far short of what black leaders desired, they were superior to what Republican regimes had supplied and were recognized as such by many blacks.

Again, more than class and economics was involved. Rhetoric also influenced the change. Some New Dealers, above all Eleanor

Roosevelt, Harold Ickes, Will Alexander, and Clark Foreman, while advising blacks to be patient and not jeopardize the New Deal by alienating whites, criticized racial discrimination and spoke of a "new democracy" in which the material status of blacks would be raised and the racial prejudices of whites would decline. New Deal appointment policy also exerted influence. It placed more blacks, including Mary McLeod Bethune and Robert C. Weaver, in important government jobs than Roosevelt's predecessors had. Although Roosevelt himself approached race questions cautiously, his departure from the discriminatory practices of Woodrow Wilson, his Democratic predecessor in the White House, was striking.

Organized Labor

Organized labor gave the Democratic presidential candidate more support than the movement had given earlier Democratic contenders. In 1932, John L. Lewis of the United Mine Workers, for one, had supported Hoover, and Sidney Hillman of the Amalgamated Clothing Workers had backed Thomas. Now, Lewis and Hillman and other leaders of the new Congress of Industrial Organizations (CIO) formed Labor's Nonpartisan League for Roosevelt. Labor, especially the CIO, liked the social welfare programs and government protection for the labor movement, a major departure from past relations between the federal government and labor, and wanted additional benefits for workers and unions. Rejecting the idea of a labor party and seeking only to establish influence in the Democratic party, the CIO's top officials worked hard and successfully to persuade union members to vote for Roosevelt. Eighty percent of them did so.

The labor movement filled a void created by the alienation of business people. A few prominent ones, including Joseph P. Kennedy, Edward Filene, A. P. Giannini, and Thomas Watson, did support Roosevelt, convinced that the New Deal was good for business. Corporations, after all, moved from losses of $2 billion in 1933 to profits of $5 billion in 1936. Nevertheless, most business leaders, including most large newspaper publishers, opposed Roosevelt's reelection, and their financial contributions to the Democratic campaign fell far below the 1932 level. Some of the unions, however, especially Lewis's United Mine Workers, compensated for this decline by contributing heavily to Roosevelt's campaign.

Rural Voters

At the same time that city people voted by a wide margin for Roosevelt, most farmers also cast their ballots for him. They did so in spite of the cultural factors that had promoted urban-rural conflicts in the 1920s and in spite of unhappiness with some features of New Deal farm programs. Farmers also supported Roosevelt even though the Farmers' Independence Council, a propaganda organ for industry, the meat packers, and some large cattle interests, preached an individualistic philosophy and tried to turn farmers against the New Deal. And farmers supported Roosevelt in spite of the strength of Republican traditions in the Middle West. In Iowa, farmers gave Roosevelt better than 60 percent of their votes compared to the less than 30 percent of their votes they had given Democratic presidential candidates during the 1920s. Obviously, the benefits of New Deal farm programs were very persuasive.

Women

Women voters also gave FDR strong support. The New Deal had not attacked discrimination against women in economic arenas, which the Depression made more severe and confining, and some programs discriminated against women. However, the New Deal did not check the growing tendency of married women to take jobs outside the home, even though jobs were scarce and the Depression intensified opposition to married women holding them. It also persuaded more wives and mothers that they must earn money to raise the standard of living of their families. (The propriety of employment for married women was a hot issue and the focus of feminist concern.) Especially important in terms of the New Deal's appeal to women voters, women occupied a substantial number of positions in the Roosevelt administration and the Democratic party. The most prominent and influential members of the female network were Frances Perkins, the Secretary of Labor and the first woman to serve in a president's cabinet, Mary (Molly) Dewson, a social worker who served as head of the Women's Division of the Democratic National Committee, and Eleanor Roosevelt, an unusually active First Lady, a liberal influence on her husband, and a frequent spokesperson for him. Products of the suffrage and social welfare movements and eager to equalize opportunities in American society, they had battled with some success for provisions aiding women in New Deal social welfare and relief programs, and for important positions for women in the administration and the party. Now, they urged women to vote Democratic, and many did so, including, one assumes, many who were grateful for direct benefits from the New Deal to their husbands and children.

Traditional Democratic Constituencies: Urban Machines and the South

In addition, two traditional props of the Democratic party, the Democratic urban machines and the South, supported Roosevelt. The Hague machine in Jersey City, the Kelly machine in Chicago, the Pendergast machine in Kansas City, and others like them backed FDR because they were interested in the enlargement of patronage that accompanied the expansion of government and because they were eager to swap votes for jobs. Organizations with good relations with the administration gained strength by staffing New Deal agencies and distributing New Deal benefits. In Pittsburgh, the New Deal actually helped the Democrats build an organization that resembled the Republican machine that had lost power in 1933. Republican organizations, like the Vare machine in Philadelphia, and Democratic combines like Tammany Hall in New York City that had bad relations with the national administration declined in the period, but the old-time bosses remained a part of American politics. FDR did not destroy them. Instead, wherever possible, the President cooperated with the bosses.

Long-time Democrats in the South also formed an important part of the Roosevelt Coalition. Most southerners supported the New Deal enthusiastically. The Speakers of the House—first Joseph W. Byrns of Tennessee and then William B. Bankhead of Alabama—were southerners, as were the Senate majority leader— Joseph T. Robinson of Arkansas—and most committee chairmen. One of the latter, Sam Rayburn of Texas, sponsored some of the most important New Deal legislation. Another Texan, Congressman Marvin Jones, jettisoned his conservative inhibitions to support New Deal programs, persuaded by the seriousness of the farm crisis. Senator James F. Byrnes of South Carolina was another influential southerner who cooperated closely with the President. Not surprisingly then, Roosevelt received 76 percent of the southern vote. The South remained solidly Democratic.

Yet, there was some dissatisfaction in the South, and southern critics of the New Deal also had representatives in Washington. Some southerners disliked the new importance of the northern cities in their party. Many also feared the new relations between Democrats and blacks, seeing them as a potential threat to white supremacy, and some believed that the new policies harmed important interests in the South and betrayed the traditions of the party. Senator Pat Harrison of Mississippi had supported Roosevelt but was uncomfortable in doing so and was moving toward a break in the late 1930s. Senators Carter Glass and Harry F. Byrd of Virginia, Walter F. George of Georgia, and Ellison D. "Cotton Ed" Smith of South Carolina had been critical of the New Deal, but all of these men recognized Roosevelt's popularity and avoided a break. Governor Eugene Talmadge of Georgia had been much less cautious in his anti-New Deal stance. Talmadge ran for the Senate in 1936 against a Roosevelt supporter, Senator Richard B. Russell, and lost, as did another one of Roosevelt's outspoken critics, Senator Thomas P. Gore of Oklahoma, who was defeated for reelection by a New Dealer, Josh Lee.

Some southerners voted for anti-New Dealers when they had a chance, as they did in North Carolina in 1936. There, voters in the Democratic senatorial primary rejected a New Dealer and endorsed a cautious anti-New Dealer, Senator Josiah W. Bailey, thereby returning to Washington a senator who recognized that his political future did not demand that he follow the President's lead. The same voters, however, supported Roosevelt.

Outside the South, some anti-New Dealers, less inhibited by party affiliation, left the party. The list included two former presidential nominees, Al Smith and John W. Davis; a former senator, James Reed; a former chair of the party's national committee, John J. Raskob. Unhappy with changes in party policies, they were convinced the party had deserted them.

THE DEMOCRATS' OPPOSITION IN 1936

The Republicans

The Democratic losses, however, were insignificant compared with the troubles of the old ruling party. The Republicans had experienced bitter frustrations since 1929, and their party was wracked by internal conflict over what response to make to the New Deal and what steps to take to regain the dominant position.

The Grand Old Party selected a moderately progressive member of its ranks to lead the ticket. Landon's ties with progressive Republicanism ran back to the days of Theodore Roosevelt, and his election victories in 1932 and 1934 in the Kansas contests for governor set him apart from most Republicans. His record in Kansas politics included support for civil liberties and social and economic reform, and he accepted much of the New Deal and promised more government help to farmers and the elderly, and a constitutional amendment permitting the states to pass social welfare legislation. He was certainly not as conservative as some of his supporters made him appear to be. Yet, Landon called for cuts in government spending and a balanced budget, criticized the growth of the central government and the presidency, and warned of dangers ahead, and other Republican campaigners emphasized Landon's disagreements with the New Deal. Landon did supply voters with a choice, but less than 37 percent of them selected the alternative he offered.

The Republican vote did dramatize the strong influence of traditions during this time of crisis. Most of the people who voted Republican were old-stock, white, Protestant Americans in the rural areas, towns, and suburbs. Nearly all had at least moderate means. Many resented the New Deal's favors to other groups. Some had been influenced by the Depression to vote for Roosevelt in 1932 but now returned to their old political home. Some had been Democrats. Some were influenced most of all by their long-standing attitude toward the Republican party, while for others, hostility toward the ways in which the country was being changed was decisive. To many of his supporters, Landon seemed to symbolize an older, simpler, and better America.

To many voters, however, the GOP seemed to be nothing more than the party of big business. Business leaders did provide very generous support for the Republican party, which reported expenditures of $14 million compared with $9.2 million for the Democrats. Republican funds financed a slick advertising campaign, which strengthened the impression that the party spoke for business leaders.

The Liberty League

The broad coalition that endorsed Roosevelt and defeated Landon also rejected other leaders and their organizations. The American

Liberty League, a bipartisan group that had emerged in 1934, united conservative politicans, mainly Democrats like Smith and Davis, and business leaders. The League, which portrayed the New Deal as an authoritarian revolution damaging America, had become increasingly active in 1935 and 1936 as members had grown more furious as a result of the legislation of those years. Its leaders had thought of forming a third party and attempted to disrupt the Democrats by supporting Al Smith. In the end, however, the Liberty League supported Landon and played a large, loud, and expensive role on his behalf, much to his embarrassment because it encouraged people to associate him with the league. The Democrats concentrated much of their fire on it.

The size of Roosevelt's victory demoralized the Liberty Leaguers. It suggested that most people liked the New Deal and wanted nothing to do with the philosophy of this right-wing group. Consequently, it ceased to function actively in 1937.

The Socialist Party

A similar fate befell the Socialist party. Sticking firmly to his principles, refusing to become merely a part of the Roosevelt Coalition and providing a Socialist critique of the New Deal, Norman Thomas received fewer than 200,000 votes. Party membership dropped nearly 50 percent after the election, falling below 7,000 in 1937.

This development owed much to the New Deal. Thomas was convinced that Roosevelt had cut the ground out from under him and his party, and one historian of the party has concluded that the "story of the decline of the Socialist party since 1933 is, for the most part, the story of the political success of the New Deal." Prominent members, such as Hillman, deserted Thomas and led others away into the Roosevelt ranks. Some Socialists had concluded that the New Deal was a fulfillment of their dreams; others realized it was not socialism but accepted it as "half a loaf," convinced that half was better than none at all. Still others concluded from the experiences of the 1930s that socialism had no chance in America and that the New Deal harmonized with American conditions. Hillman argued that the Socialist party had failed to build the labor movement and was incapable of doing so, whereas the New Deal had helped the movement make important gains. He also argued that "the defeat of

Roosevelt and the introduction of a real Fascist administration" would "make the work of building a labor movement impossible."

The New Deal's impact on potential Socialists was especially important. Millions of people who might have become Socialists, if conservatism had been the only alternative supplied by American politics, felt no need to become Socialists now. Included in this group were the working classes, who did not behave as Socialists had predicted. Consequently, as David Shannon has pointed out, "the party of Debs, which had predicted the collapse of American capitalism, itself collapsed during the worst crisis American capitalism ever had."

The National Union for Social Justice

Other forms of protest also failed. Huey Long, a Louisiana senator who had broken with Roosevelt, built a large, national Share Our Wealth Society, and seemed capable of getting several million votes as a third-party presidential candidate. In the fall of 1935, Long was assassinated. This forced others, including Father Charles E. Coughlin, the "radio priest" who also had a large following, had broken with Roosevelt, and led a National Union for Social Justice, and Dr. Francis Townsend, a popular advocate of large pensions for people over sixty, to seek a substitute to run against Roosevelt. They settled on Congressman William Lemke of North Dakota and hoped to unite behind him Long's followers in the South, Townsend's in the Far West, and Coughlin's in the Middle West and East, many of whom were middle-class people suffering from the Depression and fearful of control by centralized power. Coughlin believed that the combination would produce 9 million votes, and many assumed that it could decide a close election. But the leaders quarreled with one another; most radicals and reformers denounced them; and Coughlin encountered much criticism from the Catholic hierarchy and clergy, many of whom endorsed Roosevelt. Lemke also suffered from the party's failure to get on the ballot in fourteen states, including some in which his allies had large followings. The candidate of the Union party, Lemke ran on a rather unclear and confusing platform, and the campaign denounced the New Deal as both "bent on communistic revolution" and dominated by "international bankers." The most successful third-party candidate that year, Lemke received less than 1 million votes, about 2 percent of the total. The outcome prompted Coughlin, who had promised to take "a Communist from the chair once occupied by Washington," to announce his retirement from politics and to disband his National Union for Social Justice.

Once again, the left and others outside the two major parties had failed to gain the support of lower-income Americans, including those who did not support either the Republican or the Democratic party. Although voter turnout had increased in 1936, it remained far below its potential. Many adults—nearly 40 percent of them—did not participate actively in the politics of 1936. Turnout was especially low among the poorest people in both urban and rural areas. Educational deficiencies, restrictions on the franchise, social isolation, and other factors limited their participation, but many people apparently found nothing in the programs and proposals of the period that seemed significant to them. Roosevelt had reduced the number of the alienated by only a small percentage, but none of his rivals appealed effectively to them. His competitors were, in fact, less effective than he was in attracting people who had not voted in the past.

The Communist Party

The Communists, though numerous and active, did not challenge Roosevelt in 1936. Following guidelines from Stalin's Moscow, American Communist leaders—but not all of the rank-and-file—joined in the Popular Front against Fascism, fearing that the economic crisis in the United States, as elsewhere, provided fascists with great opportunities. Rather than run its own candidate, the Communist party endorsed Roosevelt.

In still other way, the Communists did not behave like revolutionaries in the mid-thirties. Party members devoted much of their energy to such immediate goals as the formation of industrial unions and the CIO. In these efforts, they played major roles and functioned quite effectively. While they assumed that workers would be radicalized by participation in organizing activities, union building would, in the end, integrate workers into the capitalistic system, just as other Communist efforts helped to integrate the CIO into the Democratic party.

The pursuit of revolution was not a realistic alternative for American Communists in 1936. Many workers were in a militant mood, but it was a militancy on behalf of broad-based, independent unions, collective bargaining, labor-management contracts, and a larger share of American capitalism's benefits, and Thomas's experiences suggest that Communists would have accomplished little if they had emphasized revolution. Few workers had any interest in it. American radicals, it appeared, could promote change only when they functioned as reformers.

Fascist Groups

Fascists and admirers of fascist regimes also participated in the politics of the period, but, contrary to Communist fears, they did not develop strength. Some looked to Italy for their model; others to Germany. A good many business people had admired Mussolini, but their admiration had declined before 1936. And, the fascist groups could not get the large volume of support they anticipated from Italian-Americans and German-Americans and did not get the backing from white-collar workers and farmers that they obtained in Europe. Most of the people from whom the fascists expected support voted for Roosevelt.

TRADITION AND CHANGE

The American response to the great crisis of the 1930s was influenced by desires for change and also by traditions. Almost all Americans were too heavily influenced by traditional attitudes, including political apathy and alienation, to endorse advocates of revolution on the Left and the Right, but most of the voters backed a promoter of nonrevolutionary change. To do so, millions of Americans changed their ways of behaving at election time. Clearly, the New Deal seemed significant and desirable to them.

As a consequence of widespread approval of the New Deal, relations between the two major parties changed. Roosevelt, with his program and his personality, had successfully exploited the opportunities for party realignment that existed in the 1930s. Rather than the year in which the Republicans regained their status as the majority party, as they had after the Wilsonian interlude, 1936 was the high point in what the "new political historians"—with their debts to political science and heavy use of quantification—often call a "realigning electoral era" or "a critical period of voting change." Such periods or eras have been rare in our history. This one had begun several years earlier. In 1936, the Democrats maintained and strengthened their hold on the position they had occupied in 1932. They had become the nation's majority party because most voters now felt some degree of commitment to that party. Enough people had moved away from other parties or discarded nonvoting habits to raise the Democrats from minority to majority status.

Traditions, as well as a desire for change, gave the Democrats majority status. The party had not only added voters but had also held on to most of its traditional support, doing so only in part because of the New Deal, and it needed both groups to be the majority party. Old attitudes toward the Democratic party exerted the decisive influence on some Roosevelt supporters. They voted for him, not because he was a promoter of change, but because he was a Democrat and so were they. Some Democrats voted for him even though they disliked the New Deal, apparently because his changes of the 1930s did not seem sufficiently large or threatening to them to justify change in party affiliation.

By the next presidential election, another force — war — would be competing with the New Deal for influence on American politics, but war and the forces that emerged after it would exert their influence on a political system that had been transformed by the New Deal. Its impact on American politics would be felt long after the 1930s. Just how long, in fact, would become a subject of debate among political analysts — one that need not occupy our attention here.

Another subject of recent controversy, which does deserve attention, focused directly on the 1930s and is crucial to an evaluation of the New Deal's significance for American politics. This is the New Left theory that the revolution that should have occurred in the United States during the Great Depression could have taken place. In support of this, these historians employ two quite unsatisfactory arguments. One is that a more ambitious program would have rallied the underprivileged and thereby gained the power needed to move forward. It seems unlikely, however, that a political leader, even Roosevelt, could have gained adequate support for a truly radical program. The anticapitalist left of the 1930s tried and failed dismally. The realities of the situation in the 1930s, while supporting significant change, blocked revolution.

Those who deplore the fact that Americans failed to enjoy a revolution in the 1930s also suggest that Roosevelt and the New Dealers deceived the masses and led them astray. These people did not know what was good for them, were seduced by rhetoric and style, and persuaded that they were benefiting significantly from the New Deal when actually they were not. Voter behavior at the time, however, indicates more rationality than this argument suggests. Faced with a wide range of alternatives, the voters made decisions and choices. They did not behave just as they always had. Many new voters entered the electorate, and many others moved from one party to another. These people appear to have concluded that significant changes were being made. And lower-income people were not the only ones who reached this conclusion. So did business leaders. Experiences, as well as rhetoric, apparently influenced behavior.

Perhaps Roosevelt should have pressed for revolution. He would surely have failed, however, for the voters would have rejected him. Equally important, he was incapable of doing so. If the American people wanted revolution, they should have chosen one of the revolutionaries. They did not do so; they selected instead a man who had more limited ambitions. He shared the nonrevolutionary aspirations of nearly all politically active Americans.

I wish American life and politics had become much more democratic in the 1930s, but, given the way in which so much of the world was moving at the time, I am pleased that it did not become more authoritarian. Perhaps it is foolish to imply that there was any possibility that the authoritarian right could have triumphed here. Perhaps the realities of the time dictated its defeat just as surely as they dictated the defeat of the authoritarian and the democratic lefts. Perhaps anti-authoritarian traditions were too strong and exerted too much influence even among leaders in business, the military, and the police. But repression of the forces of discontent was one of the American traditions. And what course would American politics have taken if the realities and traditions that were present had not included a reform tradition that triumphed and promoted social and economic changes? Would the points of view that Hoover and Landon represented have been strong enough to contain the forces of discontent and those alarmed by them and channel them in nonauthoritarian directions? I doubt it. It seem likely that the course that American politics followed in the 1930s was the most desirable of the real alternatives available at the time.

SUGGESTED READINGS

This essay draws upon, revises, and updates my discussion of the topic in *The United States 1929–1945: Years of Crisis and Change* (New York, 1974). See it for the bibliography on the subject up to and including the early 1970s. Since then, treatment of it has been affected by major developments in the historical profession, including the continued development of the "new political history," urban history, and black history, the rise of women's history, growing interest in ethnic groups and the working classes, and renewed interest in an old historical problem: the failure of the left (and also the right).

For me, the most influential publications of the past decade include: John L. Shover, "The Emergence of a Two-Party System in Republican Philadelphia, 1924–1936," *Journal of American History* 6 (March 1974): 985–1002; Allan J. Lichtman, "Critical Election Theory and the Reality of American Presidential Politics, 1916–1940," *American Historical Review* 81 (April 1976): 317–351; John H. Allswang, *The New Deal and American Politics: A Study in Political Change* (New York, 1978); Mark I. Gelfand, *A Nation of Cities: The Federal Government and Urban America, 1933–1965* (New York, 1975); Charles H. Trout, *Boston, the Great Depression, and the New Deal* (New York, 1977); Harvard Sitkoff, *A New Deal for Blacks: The Emergence of Civil Rights as a National Issue* (New York, 1978); John B. Kirby, *Black Americans in the Roosevelt Era: Liberalism and Race* (Knoxville, Tenn., 1980); Lois Scharf, *To Work and to Wed: Female Employment, Feminism, and the Great Depression* (Westport, Conn., 1980); Susan Ware, *Beyond Suffrage: Women in the New Deal* (Cambridge, Mass., 1981); Richard Weiss, "Ethnicity and Reform: Minorities and the Ambience of the Depression Years," *Journal of American History* 66 (December 1979): 566–585; John W. Hevener, *Which Side Are You On: The Harlan County Coal Miners, 1931–39* (Urbana, Ill., 1979); John P. Diggins, *The American Left in the Twentieth Century* (New York, 1973); Frank A. Warren, *An Alternative Vision: The Socialist Party in the 1930's* (Bloomington, Ind., 1974); James Weinstein, *Ambiguous Legacy: The Left in American Politics* (New York, 1975); Milton Cantor, *The Divided Left: American Radicalism, 1900–1975* (New York, 1978); Roger Keeran, *The Communist Party and the Auto Workers Unions* (Bloomington, Ind., 1980); John P. Diggins, *Mussolini and Fascism: The View from America* (Princeton, 1972); Sander A. Diamond, *The Nazi Movement in the United States, 1924–1941* (Ithaca, N.Y., 1974); Jurgen Kocka, *White Collar Workers in America, 1890–1940: A Socio-Political History in International Perspective* (London, 1980); Alan Brinkley, *Voices of Protest: Huey Long, Father Coughlin, and the Great Depression* (New York, 1982).

The New Deal and the Mixed Economy

Thomas K. McCraw

In the American mixed economy, as in the private economy that preceded it, most of the important economic decisions are made by business executives. The difference now, a difference that grew directly out of the New Deal, is that other powerful players also help determine the outcome of the game. Organized labor influences wage rates and working conditions. Nonbusiness interest groups help to shape social and environmental policies that have strong economic impacts. Most important of all, government now touches the pocketbooks of all citizens, through taxation, regulation, and welfare programs.

Government touches all businesses as well. It affects some in a mostly macroeconomic sense, through tax laws and interest rates aimed at controlling aggregate demand. It affects others through bureaucracies whose powers cross industry lines, such as the Environmental Protection Agency. And, it regulates still others in a microeconomic way, through agencies assigned to particular industries such as transportation, public utilities, and telecommunications.

The present situation does not represent the fulfillment of a coherent strategy designed to deal with contemporary problems. No rigorous ideology underlies the mixed economy, no socialist system from the imagination of Marx, no pure market network from that of Adam Smith. The Smithian market may be the foundation stone, but it is overlaid with a hodgepodge of government controls, many of which are inconsistent with each other.

Because of its messy intellectual underpinnings, the mixed economy is easy to attack from a theoretical viewpoint. It might be as vulnerable from a practical perspective as well were it not for the fact that it has been so successful. In the 1980s, real gross national product per capita in the United States is about four times what it was in 1933. In particular, the quarter-century that followed the New Deal and World War II was a period of uniquely high economic growth throughout the world; and that growth was led by the mixed economies of America, Europe, and Japan. The woes of the 1980s, as serious as they are, must not blind us to the stark significance of this earlier "miracle" and its connection to the arrangements that emerged from the New Deal and the war.

1. MACROECONOMIC MANAGEMENT: THE INTELLECTUAL BACKGROUND

The New Deal was not an economic revolution. Its policies were extraordinarily innovative, but they did not end the Great Depression. As late as 1939, six years after Roosevelt's inauguration, unemployment stood at the very high figure of 17.2 percent. This was an improvement over the 24.9 percent of 1933, but it was still a depression-sized number.

What did end the economic crisis was World War II. As munitions orders from abroad poured in during 1940 and 1941, and as the United States itself became an active participant following the attack on Pearl Harbor, prosperity returned with a rush. By 1944, with the economy at full-scale war mobilization, unemployment had dropped to 1.2 percent, the lowest figure in American history up to that time or since.

In the brief period of just over a decade, therefore, the American economy recorded both the worst and best growth performances in its history. For the generation then coming of age, these violent economic swings were profoundly affecting experiences. Most American presidents of the postwar generation spent their early maturity during the New Deal and World War II. (The only exceptions were Harry Truman and Dwight Eisenhower, who were too old, and Jimmy Carter, who was too young.) Between Roosevelt's inauguration in March 1933 and Japan's surrender in August 1945, John F. Kennedy went from the age of 15 to the age of 28, Lyndon Johnson from 24 to 37, Richard Nixon from 20 to 32, Gerald Ford from 19 to 32, and Ronald Reagan from 22 to 34. Hence some of their views on economic matters were shaped during an extremely atypical period of economic convulsion.

Different persons learned different lessons from the experiences of these years, of course. But of the many lessons that emerged, one was revolutionary: *a government can spend its way out of a depression.* As the popular writer Stuart Chase put it in 1942, "There is no business depression in Britain, Canada, Australia, Germany, Italy, Japan, in any nation where armament expenditures are large." Governments were spending without stint, as they had never done even during World War I. "Where's the money coming from? Nobody gives a damn. That is just the point. In the old economy, such reckless outlays would have spelled bankruptcy and ruin." But World War II had clinched the upheaval in economic thought that had begun during the New Deal. "Adam Smith may heave in his grave," Chase went on to say, "but no nation in this dangerous world of 1942 is meekly going bankrupt because some textbooks say it ought to . . . . Put your book away, my friend. The books which will explain the new world we are entering have not been written."

Actually the book had been written. It appeared in 1936, and it was entitled *The General Theory of Employment, Interest, and Money.* Its author was John Maynard Keynes. Keynes's contributions to macroeconomics made him the most important economist of the twentieth century. (Macroeconomics is the study and analysis of whole national economies as aggregates, in contrast to the microeconomic study of prices and markets for companies and industries.)

Keynes's great achievement began with the apparently simple step of dividing the effective demand for all goods and services (as recorded by the national economic statistics) into separate categories, and then scrutinizing each category. He insisted, for example, that consumption must be analyzed separately from investment, since the two were determined by different types of decisions. Expenditures by consumers on food, clothing, appliances, theater tickets, and the like were fundamentally different decisions from those by companies to invest in factories, office buildings, and capital equipment. Keynes revolutionized the way the world thought about national economies with his simple statement that

$$Y = C + I$$

in which Y (Gross National Income or Product) is determined by the sum of Consumption plus Investment.

The classification of these accounts was vital to useful analysis and diagnosis of economic problems because the elements of national income behave very differently from each other. Consumption and Investment typically rise and fall at divergent rates, and this was particularly true for the years 1929–1933. An examination of these numbers shows what was happening far more clearly than contemporaries, who did not have the numbers to work with, were able to grasp:

Table 1

	1929	1931	1933
Real GNP (Y)	$203.6b	$169.3b	$141.5b
Consumption (C)	139.6b	126.1b	112.8b
Investment (I)	40.4b	16.8b	5.3b

Source: *Economic Report of the President 1969* (Washington, D.C.: Government Printing Office, 1969), p. 228. All numbers are in billions of constant (1958) dollars. Government outlays are omitted from the table, as are imports and exports (both are included in the figures for GNP).

As the figures show, Investment declined during the Depression much more sharply than did either GNP or Consumption. GNP dropped by 31 percent from 1929 to 1933, Consumption by 19 percent, and Investment by an almost unbelievable 87 percent.

These numbers suggest the psychological as well as the economic nature of the Depression, and in so doing they point to a policy prescription. The downward spiral of Investment from 1929 to 1933 reflected an almost unanimous conviction among business executives (who made nearly all of the decisions about whether or not to invest) that conditions were not going to improve. Perceiving no upturn, they were driven by the logic of the market not to manufacture increased quantities of their products, and therefore not to invest in new plant and equipment. They were compelled by the same reasoning to lay off workers, and unemployment rose higher and higher:

Table 2

	1929	1930	1931	1932	1933
Unemployment (percent)	3.2%	8.7%	15.9%	23.6%	24.9%

Source: *Historical Statistics of the United States: Colonial Times to 1970* (Washington, D.C.: Government Printing Office, 1975), p. 135.

Keynes's diagnosis took full account of business psychology. The fundamental problem, he wrote in 1933, was not economic at all, but a "failure in the immaterial devices of the mind." Executives could not in good conscience invest their corporations' money or re-hire laid-off workers, because they sincerely believed that the business cycle was still spiraling downward. By their own standards — the standards of a private economy, not a mixed one — they were correct. In the meantime, however, the unemployed had no income and could not buy sufficient goods to stimulate national demand. And so the spiral continued, driven by its own imperatives.

But Keynes did not propose to leave it at that. Some outside force had to intervene, and the only such force possessed of the required resources was the government. "I hope the reader will feel," he wrote, "whether or not he thinks himself competent to criticise the argument in detail, that the answer is just what he would expect — that it agrees with the instinctive promptings of his common sense." If the private sector would not spend, then the public sector must. New outlays by government would alleviate unemployment, break the downward business spiral, create the prospect of recovery, and stimulate new investment by private companies. The only way to save the private market economy, in other words, was to mix public initiatives into it.

Why had such proposals not been acceptable before? For two reasons, said Keynes, both of which at first blush seemed reasonable. The two reasons, as he put them, were "the meagreness of the employment created by the expenditure of a given sum, and the strain on national and local budgets of the subsidies which such schemes usually require." In other words, governments did not have the money, and even if they did there would be only a dollar-for-dollar return on their expenditure.

It was on these two points that Keynes's logic became controversial, and a little complex. As for the first question, the lack of money, he was frank to admit that what he called "loan expenditure" (deficit financing) would be necessary. But he argued strenuously that in a downturn government's borrowing was preferable to its raising the tax rate and spending the revenues so collected. Raising taxes in order to finance increased expenditure largely "represents a redistribution, not a net increase in national spending power." Borrowing for government expenditure, on the other hand, would create new income, thus stimulating the economy. And, in any case, it was far preferable to doing nothing, a course which in the context of world depression actually threatened to bring down the capitalist system.

On the second question, the dollar-for-dollar return, Keynes proposed a breathtaking theory centered around a device which he called "the multiplier." By ingenious logic, he argued that in a situation of vast unemployment the expenditure of, say, $100 by government would ramify through the economy with the effect of an expenditure of twice that sum, or even more. The precise multiplier depended on persons' "marginal propensity to consume." If, for example, the goverment paid $100 to wealthy persons, they probably would save most of it, since they probably had purchased most of the goods they wanted already. On the other hand, if government took $100 of money which it had borrowed and paid it to a previously unemployed worker, then that worker would quickly spend the entire $100 on the necessities of life. And those to whom he paid his $100 would respend their portions too, at a rate carefully estimated by Keynes to yield at least a doubling of the original outlay by government. In the process, tax monies would be generated which would return to government, reducing the net outlay of the funds it had borrowed. This multiplier effect, therefore, meant that the total outlay necessary to return an economy to prosperity was far less than it might appear from the rest of his theory. Keynes's proposal seemed a magical remedy, if only the intellectual logjam could be broken.

"Why should this method of approach appear to so many people to be novel and odd and paradoxical?" he asked. "I can only find the answer in the fact that all our ideas about economics, instilled into us by education and atmosphere and tradition are, whether we are conscious of it or not, soaked with theoretical presuppositions which are only properly applicable to a society which [has] all its productive resources already employed." Those seeking a remedy for unemployment, said Keynes, were proceeding on a "theory which is based on the assumption that there is no unemployment."

Keynes wrote this analysis in 1933 for a newspaper audience. He published his fully argued treatise, *The General Theory*, in 1936. Many economists immediately recognized the book as a revolutionary diagnosis which explained why the depression had come, why it had stayed so long, and how it might be ended. But acceptance by some economists was one thing, adoption as public policy quite another.

2. MACROECONOMIC MANAGEMENT: THE POLICIES

It was not that Keynes's timing was wrong. Franklin D. Roosevelt was a president more than willing to experiment, and some of his actions were mildly "Keynesian" in nature. Indeed Keynes himself kept in touch with Roosevelt throughout the thirties. He offered his advice freely whenever he was asked, and often when he was not asked. Keynes wrote one of his several "open letters" to Roosevelt late in 1933, urging him toward a recovery program financed not by taxes but by loan-expenditure.

It was on the issue of deliberate deficits that the Keynesian Revolution temporarily foundered. For, in fact, there could be no greater heresy than to argue that red ink was somehow better than black. Even Roosevelt bridled at the idea. During the campaign of 1932 he had repeatedly attacked the Hoover Administration for its deficits. In his famous inaugural address of 1933, Roosevelt urged the American people to banish fear, but in the same speech he announced his own fear of unbalanced budgets: "We address ouselves to putting our own national house in order and making income balance outgo." After Keynes met Roosevelt for the first time in 1934, FDR complained that the great economist had showed him "a whole rigamarole of figures," and seemed a "mathematician rather than a political economist." Keynes himself confided that he had "supposed the President was more literate, economically speaking."

Neither Roosevelt nor the majority of his advisers, let alone most members of Congress, could ever bring themselves to contemplate deficit spending on the order Keynes was recommending. The New Deal's reputation for spendthrift policies, therefore, makes sense only when compared with what had gone before. Measured by what came afterward during the war years, not to mention the 1980s, federal budget outlays during the thirties were minuscule.

The numbers in Table 3 are overstated significantly in the later years because of inflation, but the major point is clear: the New Deal's expenditures never approached the orders of magnitude necessary for a test of Keynesian theory. Deficits five to ten times as large as those actually recorded would have been required to restore prosperity. (The deficits did not necessarily have to reach this level every year, but for at least two or three years running.) And spending on this scale was beyond the imagination of the thirties generation.

Table 3 The Federal Budget

FISCAL YEAR	RECEIPTS	OUTLAYS	DEFICIT OR SURPLUS
1929	$ 3.86 billion	$ 3.12 billion	+ $ 0.73 billion
1932	1.92b	4.66b	− 2.74b
1933	2.00b	4.60b	− 2.60b
1934	3.02b	6.65b	− 3.63b
1935	3.71b	6.50b	− 2.79b
1936	4.00b	8.42b	− 4.42b
1937	4.96b	7.73b	− 2.78b
1938	5.59b	6.77b	− 1.18b
1939	5.00b	8.84b	− 3.86b
1943	23.65b	78.53b	− 54.88b
1945	45.22b	92.69b	− 47.47b
1960	92.49b	92.22b	+ 0.27b
1970	192.81b	195.65b	− 2.85b
1981	599.27b	657.20b	− 57.93b
1983	666.12b	757.64b	− 91.52b

Source: *Economic Report of the President, 1969* and *1982* (Washington, D.C.: Government Printing Office, 1969, 1982), pp. 297 (1969), 318 (1982). All amounts are billions of current dollars. The figure for 1983 is an estimate from the Treasury Department and Office of Management and Budget; the deficit for that year exceeded the estimate by a very substantial margin. Even though federal outlays in the 1980s seem very much larger than for earlier years, in fact there has been no growth of government purchases of goods and services *as a percentage of GNP* since the early 1950s, contrary to popular mythology.

The only deliberately Keynesian policies the Roosevelt Administration implemented came after the recession of 1937–38. Believing the emergency to be over, the government reduced its spending in fiscal 1938 (as Table 3 shows), only to see another plunge of the stock market and rise in unemployment. In response to this "Roosevelt recession," outlays were increased once more and the deficit allowed to rise more than threefold during fiscal 1939. But even this was not nearly enough to bring back the good times of the twenties or to test the validity of Keynes's suggestions.

World War II, on the other hand, did provide the needed laboratory. Within the government during the early forties, a number of young economists cut their teeth on Keynesianism and applied its lessons to the tasks at hand. These included Paul A. Samuelson, John Kenneth Galbraith, and others destined for great influence later on. Working in such government agencies as the Office of Production Management and the Office of Price Administration, the young war managers saw at first hand what they believed to be a living validation of the Keynesian prescription. So dramatic was the turnaround during World War II that it was an economic lesson impossible to forget.

Nearly all economists of whatever persuasion were fearful during the early forties that once the war was over depression conditions might return. Accordingly, an enormous amount of debate and planning centered around the issue of how the postwar economy should be managed. Supporters of the kinds of "compensatory" policies associated with Keynes (that is, compensating for swings upward or downward of the business cycle) advocated an institutionalization of the new macroeconomic functions of government.

Their efforts met with partial success with the passage of the Employment Act of 1946. This legislation created the Council of Economic Advisers and the Joint Economic Committee of Congress, and required the president to submit an annual economic report setting forth the administration's plans for maintaining a healthy economy. Emphasizing aggregate measures and steeped in Keynesian assumptions, the Employment Act was a landmark in the federal government's evolving acceptance of responsibility for national prosperity. It was a fitting monument to Keynes, who died in the year it was enacted. The legislation passed both houses of Congress by very large majorities, a phenomenon that would have been unthinkable in 1929.

But it was not World War II alone that brought the intellectual revolution expressed by the Employment Act. Rather it was the New Deal and the war together, the entire turbulent experience of 1933–1945, the collective and very personal experience of that generation personified by the postwar presidents. Regardless of their rhetoric, once in office all presidents (with the exception of Ronald Reagan) consistently behaved in accordance with Keynesian principles. In 1970, Richard Nixon confirmed the fulfillment of the revolution when he said, "I am a Keynesian."

One reason for this almost unanimous embrace of the new role of government was its remarkable political appeal. For presidents, the great virtue of Keynesian-style "demand management" was that it concerned itself entirely with aggregates, and postulated that the growth of aggregate demand was the basic economic task of the federal government. In so doing, Keynesianism enlarged the purview of government, but it also begged the very much more difficult questions of distributional justice (which interest groups should get what, and at the expense of whom); and of management on the supply side (how to stimulate saving by the private sector and implement measures aimed at increasing productivity in particular industries). Instead, demand-oriented fiscal policy was calculated to enlarge the entire economic pie and thereby keep everyone happy. It did not presume to specify the size or appropriateness of individual pieces of the pie, as the New Deal had done. It did not explicitly favor one interest over another or seem to take away from some classes in order to give to others.

Compensatory fiscal management lay at the heart of the mixed economy. It steered a comfortable course between the extremes of socialism on the one hand and free market economics on the other. In the process it baffled many advocates of both. Proponents of the two extremes were able to agree with each other on very few points, but one thing that both insisted upon was the inevitability in capitalist economies of a business cycle with severe ups and downs. Keynesian economics denied this proposition. It proclaimed that government action could flatten out the business cycle and stabilize economic life. The enthusiasm with which thoughtful Americans embraced Keynesianism was based not only on its virtues as demonstrated during World War II but also on the attractiveness of the thought that a rising tide floats all ships equally. This was an extremely appealing idea to a nation that had passed through the divisive New Deal years, with the anti-Roosevelt rhetoric of the far Right matched by the antibusiness rhetoric of Socialists and of some New Dealers themselves.

The postwar embrace of Keynesianism, therefore, reflected not only a determination to avoid a new depression but also a wish to transcend the hostilities of New Deal politics. One can read this phenomenon in a number of postwar documents: John Kenneth Galbraith's *American Capitalism* (1952), which argued that "countervailing power" in the form of government and organized labor constitutes a restraint on the excessive autonomy of American business; or David E. Lilienthal's *Big Business — A New Era* (1953), a formerly militant New Dealer's paean to the American business system. The point was made especially clear in the *Economic Report of the President* for the year 1949, which drew an explicit connection between demand management Keynesian style and the American way of life. In a discussion of business-government relations within the new mixed economy, the *Report* argued:

> The particular urgency of this subject exists because there has now grown to maturity a whole generation of Americans touched by the influence of extremists who look upon conflict between business and government as normal. Conditioned by the depression era, extremists on one side have said that our business system broke down through fatal defects and that government took the whole leadership in putting it together again; while extremists on the other side have blamed government for all the tribulations of business. The new generation of Americans should always remember that the breakdown resulted from errors on the part of both government and business; that both joined in forging some of the most practical measures for recovery; and that both must admit imperfection because the recovery was incomplete until the war restored maximum production and employment. . . . We have now moved far enough away from the depression of the early thirties to start looking ahead, and to appraise the heartening evidence that free enterprise and free government have blended their varying strains into a rewarding effort. The conduct of the war was an example never to be forgotten.

The *Report* went on to describe in detail the ways in which aggregate demand management pacified the prior enmities between business and government, business and labor, big business and small business, and between other sectors and interest groups in the American economy.

3. MICROECONOMIC AND SECTORAL MANAGEMENT: THE PROGRAMS

Most New Deal programs were neither Keynesian nor otherwise macroeconomic in nature. Instead they were microeconomic, affecting particular industries and sectors. One program or another affected almost every part of the economy, but four sectors in particular merit special mention. These are banking, labor, agriculture, and regulated industries.

Banking

For most countries in most periods, a discussion of banking would belong under the heading of macroeconomics. Indeed, an influential body of opinion holds the Federal Reserve Board responsible for the severity of the Great Depression. The Board's error in contracting the money supply in 1930 and 1931 made the crisis much worse than it need have been. Conversely, Roosevelt's abandonment of the gold standard in 1933 was an extremely important step in the administration's efforts to increase the money supply, end the persistent deflation of the currency, and bring higher prices. Even so, most of the monetary significance of the New Deal is best understood by focusing not on management of the money supply (the principal macroeconomic function of central banks such as the Federal Reserve), but on the institutional structure of the banking system itself.

Both before and after the New Deal, the distinguishing characteristic of American banking was its atomization. Most other industrialized countries encouraged centralization and a system of branching out from a few very large banks. The American policy, on the other hand, was to limit branch banking severely and encourage the autonomous development of numerous independent banks. Most countries counted their banks by the dozen or the score, but Americans counted theirs by the tens of thousands. This unique policy reflected a survival of the wide-open banking practices of the American frontier and a continuing determination to prevent the creation of a centralized financial oligarchy. Most American banks were very small, regulated by the state governments, and tied only loosely into any national system. Membership in the Federal Reserve System was not mandatory, insurance of deposits was extremely casual, and in financial centers such as New York commercial banking mixed freely with investment banking. (That is, a single bank could accept deposits, make short-term loans to businesses, and help corporations create and market new issues of stocks and bonds.)

What happened during the twenties and thirties is evident from the huge number of banks that existed prior to the Great Depression, the frequency of bank failures, and the decline in banks' assets during the financial crisis of the early Depression.

It is evident from Table 4 that the Great Depression was in large measure a monetary crisis; that a destruction of depositors' con-

Table 4   American Banks and Bank Suspensions (Failures),
            1920-1980

YEAR	TOTAL NUMBER OF BANKS	TOTAL ASSETS	BANK SUSPENSIONS
1920	30,909	$53.1 billion	168
1929	25,568	72.3b	659
1931	22,242	70.1b	2,294
1933	14,771	51.4b	4,004
1934	15,913	55.9b	61
1940	15,076	79.7b	48
1950	14,676	179.2b	5
1960	14,019	282.9b	2
1970	14,187	611.3b	7
1980	14,870	1543.5b	10

Source: *Historical Statistics of the United States: Colonial Times to 1970*, pp. 1019, 1038-1039; *Statistical Abstract of the United States, 1981* (Washington, D.C.: U.S. Government Printing Office, 1981), pp. 510-511.

fidence in banks was inevitable given the frequent failures; that in 1933 or 1934 something happened to halt these failures; and that whatever it was had a permanent effect.

The New Deal actually took several different steps to restructure the banking system. The most dramatic of these was the "bank holiday" of 1933, when the new President closed every bank in the United States, ordered fresh cash from the Federal Reserve to fill their depleted vaults, then reopened the "healthy" banks a few days later. Of more importance in the long run was the creation of the Federal Deposit Insurance Corporation, a move that all but halted serious bank failures and that softened the impact on depositors even when a few banks did fail. This one change, ironically not regarded as of crucial importance at the time, did more than any other single thing to restore citizens' confidence in the system and therefore to encourage their resumption of deposits. Thousands of savers brought their currency out of socks and mattresses back to the banks, where it could be lent to businesses and other borrowers. The New Deal also separated commercial from investment banking, which ended the practice of using depositors' funds to underwrite questionable investments or stock market speculations.

Labor

Before the thirties, labor unions in America operated under heavy handicaps. Organizing efforts were often thwarted by industrialists who wanted to retain full power over their workforce. Whenever labor faced off with management, as in the Homestead strike of the 1890s or the steel strike of 1919, government either looked the other way or intervened on the side of management. The New Deal ended this pattern.

Labor recorded a significant gain with the National Industrial Recovery Act (NIRA) of 1933, but the real breakthrough came when Congress passed the National Labor Relations Act during the "Second Hundred Days" of 1935. The Wagner Act, as it was also called after its sponsor Senator Robert F. Wagner of New York, clarified and strengthened the prolabor provisions of the National Industrial Recovery Act. And it did so at an opportune time, since the Supreme Court had ruled the NIRA unconstitutional even as Congress was debating the Wagner bill. The new legislation of 1935 declared that workers engaged in interstate commerce had a "right" to join labor unions and bargain collectively with employers. The Act created a new regulatory agency, the National Labor Relations Board, and empowered it to conduct elections by secret ballot within corporations so that workers could choose their own bargaining agents. Sometimes different unions would claim the right to represent workers of a particular craft or industry, and sometimes a company itself would promote its own workers' organization. The Wagner Act insured that no worker would have to accept a company union if he or she wanted to join a different union of his or her own choosing.

The passage of the Wagner Act came at a time of rising labor militancy. With the new law behind them, workers began to organize as never before in American history. The Act required that employers recognize and bargain with unions in good faith, and the workers themselves showed their determination to win their rights in a series of novel actions such as the sit-down strike. One of these paralyzed mighty General Motors early in 1937. The strike was mounted by a small union called the United Automobile Workers (UAW), and before the year was out most Americans who read newspapers had become familiar with the UAW. Led by Walter Reuther and other militants, the auto workers' union was backed by the larger Congress of Industrial Organizations, whose colorful head, John L. Lewis, was the key figure in the impending rise of Big Labor in the United States. General Motors was led by Alfred P. Sloan, Jr., the architect of the company's great business success and one of the greatest management innovators in American history.

In effect, the sit-down strike was a test of the new national policy. Sloan, like other businessmen at the time, believed the Wagner Act might well be ruled unconstitutional by the Supreme Court, which had already invalidated much New Deal legislation. Accordingly, he took a hard line. "The real issue," he said in a statement to the workers, "is perfectly clear, and here it is: Will a labor organization run the plants of General Motors Corporation or will the management continue to do so? . . . In other words, will you pay tribute to a private group of labor dictators for the privilege of working, or will you have the right to work as you may desire? Wages, working conditions, honest collective bargaining, have little, if anything, to do with the underlying situation. They are simply a smoke screen to cover the real objective."

When the Governor of Michigan reluctantly stepped in to oust the strikers from the plants they were occupying, John L. Lewis, as he later recalled, sent back a chilling message: "I do not doubt your ability to call out your soldiers and shoot the members of our union out of those plants, but let me say that when you issue that order I shall leave this conference and I shall enter one of those plants with my own people. . . . And the militia will have the pleasure of shooting me out of the plants." Because labor violence had not been uncommon during the thirties, Lewis's message could not be taken lightly.

In the end, the union won. It was a spectacular victory, a milestone in the evolution of labor-management relations in American history. GM's Alfred Sloan, writing in his autobiography many years later, blamed it all on the government: "The UAW was able to enlist the support of the government in any great crisis [during the 1930s and afterward too]. . . . Sit-down strikes were plainly illegal—a judgment later confirmed by the Supreme Court. Yet President Franklin D. Roosevelt, Secretary of Labor Frances Perkins, and Governor Frank Murphy of Michigan exerted steady pressure upon the corporation, and upon me personally, to negotiate with the strikers who had seized our property, until finally we felt obliged to do so." Though the Supreme Court did not approve of the sit-down technique, it did uphold the Wagner Act in a ruling handed down shortly after the General Motors settlement. From that point forward the legitimacy of organized labor was confirmed, and union power stood poised for an unprecedented leap forward. Like Big Government, Big Labor was born during the New Deal, with the Roosevelt Administration serving as midwife. Statistics show the dramatic dimensions of the change:

Table 5   Labor Union Membership as Percentage of Total Labor Force

YEAR		UNION MEMBERSHIP	MEMBERSHIP AS PER-CENT OF LABOR FORCE
1930		3.6 million	6.8%
1933	(National Industrial Recovery Act)	2.9 million	5.2%
1935	(Wagner Act)	3.7 million	6.7%
1937	(Court upholds Wagner Act)	7.2 million	12.9%
1940		8.9 million	15.5%
1945		14.8 million	21.9%
1960		18.1 million	23.6%
1978		21.8 million	20.4%

Source: *Historical Statistics of the United States: Colonial Times to 1970*, p. 178; *Statistical Abstract of the United States, 1981*, pp. 379, 412. The percentages are higher for nonagricultural employment (e.g., a high of 35.5 percent in 1945). Compared with Europe, American membership is quite low, primarily because of the heavy organizing of white-collar workers in Europe.

As the numbers indicate, almost the entire modern growth of the American labor movement occurred during Roosevelt's administrations. Although collective bargaining was not one of FDR's primary interests, and although he himself never led the movement for new legislation, he did not object when union leaders invoked his name. "President Roosevelt wants you to join a union" was the most powerful organizing slogan of the thirties, and the time was so ripe for a quantum leap in union power that resistance by Sloan and other corporate executives was largely futile. The rise of Big Labor, with its huge assist from the federal government, was still another major step on the road to the mixed economy. Never again would business have quite the degree of autonomy it had enjoyed before the New Deal. From this point on, business's efforts to shape public policy would have to contend with a powerful labor movement sometimes working for very different ends.

Agriculture

"I tell you frankly," Roosevelt had said in 1933, speaking of the new Agricultural Adjustment Act (AAA), "that it is a new and untrod path, but I tell you with equal frankness that an unprecedented condition calls for the trial of new means." American farmers had been experiencing a harsh economic depression since the early 1920s. Prices of corn, wheat, cotton, and other crops had fallen to one-half or less their former levels. The government had to do something, and with the AAA, it sought to bring about a balance between production and consumption of farm products. The aim was to raise prices so that farm income might have the same purchasing power as other income — in a word, so that farmers might live on a basis of "parity" with their urban brethren. The Act gave the Secretary of Agriculture several means of achieving this elusive goal: AAA could pay farmers to take acreage out of cultivation, could allot acreage limitations for specific farms, and could thereby reduce the total production of major crops. The government could also lend to farmers, buy up surplus crops, and store, export, or sell these crops itself as conditions indicated. The initial program was to be financed by a tax on food processors, who in turn would pass along the cost to everyone who bought groceries.

In addition to AAA, the New Deal sponsored a Farm Credit Administration to make long- and short-term loans, a Resettlement Administration to address the needs of very poor farmers, and a Rural Electrification Administration to bring power to areas bypassed in the first period of development by private utilities. Some of the programs, AAA in particular, ran into serious problems. When the government ordered farmers to plow under every fourth row of cotton and to slaughter little pigs before they had grown to their customary market size, a chorus of critics objected that the New Deal was violating the laws of God and of common sense. The Socialist Norman Thomas remarked that the administration was trying to solve the problem of poverty in the midst of plenty by getting rid of the plenty. (To the protest on behalf of the little pigs, Secretary of

Agriculture Henry Wallace retorted that people seemed to be thinking that "every little pig has the right to attain before slaughter the full pigginess of his pigness.") If all this protest were not bad enough, in 1935 the Supreme Court ruled the processing tax unconstitutional, and the whole AAA program had to be reenacted in alternative form. But in this episode, as in many others, the New Dealers persisted, trying nearly any kind of remedy that might ameliorate the problem of depressed farm prices. Eventually their efforts were rewarded. Prices began to climb and agricultural prosperity began to return.

In evaluating the New Deal farm programs, it is important to keep in mind that, for better or worse, no large country in the world has an agricultural policy run entirely on the basis of free-market principles. Because farming is subject to wild swings of weather-induced periods of feast and famine, because food is of strategic importance in national development policies, and because farmers usually possess political power disproportionate to their numbers, all countries tend to make special provision for their farming sectors. The European Common Market protects its farmers against imports from North and South America, where agriculture is much more productive. The Japanese government subsidizes the cultivation of rice, paying domestic growers the astonishing figure of four times the world price and thereby insuring that an enormous crop is produced each year in the home islands.

American agricultural policy does not go to these extremes, but neither does it allow the free market to reign. Through a system of price supports, credit programs, inventory controls, and reclamation projects, the federal government reaches deep into the market relationship between producers and consumers. Most of this institutional framework grew directly out of the New Deal, and the fully developed system is a complex amalgam of public and private initiative, financing, research, control, and discretion—a microcosm of the American mixed economy. Most economists would argue that on a theoretical basis the agricultural sector today is allocated excessive amounts of resources, that prices for farm products are higher than they would be under a free-market system, and that there are still too many farmers in America. Comparatively speaking, on the other hand, American agriculture is one of the wonders of the world. It contributes mightily to American exports, helps the balance of payments, and feeds millions of people abroad. As the following table indicates, productivity has leaped forward dramatically since the New Deal, even as the total number of farms and farm workers has declined:

Table 6 Farms, Farm Workers, and Productivity in America

YEAR	NUMBER OF FARMS	NUMBER OF FARM WORKERS	PERSONS SUPPLIED PER FARMWORKER		
			TOTAL	IN U.S.	ABROAD
1910	6.4 million	13.6 million	7.1	6.1	1.0
1930	6.3 million	12.5 million	9.8	8.8	1.0
1940	6.1 million	11.0 million	10.7	10.3	0.4
1950	5.4 million	9.9 million	15.5	13.8	1.7
1960	3.7 million*	7.1 million	25.8	22.3	3.5
1970	2.7 million†	4.5 million	47.1	39.9	7.2

* Number is for 1959
† Number is for 1969
Source: Historical Statistics of the United States: Colonial Times to 1970, pp. 467, 468, 498.

The Regulation of Business

The first important federal regulatory initiatives came in the last part of the nineteenth century with the passage of the Interstate Commerce Act (1887) and the Sherman Antitrust Act (1890). Other regulatory outbursts occurred during the Progressive Era (antitrust prosecutions, food and drug legislation, enhanced power for the Interstate Commerce Commission, creation of the Federal Trade Commission), and during the early 1970s (environmental, health and safety, and consumer product regulation in the form of the Environmental Protection Agency, the Consumer Product Safety Commission, the Occupational Safety and Health Administration, and other agencies). But none of these periods quite equalled the New Deal in the number of industries brought under regulation.

The intellectual context was a conviction, born of the Great Depression, that the free market was hopelessly flawed. The same premises that underlay the Keynesian Revolution—that government should take a hand, the expert public servants were more likely than business executives to choose the wise course—also applied to microeconomic regulation. In several industries, the pattern resembled that in agriculture: government protection of the industry from overcapacity. This was true in the broadest sense in the National Recovery Administration (NRA), which sought to keep prices up by limiting the output of industrial products. (The NRA will be discussed in more detail below.) It was also true for particular industries.

Two cases in point were trucking and airlines. The New Deal brought these industries under the same kind of rate regulation and control over entry that the Interstate Commerce Commission (ICC) applied to railroads. The goal was to restore "order" by protecting existing airline and trucking companies from "excessive" or "chaotic" competition. In each case, the solution was a partial cartelization of the industry. Common-carrier trucking was subjected to the ICC's licensing and ratemaking power. Airlines were placed under a newly created Civil Aeronautics Board. And for the next forty years, the two industries operated under regimes of regulation indistinguishable from those of railroads and electric utilities.

By the 1960s, scholarly analysis had begun to conclude that neither trucking nor airlines should ever have been regulated in this manner. A number of economists held that neither industry was a "natural monopoly" like railroads and utilities. Instead, each was characterized by relatively low start-up costs, lots of willing entrepreneurs, and an industry structure like the normal run of enterprise. Accordingly, by the 1970s a "regulatory reform" movement had united a motley group of allies in opposition to trucking and airline regulation: Nader's Raiders, academic economists, liberal Democrats anxious to achieve reduced rates and fares, and conservative Republicans enamored of the free market. The upshot was the Airline Deregulation Act of 1978 and similar legislation for trucking over the next several years.

During the debates over these bills, the New Deal came in for a good deal of criticism. Skeptics argued that insofar as the regulation of trucking and airlines was protectionist in nature, then perhaps the entire New Deal was best understood as a gigantic drive for protection, not only by these two industries but also by farmers, labor union organizers, and other beneficiaries of the Roosevelt policies.

This was a penetrating and wonderfully appropriate question to raise about the New Deal. And, for the most part it was a new question. During the entire period between the thirties and the middle 1960s, the burden of scholarship in history and economics had been sympathetic to the New Deal. Most books and articles had praised Roosevelt's efforts as having at last tamed the excessive power of business. Now, however, the orthodoxy seemed turned on its head. If the patterns in agriculture, trucking, and aviation were typical, then perhaps the New Deal had not been a curb on business influence but a disguised helping hand extended by government to those very interests that it was supposed to be regulating. Had the New Deal indeed assisted business in its perennial efforts to "capture" the government?

The answer was that in some cases the system did evolve into a condition of capture (symbiosis might be a better metaphor), but that in most cases it did not. For every pattern like that in farming, aviation, and trucking, the New Deal had also taken some very different regulatory gambit. There was, for example, the prohibition of child labor and the passage of new food, drug, and cosmetics legislation. There was the strengthening of antitrust, with scores of new prosecutions. There was the Public Utility Holding Company Act of 1935 which, along with the Tennessee Valley Authority (TVA) and the Bonneville Power Administration, was anathema to the utility industry and to most businessmen in general. There were the Securities Act of 1933 and the Securities Exchange Act of 1934, which at last tamed Wall Street and brought corporate behavior into the sunshine with the requirement that all publicly owned companies submit annual reports certified by independent public accountants. Behind all these programs of microeconomic regulation stood not a particular ideology, not a single New Deal philosophy, but several competing ones.

4. MICROECONOMIC AND SECTORAL MANAGEMENT: THE PHILOSOPHIES

In both its rhetoric and its numerous programs, the New Deal affirmed the importance of particularistic management by government of the problems of individual industries and sectors. "Any neglected group," Roosevelt had said shortly before his inauguration, "whether of agriculture, industry, mining, commerce or finance, can infect our whole national life and produce widespread misery." The implication was clear: government should help each group.

From this premise, and in large part unintentionally, FDR helped to lay the basis for the legitimacy of demands by innumerable special interests, both economic and otherwise. New Dealers talked incessantly of the "public interest" even as their multitudinous new agencies laid the institutional basis for its fragmentation among particular groups. The explicit legitimization of interest groups was one thing about the New Deal that really was new, and it is possible to trace a line from the politics of the thirties to the present-day demands of an endless roster of interests: industries, labor unions, ethnic groups, feminists, farmers, and so forth. From the Left the fulfillment of some of these demands is denounced as "socialism for the rich," and from the Right as evidence that America has become a land of whiners and supplicants.

As usual, the reality is not so simple. For one thing, the New Deal obviously cannot be held responsible for the subsequent drift of American society. The generation of 1933 can no more be blamed for problems fifty years later than the generation of 1879 can be held responsible for the stock market crash of 1929. Roosevelt's remark about neglected groups was made at the very nadir of the economic depression, when nearly all groups were suffering. For another thing, it is almost impossible to generalize both broadly and accurately about the actual impact of New Deal economic policies. We have already seen the ambiguous relationship of the New Deal to Keynesian macroeconomic management. For microeconomic and sectoral issues, the record is similarly full of uncertainty. Each of the following pairs of statements, for example, is true. Yet each pair seems internally inconsistent:

1.   a. Through the National Industrial Recovery Act, the New Deal suppressed price competition among business corporations, encouraged cartelization, and suspended the antitrust laws.

b. The New Deal began the greatest antitrust campaign in American history. In the single year of 1940, the Department of Justice brought almost as many suits as had been brought during the first two *decades* under the Sherman Act.

2.   a. Most banks, large corporations, and other pillars of the economic establishment benefited enormously from the New Deal.

b. Most bankers, executives of large corporations, and other wealthy Americans detested Roosevelt personally and voted overwhelmingly against the New Deal.

3.   a. The New Deal's agricultural programs were the first in American history to address the problems of very poor farmers.

b. The New Deal's agricultural programs benefited large landowners most, sharecroppers and tenants least.

4. a. Three of the most important economic legacies of the New Deal were social security, labor legislation, and federal insurance of bank deposits.
    b. Three New Deal measures that Roosevelt cared least about and that were forced on him by his allies in Congress were social security, labor legislation, and federal insurance of bank deposits.
5. a. The New Deal sponsored the fullest range of economic planning in American history up to that time.
    b. The New Deal had no overall planning program, and foreign observers later spoke of the "antiplanning" philosophy of the system that evolved from New Deal initiatives.

Given these correct but conflicting propositions, the best generalization about New Deal economic policy was that it was plagued with inconsistency and at odds with itself intellectually. Every agency created by the New Deal had administrative conflicts among its members. Many New Dealers feuded with each other, and many resigned in protest when their policies were not implemented or when the president no longer heeded their advice. Roosevelt himself seemed unconscious of inconsistency, unworried about basing his policies on conflicting economic theories and then reversing himself in midstream. The history of the New Deal and the birth of the mixed economy, therefore, is a history of conflicting and competing ideas.

In retrospect, it is possible to see three major lines of economic thought within the New Deal. For a time one would dominate, then another, then a third. But all three persisted in significant strength throughout the thirties, right up until the time when the war in Europe began to drive economic issues from the top of the national agenda.

National Public Planning

The first line of thought advocated *national public planning*. Represented by such economists as Rexford G. Tugwell, Gardiner C. Means, and Mordecai Ezekiel (many New Dealers had marvelously unusual names), the planners tended to believe that the system had broken down beyond repair. For them the choice in 1933 was not between the free market on the one hand or a managed economy on the other. They assumed the need for economic management, and saw the essential policy decision as one of choosing the identity of the managers. Should they be private executives administering a system of gigantic trusts and monopolies, or public men devoted to genuine social and industrial planning, with participation by all affected groups? The national planners saw themselves as just such disinterested public men, and were more than willing to serve. They wanted a thorough reorganization of the industrial system, a new arrangement in which basic decisions about the allocation of resources would be made by boards of government experts. The planners were not Marxists or Fascists, though their critics called them both. They did not favor government ownership of the means of production, except that a good many of them did think that public ownership of utilities, transportation networks, and perhaps banks would be an improvement over existing regulation. A number of planners had academic backgrounds, and their heroes tended to be engineers, technicians, and other designers of rational systems.

In general, the planners had their greatest success in agricultural programs and in ad hoc experiments such as the Tennessee Valley Authority. Broader success eluded them because most citizens still believed that centralized planning went against the American grain. In the thirties, planning smacked of efficiency, but also of dictatorship. It brought to mind the radical experiments then going on in Germany, Italy, and the Soviet Union, where planning went forward at grievous cost to personal liberty.

The Business Commonwealth

The second major line of economic thought within the New Deal centered around the idea of a *business commonwealth*. Best represented by Hugh Johnson of the National Recovery Administration and private advisers such as Bernard Baruch and Gerard Swope, the proponents of the business commonwealth regarded dog-eat-dog competition as outdated. In its place they proposed the same system of industrial cooperation that had worked wonders for American mobilization in 1917 and 1918, during the Great War. In their view, the Depression had come about in part because too many businessmen had responded to the original economic downturn by cutting prices and wages, thereby forcing competitors to do the same thing, until the entire economy was swept into a downward spiral. This was "chiseling," in the idiom of the period. As the NRA's Hugh Johnson (a former army officer) put it, the economy needed to be rescued from too much "eye-gouging, knee-groining [sic] and ear-chewing in business."

If this required suspension of the antitrust laws, then so be it. The country was in crisis, and the remedy was to be found in cooperation. Each industry would be governed by a "code of fair competition," and the system as a whole would amount to "industrial self-government." Thus the frenzy of code writing in 1933 and 1934 for many hundreds of industries large and small. And thus the publicity of the NRA's symbol the Blue Eagle and its slogan "We Do Our Part." In substance, the codes called for the restriction of output in order to push up prices, and a standardization of work practices and product quality.

Despite the promising hoopla, the NRA did not work well. The clash between labor and management, consumers and producers, large companies and small ones made it a disillusioning experience. Even if the Supreme Court had not ruled the NRA unconstitutional in 1935, Congress would probably have allowed it to die. Yet the NRA had provided an important psychological boost, and it did give the appearance of action. In the largest sense its failure may have had less to do with inherent logical contradictions than with the failure of the macroeconomy to recover. Had prosperity somehow returned in 1934 and 1935, the NRA doubtless would have received much of the credit. Yet the measures in and of themselves, for good or ill, had too little impact to be held responsible for either the success or failure of the overall national economy.

Decentralization

The third major stream of thought was the philosophy of *decentralization*, expressed most vividly in the antitrust tradition. During the thirties, the custodians of this influential body of thought all seemed somehow or other to be connected with Professor Felix Frankfurter of the Harvard Law School or with Frankfurter's *éminence grise*, Justice Louis D. Brandeis. Roosevelt himself had known Frankfurter and Brandeis for many years, and within the government the decentralist tradition was represented by a large cadre of unusually talented lawyers working in the new agencies: David E. Lilienthal of the TVA, Benjamin Cohen of the Public Works Administration, James M. Landis and William O. Douglas of the Securities and Exchange Commission (SEC), Thomas Corcoran, who had assisted Cohen and Landis in drafting securities legislation, and Alger Hiss, who worked in the Agricultural Adjustment Administration with a group of other secretly radical or communist lawyers.

But if there was anything the decentralists were not, it was communists. Most of them, at this stage of their lives, disliked bigness in business, government, or any other realm of life. The Brandeisians among them put their faith in a world of small, independent units. Although institutions kept getting bigger and bigger, Brandeis once said, men kept coming in the same size and therefore had trouble handling the gigantic new institutions. To Brandeis and his disciples, big business — especially holding companies and firms in oligopolistic industries — had not grown to their large size because of superior efficiency. Instead, they had used unfair methods to drive others out of business. Centralized wealth, centralized control, and centralized location were all part of the same problem. The embodiment of all three was Wall Street. Accordingly, the antitrusters directed their most withering fire at the citadels of high finance and big business.

A spirited antitrust movement began in 1938, but the onset of World War II soon afterward meant that maximum industrial output for victory, and not the strict tenets of fair competition, was to be the national priority. In the end, the greatest achievement of the decentralist tradition was the very effective system of securities regulation built up by the SEC between 1934 and 1940. And on close examination, this system was not at all dissimilar to some of the models of ideal government which had been proposed by the advocates of the business commonwealth.

The Conflict of Principles

The same point might be made about the New Deal as a whole. Neither the decentralists, the proponents of the business commonwealth, nor the national public planners ever fully captured the New Deal or the mind of Roosevelt. There was no single New Deal policy, even at a specific time. Each of the three main streams of thought (there were several minor ones as well) retained strength through the entire decade. In the overall sense, therefore, the New Deal was a mélange of inconsistent and conflicting principles. On any one policy, FDR might blow first hot, then cold. Some of the antitrust prosecutions taken up late in the thirties attacked arrangements made earlier under the auspices of the National Recovery Administration. Even within individual agencies, all three policies might be present, strongly represented and struggling with each other. One part of the NRA or the AAA might do something another branch would attempt to undo. Within the TVA, the decentralists crusaded effectively against the holding companies that controlled local electric plants; at the same time, others in the same agency were planning for the coordinated development of the Tennessee Valley region; and still others were promoting the growth of a business commonwealth and an end to cutthroat competition.

In the end, the three lines of thought sometimes cancelled each other out. More often, and much more significantly, each one achieved a limited success and institutionalization. Thus all succeeded and all survived the thirties. Yet all failed as well, insofar as the New Deal itself failed to end the Great Depression.

In the deepest sense, the meaning of the New Deal transcends judgments of success or failure. In laying the basis for the mixed economy, it almost perfectly captured and embodied the divided lines of economic thinking present in the American people. For an administration that wanted to remain in power during an economic depression without sacrificing democratic political traditions, as the Roosevelt administration most assuredly did, an ability to be all things to all voters was a singular political virtue. Roosevelt's policies were confusing and inconsistent, but to condemn them for lack of intellectual coherence is to miss one of the main points about them. And indirectly, it is to condemn all mixed economies for their theoretical inelegance. From an ideological standpoint, the New Deal was illogical. But from a political standpoint it was marvelous. Its very inconsistency facilitated its appeal to a broad range of otherwise mutually hostile groups.

Early in the New Deal, Roosevelt had said, "What we seek is balance—balance between agriculture and industry and balance between the wage earner, the employer and the consumer. We seek also balance that our internal markets be kept rich and large, and that our trade with other nations be increased on both sides of the ledger." On this basis, Roosevelt created an amazing political coalition which kept power for decades after his own death. He himself never suffered either at the polls or in his own mind from his economic inconsistency. Indeed, he may never have grasped it.

5. THE NEW DEAL AND THE MIXED ECONOMY: AN ASSESSMENT

In retrospect, the New Deal is best understood as a political settlement involving numerous disaffected interest groups. By bringing
these groups into the mainstream of American life, Roosevelt not
only rebuilt the Democratic party and secured his own unprecedented hold on the White House but also brought the disparate
parts and classes of the country together. He legitimized the attention to their own interests given by the farmers, the elderly, the
blacks, and others hit especially hard by the depression. Again and
again he invoked the image of the "forgotten man," and he made it
his business to attend to the needs of all sectors of the economy.

In subsequent generations, this beginning, so appropriate to the
conditions of the thirties, did not always have a happy ending. The legitimization of interest groups sometimes detracted from the trans-
cendence of the overall "public interest," irrespective of how one
might define that elusive idea. The institution of federally sponsored
old age survivors' insurance, begun so tentatively under the Social
Security Act of 1935, was augmented repeatedly by ever more
generous Congresses until by the 1980s it threatened to undermine
national solvency. Big Labor, helped through adolescence by the
New Deal, in manhood took on a Jekyll-Hyde character, securing high
wages for its members at the expense of American competitiveness
against industrial powers such as West Germany and Japan. Regulation, begun in response to different kinds of crises even during the
thirties, evolved through years of war and prosperity into unimpor-
tant bureaucratic routine, only to resurface suddenly as a major national issue during the 1970s. At that time it was seen not as a solution
to the Depression-era problems of deflation and declining prices, but
as part of the intractable new problems of stagflation and rising costs.

Two points are clear from these experiences. The first is the historical truism that change is the only constant and that no problems
have permanent solutions. The New Deal solutions were specific to
the situation, and the salient situation of the thirties was the Great
Depression, with its prolonged deflation. Even if other economic aspects had been similar (which they were not, on the whole), this deflation alone would have made the thirties decisively different from
later periods. For the decade 1929–1939, the compound annual
deflation rate was 1.4 percent. By contrast, for the period 1968–

1982, the compound annual *in*flation rate was 6.7 percent. Policies set up in the thirties to deal with declining prices were certain to seem inappropriate for a reverse situation years later.

The second point is that despite the New Deal's many innovations, the American political economy remains a fragmented system and not a coherent, centralized one. Some of the state bureaucracies which were born during the thirties — in particular relief agencies such as the Public Works Administration, the Civilian Conservation Corps, and the Works Progress Administration — have long since disappeared. A great many others, however, have grown to maturity, and in so doing they have developed problems typical of institutional middle age. But they have remained competitive with each other. They vie for access to the presidential ear, just as they did during the New Deal. They compete for influence on national policy. They fight for annual appropriations from Congress. And modern presidents, like Roosevelt, do not so much direct the system as perform the role of "broker-in-chief."

This distinctive American pattern derives in large part from our historic abhorrence of centralized power. As the English scholar Andrew Shonfield remarked of the post-New Deal period, the United States "has so far appeared as the outstanding laggard in the general movement of the Western world towards the eager acceptance of a vastly enlarged role for the central government in economic affairs." In this sense a comparison with other countries is essential to a proper perspective on the nature of the New Deal and the American mixed economy. Certainly the degree of centralization and public control is less in the United States than in most democratic market economies. There is only a tiny amount of public ownership, for example, in contrast to the pervasive pattern of state-owned enterprise in other capitalist countries, not to mention socialist economies. The total tax bite from all government units in America has now reached one-third of gross national income, up enormously from about one-ninth in the years before the New Deal. But again this one-third figure pales beside the 60 percent bite in Sweden and the Netherlands, and the 45 percent in West Germany, France, and Great Britain. Against that background, the United States remains at the low end of the spectrum of state management, with a system still tilted more toward private than public influence.

The most important historical fact about the American mixed economy in the half-century since Roosevelt's first inauguration has been its outstanding performance over sustained periods. The same is true of similar systems in Europe and Japan. As the economist Paul Samuelson said at the beginning of the 1980s, "The mixed economy is *mixed*. That is its strength: to mobilize for human ends the mechanisms of the market and to police those mechanisms to see that they do not wander too far away from the desired common goals." This is what the New Dealers were trying to do, and our own generation might be well advised to emulate their efforts. As difficult as our economic problems are, theirs were far worse, and it will be to our credit if we meet ours with the boldness and creativity they brought to theirs.

SUGGESTED READINGS

Because of the centrality of economic issues during the 1930s, most of the general bibliography of the New Deal is relevant. The standard works contain a wealth of information on the economy and economic thought, especially Frank Freidel, *Franklin D. Roosevelt: Launching the New Deal* (Boston, 1973); William E. Leuchtenberg, *Franklin D. Roosevelt and the New Deal* (New York, 1963); Paul Conkin, *The New Deal* (Arlington Heights, Ill., rev. ed., 1975); and Arthur M. Schlesinger, *The Age of Roosevelt* (Boston, 1957–60).

Useful specialized histories include Lester V. Chandler, *America's Greatest Depression, 1929–1941* (New York, 1970); and Broadus Mitchell, *Depression Decade: From New Era through New Deal, 1929–1941* (New York, 1947), which is dated and flawed in other ways as well, but which contains a mass of statistical data. Charles H. Hession and Hyman Sardy, *Ascent to Affluence* (Boston, 1969) has superb interpretive coverage of the 1929–1945 period. Andrew Shonfield, *Modern Capitalism: The Changing Balance of Public and Private Power* (New York, 1965) is a superior cross-national analysis.

Martin Feldstein, ed., *The American Economy in Transition* (Chicago, 1980) is an exceptionally thorough and useful examination of recent economic trends. Glenn Porter, ed., *Encyclopedia of American Economic History*, 3 vols. (New York, 1980), contains long and very informative articles by leading scholars. Especially relevant to the New Deal are the essays on Agriculture, Antitrust, Central Banking, Economic Thought, The Economy Since 1914, Financial Intermediaries, Government Management of the Economy, Law and Political Institutions, Prices and Wages, Regulated Industries, and Savings and Investment.

The story of the revolution in macroeconomics is well told in Robert Lekachman, *The Age of Keynes* (New York, 1966), and Herbert Stein, *The Fiscal Revolution in America* (Chicago, 1969). Of special importance in understanding monetary policy during the period is Milton Friedman and Anna J. Schwartz, *The Great Contraction* (Princeton, 1965). See also Peter Temin, *Did Monetary Forces Cause the Great Depression?* (New York, 1976); and Karl Brunner, ed., *The Great Depression Revisited* (Boston, 1981).

The classic analysis of contending economic philosophies is Ellis Hawley, *The New Deal and the Problem of Monopoly* (Princeton, 1966). Useful studies of particular agencies or problems include Otis L. Graham, Jr., *Toward a Planned Society: From Roosevelt to Nixon* (New York, 1976); Susan Estabrook Kennedy, *The Banking Crisis of 1933* (Lexington, Ky., 1973); John Morton Blum, *From the Morgenthau Diaries*, 3 vols. (Boston, 1959–67); Irving Bernstein, *The Turbulent Years: A History of the American Worker, 1933–1941* (Boston, 1969); Sidney Fine, *Sit-Down: The General Motors Strike of 1936–1937* (Ann Arbor, Mich., 1969); Paul K. Conkin, *Tomorrow a New World: The New Deal Community Program* (Ithaca, N.Y., 1959); Theodore Saloutos, "New Deal Agricultural Policy: An Evaluation," *Journal of American History* 61 (September 1974): 394–416; Richard S. Kirkendall, *Social Scientists and Farm Politics in the Age of Roosevelt* (Columbia, Mo., 1966); John A. Garraty, *Unemployment in History, Economic Thought and Public Policy*, (New York, 1978); James T. Patterson, *America's Struggle Against Poverty 1900–1980* (Cambridge, Mass., 1981); Roy Lubove, *The Struggle for Social Security, 1900–1935* (Cambridge, Mass., 1968); Thomas K. McCraw, *TVA and the Power Fight, 1933–1939* (Philadelphia, 1971); Bernard Bellush, *The Failure of the NRA* (New York, 1975); Michael Parrish, *Securities Regulation and the New Deal* (New Haven, 1970); and Joel Seligman, *The Transformation of Wall Street* (Boston, 1982).

The New Deal and Social Welfare

Robert H. Bremner

The term "social welfare," denoting the common interests of private social work and public welfare, was in use in the 1930s but did not gain wide currency until after World War II. The words used in the 1930s to indicate the pressing economic concerns of the time were "recovery," "relief," and "security." Recovery remained the prime objective of the New Deal through all its permutations. New Deal efforts to provide relief for the unemployed and security for workers determined the form and direction of American social welfare for a half century after 1933. This essay examines Franklin D. Roosevelt's attitudes toward relief and security as expressed in his public messages and addresses, the development of New Deal programs for relief and social security, and evaluations of those programs at the end of the New Deal era. In the concluding section the significance of the New Deal's achievements and shortcomings in social welfare are viewed from the perspectives of both fifty years earlier and fifty years later.

ROOSEVELT'S ATTITUDES TOWARD SOCIAL WELFARE

In August 1931, at a time when President Hoover was seeking to assist the unemployed by mobilizing and coordinating the charitable resources of the nation, Governor Franklin Roosevelt told a special session of the New York state legislature that "aid must be extended [to the unemployed] by Government, not as a matter of charity but as a matter of social duty." Roosevelt acknowledged that in normal times and under ordinary conditions relief of the poor was a function of local government and private agencies. He emphasized that the $20 million he proposed to take from state funds for apportionment among counties and cities was to supplement amounts raised locally. As if to reiterate the extraordinary circumstances that made state action necessary, he proposed the name "Temporary Emergency Relief Administration" for the commission responsible for distributing the fund. Roosevelt made clear his own preference for work relief as opposed to "the dole" and recommended that if local officials were unable to find or provide work for public service, relief should take the form of food, clothing, and shelter. "Under no circumstances," he declared, "shall any actual money be paid in the form of a dole . . . by the local welfare officer to any unemployed [man] or his family."

Early in 1932 Roosevelt commended Senator Robert Wagner for his efforts to get federal appropriations for relief. Federal aid was justified and sorely needed in the present crisis, said Roosevelt, "although it should not be regarded as a permanent Government policy." Roosevelt's speech accepting the Democratic nomination for President had little to say on the subject of relief except that "while now, as ever" primary responsibility rested with localities, the federal government "has always had, and still has a continuing responsibility for the broader public welfare." During the closing weeks of the campaign he declared that when states and communities were unable to provide necessary relief "it then becomes the positive duty of the Federal Government to step in to help." This was, in fact, the course reluctantly adopted by the Hoover Administration in the summer of 1932 when the Reconstruction Finance Corporation began to make loans to states for relief and public works. In his inaugural address of March 4, 1933, Roosevelt indicated he was willing to go substantially further, including "direct recruiting" of the unemployed by the federal government for work on "projects to stimulate and reorganize the use of our natural resources."

Scarely a month after taking office, President Roosevelt signed the executive order establishing the Civilian Conservation Corps (CCC), the first and longest-lived New Deal unemployment relief agency. Within three months the CCC had enrolled 250,000 young unemployed men, 25,000 World War I veterans, and 25,000 experienced woodsmen and put them to work on reforestation, soil conservation, and similar projects in parks and forests at more than 1,400 camps across the nation. In Roosevelt's words, "It was the most rapid large-scale mobilization in our history." Enrollees received $30 a month (of which all but a small allowance was ordinarily sent home to their families), plus food, shelter, clothing, transportation, medical and dental attention, and, after the program had been in operation for some time, the opportunity for general educational and vocational training. During the life of the program enrollees sent a total of $670 million in allotments to their families. After 1937 family need was given less consideration in selection of enrollees and, in 1939, the director of the Corps announced, "The CCC as a monetary relief and job-giving agency has been replaced by the CCC as a work-training agency." When the program came to an end in June 1942 more than 2.5 million youths had served in the CCC; enrollment hit a peak of 500,000 in August 1935 and a low point of 240,000 in March 1937. As late as 1940, more boys entered the Corps each year than entered colleges and universities as freshmen.

In the message to Congress proposing the CCC, Roosevelt also pointed out the need for grants to the states for relief and recommended establishment of an office of Federal Relief Administration "to scan requests for grants and to check the efficiency and wisdom of their use." The Federal Emergency Relief Act, adopted on May 12, 1933 in response to Roosevelt's request, was a landmark in the development of federal-state cooperation in the relief of distress. It authorized outright grants, instead of loans, to the states, transferred administration of the grants from the Reconstruction Finance Corporation to a new social agency, the Federal Emergency Relief Administration (FERA) and, by giving the agency authority to make or withhold grants, allowed the federal government to exert some influence over the kind and quality of relief offered in the states. Roosevelt's remarks on signing the measure emphasized that localities and states must do their utmost to relieve the needy before the federal government would make funds available. In fact, the need for immediate assistance was so well recognized that Harry L. Hopkins, former director of the New York State Relief Commission, approved grants to seven states on the day he took office as head of FERA.

Under Hopkins' leadership, and partly because there were few precedents to follow, the FERA proved one of the most resourceful and innovative of all New Deal executive agencies. In theory it simply supplemented the work of local and state governments, by providing funds dispensed by local officials with a minimum of federal direction. One of the FERA mandates was that its funds should be spent only through public agencies, a requirement that strengthened public agencies and, in some communities, brought them into existence. In addition to making funds available (or withholding them and thereby stimulating laggard states to bestir themselves), the FERA maintained programs for transients, distributed surplus commodities supplied by the Agricultural Adjustment Administration to people on relief, instituted a rural rehabilitation program for the needy in rural areas, and granted funds to colleges and universities for the employment of students on part-time work projects.

Both Roosevelt and Hopkins vastly preferred work relief to direct cash relief, which Roosevelt often referred to, always slightingly, as "the dole." Hopkins recognized that direct relief might tide the unemployed over a period of a few months or even a year, but he believed that when people were out of jobs for a long time, worklessness was as destructive as physical want. Hopkins also distinguished between work relief of the leaf-raking or snow-shoveling kind, favored by some local governments, and employment on a federally financed work project. "To the man on relief," Hopkins observed, "the difference is very real." He went on to note:

> On work relief, although he gets the disciplinary rewards of keeping fit, and of making a return for what he gets, his need is still determined by a social worker, and he feels himself to be something of a public ward, with small freedom of choice. When he gets a job on a work program, it is very different. He is paid wages and the social worker drops out of the picture. His wages may not cover much more ground than his former relief budget but they are his to spend as he likes.

In November 1933 Roosevelt announced the establishment of the Civil Works Administration (CWA), a branch of the FERA, which was intended to take 4 million persons off relief rolls and convert them, for the winter of 1933–34, into "self-sustaining employees" on small public works projects. During the four and a half months that the CWA operated, Hopkins and his lieutenants devised 180,000 work projects which, at their peak in mid-January 1934, employed slightly more than 4 million persons. Most of the jobs were in construction projects but the CWA also set up projects for teachers, engineers, architects, artists, nurses, and other white-collar workers. The total cost of the CWA was just under $1 billion, nearly 80 percent of which went for wages.

Both during and after the CWA experiment with federally controlled work projects, FERA continued to make grants to states for direct relief of persons who could not be employed on the work projects. After the dissolution of the CWA in the spring of 1934, the FERA supported an Emergency Works Relief Program, transferring to it a number of CWA projects and employees. The FERA continued efforts begun under the CWA to adapt work relief to the occupational skills and backgrounds of people from all walks of life.

In the State of the Union message of January 1935, Roosevelt distinguished between the 1.5 million relief recipients who, for reasons of age or physical or mental incapacity, were unable to maintain themselves independently, and the 3.5 million employable persons then on relief rolls who were victims "of a nationwide depression caused by conditions which were not local but national." Care of the former group, "the unemployables," had traditionally been a local responsibility. In declaring that "the Federal Government must and shall quit this business of relief," Roosevelt signified his intention to return responsibility for their care to local and state officials, justifying the decision by "the dictates of sound administration." "The dictates of sound policy," strongly influenced by the President's reverence for "the moral and spiritual values of work," determined his prescription for the employables: "Work must be found for able-bodied but destitute workers," he declared. "We must preserve not only the bodies of the unemployed from destitution but also their self-respect, their self-reliance and courage and determination."

The Emergency Relief Appropriation Act of 1935, passed at Roosevelt's recommendation, authorized a massive federal works program with an initial appropriation of nearly $5 billion. The Works Progress (after 1939 Projects) Administration, headed by Harry Hopkins, replaced the FERA as the key agency in the fight against unemployment. Over the next eight years the WPA received a total of $11.4 billion in appropriations and gave work and wages to 8.5 million people. WPA employment rolls varied from month to month and year to year in accordance with the availability of funds and the administration's not always accurate prediction of economic conditions. In September and October 1937, when a deep recession was commencing, the number of WPA workers fell below 1.5

million; during the latter half of 1938, when the recession was easing, there were more than 3 million WPA workers.

One of the WPA's tasks was to coordinate and report on the progress of the forty other federal agencies, including the CCC, the Public Works Administration, and the National Youth Administration (NYA), a subsidiary of the WPA, all of which participated in the works program. The NYA, for example, gave employment on work projects to 2.5 million out-of-school youth aged 16 to 25, and funded part-time work projects that allowed 2 million young people to remain in school. The WPA approved and supervised "small useful projects"— mainly in the fields of construction, reclamation, rehabilitation, and conservation—sponsored by state and local governments, which paid for most of the nonlabor costs. The 1935 Appropriation Act included "assistance for educational, professional, and clerical persons" among the projects authorized for support by the WPA. Drawing upon the experience of both the FERA and the CWA, Hopkins funded projects capable of using the labor or talent of people in fields as diverse as equipment operating, acting, dancing, painting, music, and historical research. WPA projects enhanced the quality of life in countless communities, not only in tangible, brick-and-mortar ways, but by supporting educational, cultural, and recreational opportunities and amenities. The projects promoted literacy programs, surveyed and preserved historical and architectural records, and fostered awareness and respect for the diversity and richness of American culture. In 1943, when Roosevelt awarded the WPA an "honorable discharge," he saluted its record in rendering "almost immeasurable kinds and quantities of service," and "reaching a creative hand into every county" of the nation. "It has added to the national wealth," he said, "has repaired the wastage of depression, and has strengthened the country to bear the burden of war."

The contributions of New Deal work projects to the morale of workers employed on them is harder to measure than the physical and social results of the programs. It is important to keep in mind that their purpose was not to rehabilitate the unemployed but to rescue them from idleness and to foster a sense of self-respect among people not deemed responsible for their misfortune. The distinction Roosevelt and the New Deal made between the unemployed and chronic dependents, and the special status accorded the "employables," made for a more favorable public attitude toward, and a better self-image among, the unemployed. But, as the years passed and the Depression dragged on, the difference between the "new poor" and the "old" became less apparent. The distinction between employables and unemployables, always sharper in principle than in application, became thoroughly blurred before the end of the 1930s.

A *Fortune* survey of unemployment and relief, made in 1937 under the mistaken impression that the Depression was over, concluded "the despised WPA" had worked, even if expensively. Most of the countless criticisms of the works program alleged waste, extravagance, and inefficiency on the part of project management and loafing on the part of employees. Hopkins, however, in a book appropriately entitled *Spending to Save* (1936), maintained that the most telling and truthful criticism was "We have never given adequate relief." In 1934–35 under FERA, the average *monthly* grant paid to an unemployed worker and his family (less than $30) was about the same as the average *weekly* wage of an industrial worker before the Depression. WPA workers received a "security wage," higher than direct relief under the FERA but less than the prevailing wage in the community for a comparable job in private industry. In 1941 WPA monthly earnings for the country as a whole averaged $60, somewhat less than the total benefits (cash allowance, clothing, shelter, subsistence, and medical care) received by CCC enrollees, which amounted to $67 a month.

Hopkins once acknowledged that the Roosevelt Administration, in its eagerness to win acceptance for the federal works program, "overemphasized the undesirability of relief." Roosevelt's 1935 State of the Union message denounced relief as "a narcotic, a subtle destroyer of the human spirit." Later in 1935, he admitted "a dole would be more economical than work relief," but added, "Most Americans want to give something for what they get. That something, in this case honest work, is the saving barrier between them and moral disintegration. We propose to build that barrier high." The WPA's official *Workers' Handbook* (1936), distributed to new employees, asked and answered a loaded question:

> What happens to us when we are on the dole?
> We lose our self-respect. We lose our skill. We have family rows.
> We loaf on street corners. Finally, we lose hope.

Such attacks on direct relief were unfortunate, as Hopkins conceded, "inasmuch as we have not been able to remove from hundreds of thousands of people the inescapability of accepting it." "Seeking" would have been a better word than "accepting" because New Deal work projects, despite their number, variety, and the large appropriations supporting them, were never adequate to care for all of the needy unemployed. There was always a pool of employable persons, certified to be in need and eligible for assignment to federal work projects or special youth programs, who were not added to the rolls because funds were not available for their employment. At various times after 1935, the number of these unfortunates ranged from 600,000 to 1.3 million a month.

After 1935, except for subsistence grants to poverty-stricken farmers, distribution of surplus commodities, and grants-in-aid for groups covered by the Social Security Act, the federal government left relief of the poor (often called general assistance) entirely to local communities, with such assistance as the states chose to provide. With federal aid withdrawn and with either no state funds or inadequate ones, local authorities faced, but seldom met, the need for helping both the unemployables and many of the employables. The federal relief administration no longer, as under the FERA, had any leverage for inducing or compelling states to bolster local efforts. Had Roosevelt and Hopkins chosen to do so, they might have diverted some funds from work relief to direct relief since all the emergency relief appropriation acts from 1935 through 1939 stated that the appropriated funds might be used for "relief" as well as "work relief." Their refusal to do so, despite clear need for such action, shows how strongly committed a supposedly pragmatic administration was to certain moral assumptions and to traditional assignments of responsibility for poor relief.

SOCIAL SECURITY

In 1928, while campaigning for the governorship of New York, Roosevelt endorsed his party's platform pledge for a study of old-age pensions, a subject then as radical and socialistic, he joked, as factory inspection and workmen's compensation had seemed twenty years earlier. After the election a commission jointly appointed by legislative leaders and Governor Roosevelt studied the problem, issued a report, and early in 1930 the chairman of the commission introduced an old-age pension bill in the legislature. Roosevelt was disappointed in the report and unenthusiastic about the bill which, instead of providing for a contributory system with uniform application throughout the state, made old-age pensions an extension of the poor laws and allowed local authorities wide discretion in administering them. "Our American aged do not want charity," Roosevelt asserted, "but rather old age comforts to which they are rightfully entitled by their own thrift and foresight in the form of insurance." Despite his objections he accepted the measure as a stopgap and a possible beginning toward something better: "We can only hope that this will be a forerunner of a proper system of security against old-age want in the years to come."

In accepting the Democratic nomination in 1932, Roosevelt cited "work and security" as the goals toward which he and the party should strive. After a little more than a year in the presidency, he declared that the first objective of the administration was security for individuals and families and announced his intention of furthering the objective through social insurance. In June 1934, Roosevelt told Congress that he was looking "for a sound means which I can recommend to provide at once security against several of the great disturbing factors in life—especially those which related to unemployment and old age." Roosevelt made it clear that he believed the funds necessary to provide the insurance should be raised by contributions of workers and employers rather than by general taxation, and that the insurance system should be national in scope. To study the matter further and recommend a "sound means," he appointed a Committee on Economic Security, which he directed to report its findings and recommendations no later than December 1, 1934.

The committee consisted of the secretaries of the Departments of Labor (chairman), Treasury, and Agriculture, the Attorney General, the Federal Emergency Relief Administrator, an advisory council composed of representatives of industry, labor, and social welfare, a technical board made up of officials from interested federal agencies, and a staff directed by Edwin E. Witte, an expert on social legislation and chairman of the Department of Economics at the University of Wisconsin. The members and staff of the committee worked under the pressure of time; against the background of agitation for proposals such as the Townsend Plan and Huey Long's

Share-Our-Wealth Plan,* which the President considered unsound and too radical to be considered; in receipt of contradictory testimony from expert witnesses; and amidst uncertainty whether the Supreme Court would recognize the constitutionality of any national system of social insurance. Committee members were divided in their opinions about the relative importance of unemployment and old-age insurance. Those who thought unemployment insurance was the most urgent issue were further divided between supporters of a national system under federal control and a federal-state system permitting the states greater freedom for experiment and innovation. The President's views, possible congressional reaction, and questions of administrative feasibility all had to be taken into consideration in weighing alternatives. As a result, a key member of the group, Arthur J. Altermeyer, recalled, "the committee did not arrive at its final recommendations without considerable travail." The legislative program recommended by the committee included:

1. a federal-state system of unemployment insurance;
2. a compulsory, federally administered old-age insurance system, financed by contributions from employees and employers, with benefits payable to insured workers at age 65; and
3. federal grants-in-aid to the states for old-age pensions (for people too old to benefit from the old-age insurance system), for the support of dependent children, for an expanded public health program, and to finance maternal and child health and welfare programs.

In January 1935, Roosevelt transmitted the committee's report to Congress with a message that strongly endorsed the proposed Economic Security Act and warned against discrediting "the sound and necessary policy of Federal legislation for economic security" by applying it, at the outset, on too ambitious a scale. He specifically noted that the measure he recommended for adoption did not include health insurance. During congressional consideration of the economic security bill, witnesses referred to it as the "social security bill" and it was the Social Security Act that finally received the ap-

---

* The Townsend Plan proposed paying a pension of $200 per month to everyone over the age of sixty who promised to spend the sum within a month. Long's Share-Our-Wealth plan advocated the liquidation of private fortunes so that the government could distribute enough money for each family to buy a home, a car, and a radio.

proval of Congress and, on August 14, 1935, Roosevelt's signature. Social security, a more inclusive term than economic security, covered the three areas or kinds of programs provided for in the act: protection against some of the "hazards and vicissitudes of life" by social insurance; provision of public assistance for certain categories of the needy; and extension of public services to promote public health, child and maternal health and welfare, and rehabilitation of the handicapped. The act created a new federal agency, the Social Security Board, to keep the records and make payments to the millions of workers to be covered by the old-age insurance program, to exercise general responsibility for the federally subsidized (but state-administered) unemployment insurance plans, and to supervise the program of grants-in-aid to states for old-age assistance, aid to dependent children, and aid to the blind.

Roosevelt's statement on signing the Social Security Act sounded a note between pride in its enactment and modesty in recognition of its limitations. The measure, in his words, would give "at least some measure of protection" to an estimated 30 million persons who would benefit from unemployment compensation, the public assistance programs, and services for children and public health. It would give "some measure of protection to the average citizen and to his family against the loss of a job and against poverty-ridden old age." Most important, in the President's view, the law represented "a cornerstone in a structure which is being built but is by no means complete."

Knowledgeable contemporary observers mixed criticism of shortcomings of the act with recognition of its significance and optimism about possibilities of improving it. The economist Paul Douglas, a long-time advocate of social insurance, called it "a worthy effort to protect better the lives of wage-earners and salaried employees," but "full of weaknesses" and "merely a first step which must soon be followed by others." Edith Abbott, a noted social-work educator, criticized the act's failure to provide grants-in-aid for general relief, for low benefits, gaps in coverage, and absence of a health insurance program. On balance, however, she concluded: "We can also count great gains. In the first place, and of tremendous significance, the responsibility of government and industry to insure security will be recognized for the first time. The system can and will be improved in the light of experience."

In contrast to the CCC, the FERA, and the WPA, the Social Security Act was intended to launch a permanent, rather than a temporary, program. Appropriations to carry out its provisions were the first—with the exception of the Railroad Retirement Act of 1934, which was declared unconstitutional in 1935—in the area of relief and public welfare without the prefix "emergency." Adoption of the act inaugurated a lasting commitment, as well as a significant involvement, on the part of the federal government in social welfare. Supreme Court decisions in 1937 made possible continuance and further development of the federal government's activity in programs for protection against economic insecurity. In *Steward Machine Co.* v. *Davis,* a case involving the unemployment insurance titles of the act, Justice Benjamin Cardozo, noting the billions of dollars spent on unemployment relief between 1933 and 1936, declared "the *parens patriae* [the state as parent and protector] has many reasons—fiscal and economic as well as social and moral—for planning to mitigate disasters that bring these burdens in their train." In *Helvering et al.* v. *Davis,* Justice Cardozo, again speaking for the majority of the Supreme Court, unequivocally endorsed the constitutionality of the old-age insurance titles: "The problem [old-age poverty] is plainly national in area and dimensions. Moreover, laws of the separate states cannot deal with it effectively. . . . Only a power that is national can serve the interests of all."

On the same day the Supreme Court sustained the Social Security Act, the President sent a special message to Congress stating, "The time has arrived for us"—meaning the three branches of the federal government—"to extend the frontiers of social progress, by adopting a minimum wage law." Roosevelt presented the measure, which revived some of the wage, hours, and child-labor provisions of the NRA codes, overthrown by the Supreme Court in 1935, as essential to economic recovery. Its objectives were "to reduce the lag in purchasing power of industrial workers and to strengthen and stabilize the markets for the farmers' products." In calling for a floor under wages and a ceiling over hours, he appealed to the nation's sense of fairness but not to pity: "A self-supporting and self-respecting democracy can plead no justification for the existence of child labor, no economic reason for chiseling workers' wages or stretching workers' hours."

In the year that elapsed, and during the three sessions of Congress that met while the wage-hour bill was under consideration, opponents offered numerous amendments and the House Rules Committee attempted to prevent a vote on the measure. Most of the seventy-two amendments sought to weaken the act by broadening the industries and occupations exempted and by narrowing the coverage of workers to whom it applied. Roosevelt vigorously supported the bill, always emphasizing economic rather than humanitarian arguments for its passage. In January 1938, referring to underpaid industrial workers, he said, "Aside from the undoubted fact that they thereby suffer great human hardship,"—and apparently of equal or greater import in Roosevelt's view—"they are unable to buy adequate food and shelter, to maintain health or to buy their share of manufactured goods." His approach may have been influenced by the sharp economic recession of 1937–38, but it was consistent with his general tendency to look at social problems from what he called "the practical, dollars-and-cents point of view" and to justify social legislation on the grounds of common sense and fair play.

As finally adopted in June 1938, the Fair Labor Standards Act provided, at the start—in those industries and occupations not exempted from its provisions—for a minimum wage of 25 cents an hour to go into effect at once and gradually to be increased to 40 cents; a maximum workweek of 44 hours (to be reduced within three years to 40 hours) with time-and-a-half pay for overtime work; a prohibition of the shipment in interstate commerce of goods produced by children under 16 years of age (18 in hazardous industries); and the establishment of a Wage and Hour Division in the Department of Labor to supervise application and enforcement of the Act.

Like the Social Security Act, the Fair Labor Standards Act represented only a modest beginning toward realization of its objectives. Roosevelt recognized that the rudimentary standards established by the Act fell far short of the ideal. "Backward labor conditions and relatively progressive labor conditions," he explained, "cannot be completely assimilated and made uniform at one fell swoop without creating economic dislocations." For constitutional reasons, the Act applied only to employees in manufacturing establishments that shipped their products in interstate commmerce, and for political and/or expedient reasons it exempted agricultural workers, employees in intrastate retail and servicing establishments, seamen, fisherman, and employees in a number of other industries. Of the approximately 850,000 children under 16 years of age who were gainfully employed in 1938, only about 50,000 came within the purview of the act. Children in agriculture, the street trades (selling newpapers or other merchandise in the streets), messenger and de-livery service, stores, hotels, restaurants, bowling alleys, filling sta-tions, and similar intrastate enterprises were not subject to the law. As in the case of the Social Security Act, a favorable decision by the Supreme Court on the constitutionality of the Fair Labor Standards Act — *United States* v. *Darby Lumber Co.* (1941) in which the court endorsed a broad interpretation of the powers of Congress under the interstate commerce clause — permitted subsequent broaden-ing of coverage and elevation of standards.

In 1939 Congress passed the first of a series of amendments to the Social Security Act, which extended its coverage to more workers and improved benefits to the insured and their dependents. The 1939 amendments incorporated recommendations developed over a period of two years by the President, the Advisory Council on Social Security, and the Social Security Board, which was given the task, in the 1935 Act, of conducting studies and making recommendations for legisla-tion and policies to improve economic security through social insur-ance. The most important of the numerous changes made by the 1939 amendments converted old-age insurance into Old Age and Survivors' Insurance (OASI) by making wives and young children of insured workers eligible for monthly benefit payments in the event of the work-er's death either before or after retirement. OASI thus became a system offering protection both to individual workers and their families. The amendments also improved benefits under the public assistance pro-gram for Aid to Dependent Children by increasing the federal match-ing ratio from one-third to one-half of the aid granted. The amend-ments also provided for larger federal contributions to federal-state pro-grams in public health, maternal and child health, child welfare ser-vices, care of crippled children, and vocational rehabilitation.

Almost a decade earlier, disappointed in the New York State old-age pension law, Roosevelt admitted "progress comes slowly." He could point to the 1939 amendments with some pride as a further advance toward the "kind of old-age insurance . . . our most progressive thought demands" and as evidence that progress is possible, even if slow.

RELIEF

In any single month between 1933 and 1940 at least 10 percent, and at times more than 20 percent, of the American population received aid from one or another of the New Deal relief or work programs, and general relief furnished by local and state governments. The high point came in February 1934 when the CCC, the FERA, the CWA, and general relief provided work or direct relief for 28 million people (22 percent of the population) in 8 million households. The low came in September 1937 when the WPA, the CCC, the NYA, and other work and public assistance programs aided 13.5 million people (10 percent of the population) in 4.5 million households. Even in June 1940, after the defense and war boom was under way, at least 6.5 million households still relied on federal work and construction projects and other forms of public aid.

Distribution and control of the expenditure of funds made available for grants-in-aid and work projects made it necessary for the federal government to create an administrative organization in Washington and in the field, and to devise regulations to ensure that funds were spent for the purposes intended. Consequently, after 1933, the federal government came to exercise greater authority than ever before over the kinds of public aid provided and the methods used to distribute it. *Security, Work and Relief Policies* (1942), an analysis prepared by the Committee on Long-Range Work and Relief Policies of the National Resources Planning Board, concluded that the FERA, through its policies governing the expenditure of federal funds in states and localities, profoundly and favorable influenced local relief policies. Under the FERA, and despite Roosevelt's earlier objections, cash relief gradually supplemented relief in kind. In keeping with Roosevelt's and Hopkins' convictions, the FERA encouraged work relief rather than the dole. The FERA rules and regulations, promulgated in July 1933, specified that in the distribution of relief funds "there shall be no discrimination because of race, religion, color, noncitizenship, political affiliation, or because of membership in any special or selected group." The FERA provided the only nationwide, federally supported program for "nonresidents," 200,000 or more unattached individuals and 50,000 family groups who could not meet state settlement requirements.

When the FERA ceased at the close of 1935, federal administrative and financial participation in general relief came to an end. Some states and communities retained methods and standards established under the FERA; others imposed more stringent eligibility requirements, restored harsh administrative practices, and reverted to the meager standards of poor law relief. Few were ready or able to give adequate assistance to the migrants, the sick, the disabled, and the hundreds of thousands of unemployed employables left on their hands by the demise of the FERA. Grace Abbott, professor of social work at the University of Chicago, former chief of the Children's Bureau, and one of the framers of the children's provisions of the Social Security bill, was among the many social workers who criticized the New Deal for its decision to "quit this business of relief." In a lecture delivered in 1939, Abbott asserted: "The end of federal aid for the general relief program has been a continuing tragedy for all the destitute — whether employable or unemployable. We are told that work is the American way of caring for the 'employables,' but is there any reason why the nonemployables should not be cared for in the American way, and does anyone think that the American way has been followed since the federal grants-in-aid for relief came to an end in 1935?" Although appreciative of the objectives and many of the results of the federal works projects, Abbott maintained experience had demonstrated that the WPA's goal of providing work for all the unemployed was unattainable. "It is not now politically possible or administratively practical," Abbott said, "to guarantee employment to all those who are able to work but who are or will be unemployed."

Partly because the federal government contributed nothing to general relief after 1935, its share of the nation's total relief bill dropped from 75 percent in 1934 and 1935 to 60 percent in 1940 and 1941. Even after 1935, however, national programs and policies, particularly the tax-offset and grant-in-aid provisions of the Social Security Act, continued to influence social welfare in the states. Only one state had passed an unemployment compensation law before 1935 and four more states passed such laws in 1935 in anticipation of the adoption of the Social Security bill. Under the stimulus of the Act, and often with the advice of the Social Security Board and using draft bills provided by it, all states, territories, and the District of Columbia had adopted unemployment compensation laws before July 1937. There was no precedent for such rapid, nationwide adoption of major social legislation. The categorical assistance programs were also adopted with unusual dispatch: old-age assistance was in effect in all states by the end of 1937, and aid to the blind and aid to dependent children were adopted in forty of the states. These three programs allowed states freedom to establish eligibility and the amount of assistance but laid down requirements that states had to meet in order to quality for grants. Officials of the Social Security Board's Bureau of Public Assistance supervised the programs to ensure compliance with the general requirements — for example, that programs be uniform throughout a state. The 1939 amendments empowered the Social Security Board to require that states and local communities use the merit, rather than the spoils, system in making appointments to administer the programs.

In the late 1930s, Congress, responding to or reflecting anti-New Deal or anti-"Washington" sentiment in states and communities, imposed increasing tight limitations on the kinds and numbers of people the WPA could employ, the kinds of projects to which the workers could be assigned, conditions of employment, and quantities of materials, supplies, and equipment available to the works program. A poll conducted in 1939 by the Institute of Public Opinion revealed public ambivalence toward the WPA: people in all walks of life and every state answered "WPA" most often when asked to name "the greatest accomplishment" of the Roosevelt Administration and also when asked to name "the worst thing" the New Deal had done.

Donald S. Howard noted both the sharp division in public opinion and the adverse effect of congressional restrictions in his generally favorable, but not uncritical, study, *The WPA and Federal Relief Policy* (1943). The book opened with the statement: "Never before in the history of the human race has a public works program, whose principal object was the mitigation of need due to unemployment, reached the magnitude of the Works Projects Administration." Howard shared the view of those who regretted and criticized the administration's refusal to participate in "a really decent national program of direct assistance to help meet needs arising from any cause and in any section of the country." Nevertheless, he recognized the "inestimable value" of the WPA in saving millions of people from idleness, acknowledged that the work accomplished by the WPA represented "priceless gains" to the American people as a whole, and paid tribute to Roosevelt and Hopkins for their social vision, human sympathy, energy, and leadership.

The New Deal response to unemployment relief, economic insecurity, and public assistance was part of, and inevitably influenced by the general response of the American people to these problems. In this country, as Howard and others have pointed out, relief measures are generally hampered by public resistance to increased taxation and suspicion of bureaucratic inefficiency, political corruption, and bossism. Generous sympathy for those known to be in need mingles with fear of being duped and misgivings about the need and consequences of heavy outlays for the unknown and faceless poor. Even in times of severe economic depression, some people cling stubbornly to individualistic theories of the causes and cure of want. In providing relief and work projects for large numbers of the unemployed, Roosevelt overcame some of the traditional fears and misgivings about public aid, but these reservations acted as a brake on developing more adequate provision of public assistance for all who needed it. In social welfare, as in other fields, the New Deal followed a middle course abominated by traditionalists, scorned by radicals, and not entirely satisfactory to the more forward looking of the President's own supporters.

SOCIAL WELFARE

A year before Franklin Roosevelt was born and fifty-one years before his election to the presidency, William Graham Sumner, a Yale political economist, asserted that the task of dealing with social ills was not a new ideal but a continuation of humankind's age-old struggle with the problems of social welfare. Sumner, like Benjamin Franklin, regarded individualism and self-help as the only effective methods of securing improvement in human affairs. He was both pessimistic and cynical about the possibilities of social reform: "It would be hard to find a single instance of a direct assault by positive effort upon poverty, vice, and misery," he declared, "which has not either failed or, if it has not failed directly and entirely, has not entailed other evils greater than the one which it removed." In Sumner's opinion "the only two things which really tell on the welfare of man on earth are hard work and self-denial . . . , and these tell most when they are brought to bear directly upon the effort to earn an honest living, to accumulate capital, and to bring up a family of children to be industrious and self-denying in their turn."

In 1883 the single-tax philosopher and reformer Henry George responded to Sumner in a series of magazine articles published in book form under the title, *Social Problems*. (Sumner's articles in a rival periodical were also published in 1883 under the title, *What*

Social Classes Owe to Each Other.) George scoffed at Sumner's "Gospel of Selfishness," the teaching that "the saving word for society" was for each to mind his own business. Instead of individualism and self-help, George stressed the interdependence of individuals and classes imposed by modern technology and economic arrangements: "Social progress makes the well-being of all more and more the business of each . . . . He who observes the law and the proprieties, and cares for his family, yet takes no interest in the general weal, . . . is not a true Christian. Nor is he a good citizen."

Sumner and George differed not only on the methods of social progress but on the possibility of overcoming want. Sumner assumed that the pressure of population on scarce resources and the competitive struggle for existence circumscribed opportunities for wholesale improvement in economic conditions and restricted the enjoyment of wealth to the prudent, energetic, and lucky. George maintained that it was not the scarcity of resources but their waste, monopolization, and mismanagement that caused poverty. He believed that by adopting a comparatively simple reform—the single-tax on land values—society could unlock the bounty of nature and make it possible for all to live in comfort, decency, and security.

Sumner's and George's attitudes and approaches to social welfare represent the two sides of the American coin. In any period of American history each has its adherents; sometimes one view is dominant, sometimes the other. Although it is unlikely that Roosevelt consciously made a choice between them, his outlook in most respects was closer to George's than to Sumner's. Roosevelt was not a utopian. Unlike George, he had no panacea—except work—to cure social ills, and he did not expect social gains to be scored all at once and once and for all, but he did believe that American abundance in human and natural resources made hope and confidence more appropriate than despair. Roosevelt saw and always presented the nation's problems as man-made rather than imposed by providence; he not only accepted but welcomed the need for action to correct social ills; and he never doubted the possibility of achieving changes that would promote the common welfare. In his message to Congress proposing the minimum-wage, maximum-hours bill he cited cogent reasons why "exponents of the theory of private initiative as the cure for deep-seated national ills" were wrong:

... first, they see the problem from the point of view of their own
business; second, they see the problem from the point of view of
their own locality or region; third, they cannot act unanimously
because they have no machinery for agreeing among themselves;
and, finally, they have no power to bind the inevitable minority of
chislers within their own ranks.

As Roosevelt saw it supporters of the private enterprise theory of
reform had always resisted legislation to advance social progress. "In
actual practice," he said, [social progress] "has been effectively advanced only by the passage of laws by state legislatures or the National Congress."

Sumner devoted two chapters of *What Social Classes Owe to
Each Other* to "The Case of a Certain Man Who Is Never Thought
Of" and made "The Forgotten Man" the subject and title of one of
his most popular essays. The man (and woman) Sumner had in mind
was the ordinary worker and taxpayer who, in Sumner's opinion,
had been neglected by philanthropists and reformers; the latter
seemed to think the only people worth attention were the poor and
the weak, described by Sumner as "the nasty, criminal, whining,
crawling and good-for-nothing people." Roosevelt, in a preconven-
tion radio address in 1932, borrowed Sumner's phrase, "the forgotten man," and applied it to the same commonplace folk with whom
Sumner had sympathized—homeowners, farmers, workers and
would-be workers, "the infantry of our economic army"—but
Roosevelt alleged they had not been forgotten by reformers, but by
the Hoover Administration.

As President, Roosevelt used "the average man" or "the average
citizen and his family" rather than "the forgotten man" to denote the
segment of the population the New Deal meant to serve. After the
policies of the Republican administrations of the 1920s, champion-
ship of the common man was novel enough to win Roosevelt the
reputation of a radical among the groups he dubbed "economic
royalists." New Deal programs were broad enough to bring a great
many, varied people in different kinds of activities and representing
different economic interest groups within the meaning of "the
average man." Under the broader definition, the ordinary American
came to seem a much more interesting and attractive figure than
Sumner's prosaic "forgotten man," or the boobs and Babbitts who
were thought by some to typify the population in the 1920s.
Whether because of the New Deal or for other reasons, the 1930s

was one of the few times in recent American history when intellectuals and artists treated the lives and experiences of everyday Americans with respect rather than contempt and derision.

Roosevelt's Second Inaugural Address, which contained the moving sentence, "I see one third of a nation ill-housed, ill-clad, ill-nourished," hinted that the New Deal might broaden its concern from the average to the less-than-average Americans, the people who were not so much forgotten as routinely overlooked and whose interests were seldom taken into consideration by shapers of public policy. Roosevelt declared, "We are determined to make every American citizen the subject of his country's interest and concern; and we will never regard any faithful, law-abiding group within our borders as superfluous."

Through various programs carried out under the FERA, the Resettlement Administration, and the Farm Security Administration, the New Deal expressed at least intermittent concern for the plight of the desperately poor. Other New Deal decisions, such as the distinction drawn between employables and unemployables and the cessation of federal grants for direct relief, signified that the administration was willing to sacrifice the interest of marginal people to the welfare of people deemed more deserving of help from the federal government. Even being self-supporting was not enough to bring workers in low-status jobs under the coverage of the Social Security and Fair Labor Standards Acts, both of which, as originally adopted, excluded domestic and agricultural labor. Ten years after the passage of the Social Security Act, one-third of black male workers and two-thirds of black female workers were in jobs not covered by the act.

In the early years of Social Security, when contributions far exceeded disbursements, critics complained of the large reserves accumulating in the OASI trust fund. During World War II, against strenuous objections from Roosevelt, Congress postponed scheduled increases in contributions and limited taxes collected from employers and employees to 1 percent. The Revenue Act of 1944, which Roosevelt denounced as "a tax relief bill providing relief not for the needy but for the greedy," contained a provision (strongly backed by Republicans) authorizing appropriations to the trust fund of "such additional sums as may be required to finance the benefits and payments" provided under the OASI title of the Social Security Act. The provision was removed by the Social Security

Amendments of 1950 which, for the first time, increased OASI contribution rates. Subsequent expansion of coverage and liberalization of benefits, like the original Act, were based on the assumption that the contributory method of financing old-age, survivors, and (after 1956) disability insurance was preferable to the so-called "charity method" of supporting the programs by appropriations from general revenue. In practice, payment to retirees, survivors, and the disabled depended on a steady flow of contributions from people still working. By the 1980s, demographic developments and projections, as well as widespread unemployment, made changes in financing the Social Security system imperative.

Fifty years after the start of the FERA, the federal government was still deeply involved in the "business of relief." One of the main reasons was the program of grants-in-aid to states for Aid to Dependent Children inaugurated by the Social Security Act. Roosevelt never endorsed the view advanced in 1934 by a veteran social worker, Homer Folks, that receiving relief when it is needed and properly administered is less demoralizing for recipients and a sounder policy for society than allowing need to go unrelieved. Long before 1935, however, he supported the idea of public assistance for children "thrown on the mercy of the community by the death, the insanity, the desertion, or the incapacity of their fathers." Instead of institutionalizing the children, Roosevelt favored the mothers' pension method of helping mothers to raise the children at home. "Money used to give these children a mother's love and a mother's rearing can never be wasted," Roosevelt announced in a campaign address in 1928.

Aid to Dependent Children was included in the Social Security Act because the framers recognized that fatherless children would not benefit from other provisions of the act, from work projects, or even from economic recovery. It was believed, however, that need for the program would gradually decline as more and more families came under the protection of Social Security. Contrary to expectations, and largely because of the general increase in the child population in the 1950s, the survival of poverty, and high rates of illegitimacy and desertion, the number of children and adult caretakers served by Aid to Families with Dependent Children (AFDC) expanded rapidly during the 1960s and 1970s. In 1980 the program assisted nearly 4 million families and more than 11 million individuals, of whom 7.6 million were children. The federal share of the cost of the program was $7.8 billion in 1981, $7.7 billion in 1982.

Despite acknowledged shortcomings—low benefits, benefits that vary from state to state and from section to section, sometimes insensitive administration, and failure to provide for many poor families in which the father is present—AFDC continues as an important example of federal-state cooperation in the relief of need. It is an essential source of support for poor, female-headed households. The original justification for the program—"to make universally available throughout the United States certain minimum standards of public protection, without which any private effort or any purely local effort is bound to be uneven and most inadequate in the places and areas where children are in the greatest need"—is still valid and has not yet been fully realized. That the nation has not yet been able to agree upon any better way of providing for its most deprived and unfortunate children is a reminder both of the New Deal's lasting significance and limited achievement in social welfare.

SUGGESTED READINGS

Samuel I. Rosenman, comp., *The Public Papers of Franklin D. Roosevelt,* 13 vols. (New York, 1938–1950) contains texts of FDR's campaign addresses, messages to Congress, statements on signing legislation, news conferences and miscellaneous correspondence relating to public events. Explanatory notes are provided for many documents.

James Leiby, *A History of Social Welfare and Social Work in the United States* (New York, 1978) presents New Deal relief and economic security measures in the perspective of American social welfare history; the three chapters dealing with the period 1930–1961 offer more detailed treatment of topics covered in this essay. John A. Garraty, *Unemployment in History, Economic Thought and Public Policy* (New York, 1978) compares the New Deal attack on unemployment with policies and programs followed in other countries, including Nazi Germany. William E. Leuchtenburg, *Franklin D. Roosevelt and the New Deal: 1932–1940* (New York, 1963) provides the most reliable and judicious brief history of the New Deal as a whole. James T. Patterson, *America's Struggle Against Poverty, 1900–1980* (Cambridge, Mass., 1981) contrasts New Deal relief and work projects with the War on Poverty programs of the 1960s. Patterson's *The New Deal and the States, Federalism in Transition* (Princeton, 1969) deals with conflicts and cooperation between relief administrators and state officials. John Braeman et al., eds., *The New Deal,* 2 vols. (Columbus,

Ohio, 1975), devotes one volume to development of New Deal policies at the national level, the other to the operation of the programs at the state and local levels.

Harry L. Hopkins, *Spending to Save, The Complete Story of Relief* (New York, 1936) is a lively and moving account of the author's experiences as New York State and federal relief administrator, dealing mainly with the FERA and the CWA. Raymond Moley, *The First New Deal* (New York, 1966) is informative on the origins of the WPA. Paul H. Douglas, *Social Security in the United States* (New York, 1939) surveys the background, provisions, and needed improvements in the Social Security Act. Edwin E. Witte, *The Development of the Social Security Act* (Madison, Wis., 1963) and Arthur J. Altmeyer, *The Formative Years of Social Security* (Madison, Wis., 1966) deal respectively with the planning and legislative history of the Act and developments in the Social Security program, 1934–1954.

The most informative, detailed, and balanced contemporary analyses and appraisals of New Deal social welfare programs are U.S. National Resources Planning Board, *Security Work, and Relief Policies* (Washington, D.C., 1942) and Donald S. Howard, *The WPA and Federal Relief Policy* (New York, 1943); both are sympathetic to New Deal aims but point out faults in execution and instances of unmet need. Two important articles emphasizing the necessity for change in public attitudes toward relief are Grace Abbott, "The Social Services a Public Responsibility" (1939) in *From Relief to Social Security* (Chicago, 1941) and Homer Folks, "Making Relief Respectable" (1934) in Savel Zimand, ed., *Public Health and Welfare, The Citizen's Responsibility, Selected Papers of Homer Folks* (New York, 1958).

Monographs treating particular New Deal agencies include John A. Salmond, *The Civilian Conservation Corps, 1933–1942: A New Deal Case Study* (Durham, N.C., 1967); Forrest A. Walker, *The Civil Works Administration, An Experiment in Federal Work Relief* (New York, 1979); Sidney Baldwin, *Poverty and Politics, The Rise and Decline of the Farm Security Administration* (Chapel Hill, N.C., 1968); William Francis McDonald, *Federal Relief Administration and the Arts* (Columbus, Ohio, 1969); and Jerre G. Mangione, *The Dream and the Deal: The Federal Writers' Project, 1935–1943* (Boston, 1972). Sar Levitan and Robert Taggart, *The Promise of Greatness* (Cambridge, Mass., 1976) examines post-1962 developments in the AFDC in a favorable light.

The New Deal and Race Relations

Harvard Sitkoff

Perhaps no aspect of the New Deal appears more anomalous or paradoxical than the relationship of Afro-Americans and the administration of President Franklin Roosevelt. On the one hand are the facts of pervasive racial discrimination and inequity in the recovery and relief programs, coupled with the evasiveness of New Dealers on civil rights issues. On the other hand, there is the adoration of FDR by blacks and the huge voting switch of Afro-Americans from the party of Lincoln to the Roosevelt coalition between 1932 and 1940. Faced with this enigma, some historians have concluded that Roosevelt gulled blacks in the 1930s, seduced them with rhetoric and gestures that left untouched the actual harm perpetuated by New Deal neglect and political cowardice. Others conjecture that the blacks' positive opinion of Roosevelt in the thirties had little to do with any effort the New Deal made to improve race relations and everything to do with the desperate need of Afro-Americans for the New Deal programs designed to aid the unemployed and the poor, regardless of color. As Congressman Jack Kemp of New York recently surmised: "Hoover offered a balanced budget, and FDR offered buttered bread." Both interpretations have greatly enriched our historical understanding of blacks and the New Deal. Together they give us a more accurate assessment of Roosevelt's shortcomings and his image as a savior. But, both interpretations omit the impact of the New Deal on civil rights in the context of the prevailing racial conservatism of the period. However limited and tentative they may seem in retrospect, the New Deal's steps toward racial justice and equality were unprecedented and were judged most favorably by blacks at the time. Their significance is the theme of this essay.

A RAW DEAL

Certainly no racial issue or matter had greater priority for blacks in the 1930s than the opportunity to earn a living or to receive adequate relief. The Great Depression devastated Afro-Americans, who were disproportionately mired in farm tenancy or who were the "last hired and first fired" in industry. At the bottommost rungs of the economic ladder, no group was in greater need of governmental assistance simply to survive. Accordingly, every civil rights organization and Afro-American leader scrutinized the various New Deal programs for their material effect on blacks. They found much to condemn. Blacks were never aided to the full extent of their need. New Deal legislation and local administration often resulted in discrimination against blacks or their exclusion from benefits. And, at times, the New Deal augmented the educational, occupational, and residential segregation of Afro-Americans.

However much blacks hoped for a new deal of the cards from Roosevelt, they found the deck stacked against them. The heritage of black poverty and powerlessness brought them into the Depression decade without the wherewithal to overcome at the local level those insisting that they remain the lowest social class or to prevail over their opponents at the national level in a political system granting benefits mostly on the power of the groups demanding them. Largely due to the measures taken by Southern state legislatures at the turn of the century to disenfranchise blacks, they could do little to lessen the President's dependence for New Deal legislation and appropriations on the white southerners who held over half the committee chairmanships and a majority of the leadership positions in every congressional session during the thirties. The very ubiquity of the worst depression in American history, moreover, limited the possibility of a major New Deal effort to remedy the plight of blacks. Hard times defined Roosevelt's mandate and kept the pressure on the New Deal to promote the economic recovery of middle-class America rather than to undertake either the long-range reform of the structural bases of poverty or to engage in a protracted effort to vanquish Jim Crow. In addition, the traditions of decentralization and states' rights further undermined the effort of blacks to gain equitable treatment from the New Deal. Despite the laudable intent of many Roosevelt appointees in Washington, those who administered the New Deal at the state and local levels, especially in the South, saw to it that blacks never shared fully or fairly in the relief and recovery projects.

Thus the National Recovery Administration (NRA) quickly earned such epithets as "Negroes Ruined Again," "Negro Run Around," and "Negro Rights Abused." The NRA wage codes excluded those who toiled in agriculture and domestic service — three out of every four employed blacks — and the administrators in Washington connived to accept spurious occupational classifications for black workers, or their displacement by white employees. Denied the benefits of the NRA's effort to raise labor standards, blacks nevertheless felt the impact of the NRA as consumers by having to pay higher prices for most goods. Similarly, the Agricultural Adjustment Administration (AAA) cotton program achieved about as much for the mass of the nearly 3 million black farm tenants as a plague of boll weevils. The AAA eschewed safeguards to protect the exploited landless black peasantry and acquiesced in the widespread cheating of croppers out of their share of the subsidy to planters, or the wholesale eviction of tenants whose labor was no longer needed. Those who had traditionally oppressed blacks in the South also controlled the local administration of the Tennessee Valley Authority (TVA), and the consequences were the same. Blacks were initially excluded from clerical employment and from living in the TVA's new model town of Norris, Tennessee. Local officials segregated work crews and relegated blacks to the least-skilled, lowest-paying jobs. They refused to admit blacks to TVA vocational schools or to training sessions in foremanship. And, everywhere in the Tennessee Valley, white southern administrators insisted upon Jim Crow housing and recreational facilities, and on segregated drinking fountains and employment offices in the TVA.

The early relief and welfare operations of the New Deal proved to be only marginally more beneficial to blacks. The Civilian Conservation Corps (CCC) allowed local officials to choose the enrollees, and, not surprisingly, young black men were woefully underrepresented. They were also, in the main, confined to segregated CCC units and kept out of the training programs that would lead to their advancement. Moreover, despite the laudable intentions of Harry Hopkins, the Federal Emergency Relief Administration and the Civil Works Administration succumbed to the pressure brought by angry whites who thought that blacks were being spoiled by direct relief or were earning more on work-relief than white laborers in private enterprise. New regulations lowered the minimum wages on work-relief and prohibited relief payments from exceeding prevailing wages in a region. They also gave greater discretion to state and local relief officials in the administration of their programs. Consequently, blacks saw both their chances for obtaining relief and the amount of relief drop. Especially in 1933 and 1934, discrimination was rife and blacks depended on the mercy of the lily-white personnel in local relief offices. Similarly, the New Deal's capitulation to racial prejudice became manifest in the refusal to admit blacks in the subsistence homestead program; the failure to prohibit racial discrimination in unions protected by the National Labor Relations Act; the passage of a Social Security Act with enough loopholes to exclude two-thirds of all Afro-American workers in 1935; and the encouragement of residential segregation by the Federal Housing Administration.

PRESSURE FOR CHANGE

Gradually, however, counterforces pushed the New Deal toward a more equitable treatment of blacks. A clear demonstration by blacks of their determination to achieve full, first-class citizenship seemed foremost among the interrelated reasons for that transformation. On a scale, and with an intensity, unknown in any previous decade, a host of black advancement and protest organizations campaigned for racial justice and equality. More blacks than ever before marched, picketed, rallied, and lobbied against racial discrimination. They boycotted businesses with unjust racial practices. The National Association for the Advancement of Colored People (NAACP) and the National Urban League adapted to the mood of militance. They forged additional weapons of struggle, developed greater skills and sophistication, and acquired powerful allies and sources of support. New militant organizations such as the National Negro Congress and Southern Negro Youth Congress prodded the more moderate black groups to greater aggressiveness and amplified the volume of the growing movement for black rights. Simultaneously, the Negro vote in the 1930s developed into a relatively sizable and volatile bloc that politicians of both major parties in the North could no longer ignore. A marked upsurge in the number of blacks who registered and voted resulted from the continuing migration of Afro-Americans from the South to the cities above the Mason-Dixon line, and from the new immediacy of government to the life of the common people during the New Deal. Concentrated in the states richest in electoral votes, the black vote began to be ballyhooed as a balance of power in national elections, a swing bloc that would go to whichever party most benefitted blacks. Northern big-city Democrats became especially attentive and displayed unprecedented solicitude for black needs. At the same time, the power of the South within the Democratic party declined; Dixie Democrats prominently joined in the conservative criticism of the New Deal; and racism became identified with fascism. One result was that northern Democrats ceased to support their southern brethren in opposing black rights.

Augmenting these developments, members of the radical left and the labor movement in the thirties preached the egalitarian gospel to millions of white Americans. Communists and the Congress of Industrial Organizations, in particular, advocated an end to racial discrimination and insisted on the necessity for interracial harmony. Their desire for strong labor unions or class unity, unhampered by racial divisions, propelled them into the forefront of mainly white organizations pressing for civil rights. White southern race liberals, although few in number, joined the fray, stressing the connections between economic democracy in the South and the cause of black rights. What George Washington Cable once called the "Silent South" grew vocal, shattering the image of a white South that was solidly united on racial matters. These trends, in turn, gained from the changes in the 1930s in the academic and intellectual communities. Biologists refuted the doctrines of inherent and irremediable racial differences. Social scientists started to undermine white racism by emphasizing environment rather than innate characteristics; by stressing the damage done to individuals by prejudice; and by eroding the stereotype of the Afro-American as a contented buffoon. A new ideological consensus began to emerge, an American creed of treating all people alike, of judging each person as an individual.

Roosevelt could neither ignore what these occurrences portended, nor disregard the strength of the forces arrayed against racial reform. He understood that however much black powerlessness had decreased and white hostility to blacks had begun to diminish, the majority of white Americans still opposed desegregation and equal opportunities for blacks. He knew that to combat the worst depression in the nation's history he needed the backing of the southern Democrats who wanted no modification of traditional racial practices. Roosevelt, the consummate politician and humanitarian, therefore, husbanded his political capital on racial matters, doing what he thought was right, if it would not cost him dearly. Above all, he avoided an all-out confrontation with those whose support he deemed necessary. Always the fox and never the lion on civil rights issues, Roosevelt nevertheless acted in ways that had the unintended consequence of laying the groundwork for the Second Reconstruction.

A BETTER DEAL FOR BLACKS

After 1934, although Jim Crow remained largely intact, blacks gained a much fairer, but still far from fully adequate, share of New Deal benefits and services. In the CCC the percentage of black enrollees rose from 3 percent in 1933 to 6 percent in 1936, to nearly 10 percent in 1937, and to over 11 percent in 1938. In that same year about 40,000 young blacks were sending $700,000 a month home to their parents and dependents. By the start of 1939, some 200,000 blacks had served in the Civilian Conservation Corps, and when the CCC ended in 1942 the number stood at 350,000. In addition, over 40,000 blacks who had entered the Corps as illiterates had learned to read and write.

The National Youth Administration (NYA) directly aided another 300,000 black youths. Like other New Deal agencies, the NYA accepted segregated projects in the South, employed a disproportionate number of blacks in servile work, and lacked the resources to assist Afro-Americans to the extent their privation required. Yet the fervor of Aubrey Williams, head of the NYA until it ended in 1943, led that agency to hire black administrative assistants to supervise black work in every southern state, to forbid either racial or geographic differentials in wages, and to an insistence that black secondary and college students in every state receive aid at least in proportion to their numbers in the population. The NYA also employed more blacks in administrative posts than any other New Deal program, and Afro-Americans annually received between 10 and 20 percent of NYA's appropriations.

With a zeal similar to that of Williams, Dr. Will Alexander, the chief of the Farm Security Administration (FSA) managed to insure benefits for black farmers that were roughly proportionate to their percentage of farm operators. Overall, blacks received about 23 percent of the New Deal's farm security assistance. This was achieved only because FSA officials in Washington kept constant pressure on local authorities to prevent racial discrimination. But the FSA could never convince Congress to appropriate the funds needed to make more than the slightest dent in the problem of needy and displaced tenant farmers. By 1940, despite its egalitarianism, the FSA had placed a mere 1,393 black families on its resettlement communities and had provided tenant purchase loans to only 3,400 blacks. Even this minimal effort, however, earned the FSA a reputation as a "disturber of the peace," and the top place on the southern conservative's "death list" of New Deal programs.

Equally vigilant on matters of race, Secretary of Interior Harold Ickes, who ran the Public Works Administration (PWA), employed a quota system on government construction projects to root out discrimination against black laborers. Beginning in 1934, the PWA included a clause in all its construction contracts stipulating that the number of blacks hired and their percentage of the project payroll be equal to the proportion of blacks in either the local labor force or in the 1930 occupational census. The quota was effective in diminishing discrimination. It led to the admission of hundreds of skilled blacks into previously lily-white southern construction trade unions, and resulted in over $2 million, nearly 6 percent of the total payroll to skilled workers, being paid to blacks—a portion considerably greater than that warranted by the occupational census. Similar quota systems would later be adopted by the U.S. Housing Authority, the Federal Works Agency, and the President's Committee on Fair Employment Practices.

Ickes' concern for racial fairness also led to the PWA expenditure of over $45 million for the construction and renovation of Afro-American schools, hospitals, and recreational facilities. The nearly $5 million granted for new buildings at black colleges increased their total plant value by more than 25 percent. In addition, the PWA loaned municipalities and states more than $20 million to build and repair scores of schools, dormitories, auditoriums, and gymnasiums for blacks. Of the 48 PWA housing projects completed by 1938, 14 were solely for Afro-Americans and 15 for joint black-white occupancy. Blacks occupied one-third of all PWA housing units and 41,000 of the 122,000 dwelling units built by the U.S. Housing

Authority (USHA). The determination of the PWA and USHA to be racially fair and to meet the black demand for public housing also led them to charge blacks a lower monthly average rent than they did whites, and to set a higher maximum family income for blacks than whites as the cut-off for admission to the housing projects.

Likewise, the concern for black welfare of Harry Hopkins was manifest in the constant efforts of officials in the Works Progress Administration (WPA) to forbid racial discrimination by local relief authorities in assigning jobs to the unemployed and in establishing wage rates. Hopkins did not succeed in ending such practices in the South, but as the Urban League proclaimed: "It is to the eternal credit of the administrative offices of the WPA that discrimination on various projects because of race has been kept to a minimum and that in almost every community Negroes have been given a chance to participate in the work program." Indeed, during Roosevelt's second term, roughly 350,000 blacks were employed by the WPA annually, about 15 percent of the total in the work-relief program. For the most part, blacks received their proper job classifications from the WPA, gained the equal wages promised them, and were included in all special projects. Over 5,000 blacks were employed as teachers and supervisors in the WPA Education Program, where nearly 250,000 Afro-Americans learned to read and write. Tens of thousands of blacks were trained for skilled jobs in WPA vocational classes. The Federal Music Project performed the works of contemporary Afro-American composers; featured all-black casts in several of its operas; made a special effort to preserve, record, and publish Negro folk music; and conducted music instruction classes for blacks in more than a score of cities. The Federal Art Project, the Federal Theatre Project, and the Federal Writers' Project also employed hundreds of blacks and made special efforts to highlight the artistic contributions of Afro-Americans.

Blacks, long accustomed to receiving little more than crumbs, largely accepted the New Deal's half a loaf. The continuance of discrimination and segregation appeared secondary to the vital importance of work-relief, public housing, government-sponsored health clinics and infant care programs, NYA employment to keep a child in school, a FSA loan to purchase a farm, or new educational facilities in the neighborhood. Primarily because of the PWA and WPA, the gap between both black unemployment rates and black median family income relative to whites diminished during the

1930s, and the percentage of black workers in skilled and semiskilled occupations rose from 23 to 29 percent.

In no small part because of the myriad of New Deal programs that improved the nutrition, housing, and health care available to Afro-Americans, black infant and maternal mortality significantly decreased, and black life expectancy climbed from 48 to 53 years in the 1930s. Over 1 million blacks learned to read and write in New Deal-sponsored literacy classes. Federal funds and New Deal guidelines for the expenditure of those funds also resulted in a lengthening of the school term for blacks, and a significant growth in the number of schools for blacks. The percentage of Afro-Americans, aged 5 to 18, attending school jumped from 60 to 65 percent, and the gap in expenditures per black pupil narrowed from 29 percent of the average for white students in 1930 to 44 percent in 1940. In addition, the average salary paid to black teachers, only one-third of that paid to white teachers in 1930, increased to about one-half in 1940.

Summing up the prevailing Afro-American response to the New Deal efforts to relieve black distress, the *Pittsburgh Courier* editorialized that "armies of unemployed Negro workers have been kept from the near-starvation level on which they lived under President Hoover" by the work provided by the WPA, CCC, PWA, and other federal projects. It acknowledged the unfortunate continuation of racial discrimination and the New Deal's failure to end such practices. "But what administration within the memory of man," the *Courier* concluded, "has done a better job in that direction considering the very imperfect human material with which it had to work? The answer, of course, is none."

DIMINISHING RACISM

Blacks expressed their thankfulness for the uncommon concern the Roosevelt Administration showed for their well-being, and for the direct material assistance that enabled them to endure the Depression. The very novelty of simply being included—of being considered and planned for—elicited praise in hundreds of letters written to the White House and to New Deal agencies. As a group of black social workers visiting Hyde Park proclaimed: "For the first time Negro men and women have reason to believe that their government does care." That sentiment was bolstered time and again by the battles that Alexander, Ickes, Williams, and other New Dealers waged in pursuit of a more equitable deal for blacks, by their overt disdain for racist attitudes and practices, and by their public championing, in articles and speeches, of the cause of racial justice and equality. Blacks viewed their actions with hope as symbolic of a new high-level governmental disposition to oppose racial discrimination.

Blacks in the 1930s also applauded the success of these New Dealers in enlarging the roster of Afro-Americans working for the government. The number of blacks on the federal payroll more than tripled during the Depression decade. The proportion of black government employees in 1940 was twice what it had been in 1930. In addition, the Roosevelt Administration unprecedently hired thousands of blacks as architects, engineers, lawyers, librarians, office managers, and statisticians. This was viewed at the time as "the first significant step toward the participation of Negroes in federal government activity," and as "representing something new in the administration of our national affairs." To insure further steps, the Administration also abolished the Civil Service regulations that had required job seekers to designate their race and to attach a photograph to their application forms. Some New Deal officials desegregated the cafeterias, restrooms, and secretarial pools in their agencies and departments; others highlighted their abhorrence of Jim Crow by having blacks and whites work at adjoining desks.

Roosevelt also reversed two decades of diminishing black patronage. He appointed over one hundred blacks to administrative posts in the New Deal. Previous administrations had, at best, reserved a handful of honorific and innocuous positions for loyal Negro party leaders. Roosevelt selected a large number of nonpartisan black professionals and veterans of the civil rights movement and placed them in formal positions of public importance so that both government officers and the Afro-American community regarded their presence as significant. Popularly referred to as the Black Cabinet or Black Brain Trust, these black officials had considerably more symbolic value than actual power. They rarely succeeded in pushing the New Deal further along the road to racial equality than it wished to go. Most of their efforts to win greater equity for blacks were defeated by interest groups that were better able to bring pressure to bear on Roosevelt. But their very being and prominence, Roy Wilkins of the NAACP noted, "had never existed before." This fact alone elicited howls from white southerners that "Negroes were taking over the White House," which was hardly the case. Still, the presence of the Black Cabinet, like Roosevelt's selection of William Hastie as the first Afro-American federal judge in American history, hinted at a New Deal determination to break, however timorously, with prevailing customs of racial prejudice. As Mary McLeod Bethune, director of the NYA's Division of the Negro Affairs, emphasized during the thirties, such appointments were not "tokenism" but the essential first steps in making the government aware of black needs and in planning policies that would help the race.

The Black Cabinet certainly did raise the level of national awareness of racial issues. The race advisers appointed by Roosevelt articulated the problems of blacks, the ultimate goal of integration, and the specific responsibility of the federal government in the area of civil rights, both within the corridors of the various agencies in which they worked and in the public conferences and reports they generated. "At no time since the curtain had dropped on the Reconstruction drama," wrote Henry Lee Moon of the NAACP, "had government focused as much attention upon the Negro's basic needs as did the New Deal." For example, the NYA convened a three-day National Conference on the Problems of the Negro and Negro Youth in 1937, for the purpose of increasing support for greater governmental assistance to blacks. It was addressed by four Cabinet members, half-a-dozen agency chiefs, and Eleanor Roosevelt. Such a conference would have been inconceivable before the New Deal. As Mary Bethune noted in her opening remarks: "This is the first time in the history of our race that the Negroes of America have felt free to reduce to writing their problems and plans for meeting them with the expectancy of sympathetic understanding and interpretation." Even Ralph Bunche, who was perhaps the New Deal's severest black critic, admitted at the end of the 1930s that the New Deal was without precedent in the manner in which it granted "broad recognition to the existence of the Negro as a national problem and undertook to give specific consideration to this fact in many ways."

A NEW HOPE

Roosevelt appointees also stirred the hopes of Afro-Americans by establishing precedents that challenged local white control over blacks. The National Advisory Committee on Education, which was appointed by Roosevelt, called in 1938 for specific guarantees that federal grants to states for education would be spent equitably for black as well as white schooling. No government body had said that before. Less than a decade earlier, in fact, that exact proposition had been overwhelmingly rejected by President Hoover's National Advisory Committee on Education. In fact, only the blacks on the Hoover committee supported it. But, during the New Deal, the earlier all-black minority opinion became a part of the official proposal, and the committee's recommendation appeared verbatim with Roosevelt's support in the Harrison-Fletcher-Thomas federal aid to education bill submitted to Congress.

The New Deal, indeed, substantially expanded the scope of the federal government's authority and constricted traditional states' rights. The states' failures to cope with the economic crisis enlarged the responsibilities of the national government, and the New Deal involved the states in joint programs in which the federal government increasingly imposed the standards and goals. This alteration in the system of federalism augured well for black hopes of future federal civil rights actions, as did the emergence of a new conception of positive government, the "powerful promoter of society's welfare," which guaranteed every American a minimally decent economic existence as a matter of right, not charity, and which assumed the role of the protector of weak interests that could not contend successfully on their own.

Roosevelt's appointments to the Supreme Court immediately sanctioned the expansion of federal power over matters of race and strengthened the rights of blacks. After FDR's abortive attempt at "court packing" in 1937, the personnel on the Supreme Court changed swiftly and power passed into the hands of New Dealers, who articulated a new judicial philosophy which championed the rights of racial and religious minorities and formulated new constitutional guarantees to protect civil rights. As a result, both the number of cases involving black rights brought before the federal courts and the percentage of decisions favorable to black plaintiffs leaped dramatically. What would culminate in the Warren Court clearly began in the Roosevelt Court. With the exception of James Byrnes, Roosevelt's eight appointees to the Court were truly partisans of the cause of civil rights. Together, men who had long been associated with the NAACP and issues of racial justice, such as Felix Frankfurter, Wiley Rutledge, and Frank Murphy, joined with new converts like Hugo Black and William O. Douglas to begin dismantling a century of legal discrimination against blacks. Their decisions in cases involving the exclusion of blacks from juries, the right to picket against discrimination in employment, racially restrictive covenants, inequality in interstate transportation, peonage, disfranchisement, and discrimination in the payment of black teachers and in graduate education signaled the demise of the separate-but-equal doctrine established by *Plessy* v. *Ferguson* (1896).

Such decisions, according to legal scholar Loren Miller, made the Negro less a *freedman* and more a *free man*. The federalizing of the Bill of Rights left blacks less at the mercy of states' rights. The inquiry into the facts of segregation, rather than just the theory, diminished the possibility of anything racially separate meeting the test of constitutionality. And, the expansion of the concept of state action severely circumscribed the boundaries of private discrimination. Perhaps most importantly, the decisions of the Roosevelt Court had a multiplier effect. They stimulated scores of additional challenges to Jim Crow, both in court and out. Fittingly, in 1944, when the Supreme Court struck down the white primary, the only dissenter was Owen Roberts, the sole justice then sitting whom Roosevelt had not appointed.

ELEANOR ROOSEVELT

Although not a presidential appointee, Eleanor Roosevelt certainly made the most of her position as First Lady to link the civil rights cause with the New Deal. Working quietly within the administration, at first, Mrs. Roosevelt influenced her husband and numerous agency heads to be more concerned with the special needs of blacks. Gradually her commitment became more open and visible. Functioning as an unofficial ombudsman for blacks, she goaded bureaucrats and congressmen into lessening racial discrimination in federal programs, and acted as the main conduit between the civil rights leadership and the higher circles of the New Deal and the Democratic party. Repeatedly breaking with tradition, Eleanor Roosevelt openly entertained Afro-American leaders at the White House, posed for photographs with blacks, and publicly associated herself with most of the major civil rights organizations and issues. The peripatetic Mrs. Roosevelt spoke out for National Sharecroppers Week, addressed conventions of the Brotherhood of Sleeping Car Porters and National Council of Negro Women, candidly backed the civil rights activities of the American Youth Congress, and frequently pleaded for racial tolerance and fairness in her syndicated newspaper column, published articles, and radio broadcasts.

"Nigger Lover Eleanor," as some whites derided her, squarely placed her authority and prestige behind the drive for civil rights legislation in President Roosevelt's second term. Delivering the keynote address at the first meeting of the Southern Electoral Reform League, she emphasized the necessity for a federal act to end all poll tax requirements for voting. Mrs. Roosevelt also publicly endorsed the quest for antilynching legislation, and sat prominently in the Senate gallery during the efforts of northern liberals to invoke cloture and shut off the southern filibuster of the 1938 Wagner-Van Nuys-Gavagan antilynching bill. In the same year Eleanor Roosevelt also helped to organize the Southern Conference for Human Welfare. At its opening session in Birmingham, Alabama, she defied the local segregation ordinance, conspicuously taking a seat on the "Colored" side of the auditorium. White supremacists immediately condemned the First Lady's act as "an insult to every white man and woman in the South." But in the Negro press, Eleanor Roosevelt's disdain for Jim Crow was a "rare and precious moment in the social history of America." Further stirring the wrath of white supremacists and gaining the admiration of blacks, Mrs. Roosevelt began to denounce racial discrimination in the defense program. In 1939, she publicly decried the bigotry of the Daughters of the American Revolution when that organization refused to rent its Constitution Hall for a concert by the famous black contralto, Marian Anderson. Mrs. Roosevelt then used her "My Day" newspaper column to explain why she could no longer remain a member of a group practicing such discrimination and, working with her husband and the NAACP, she arranged for Marian Anderson to sing her concert in front of the Lincoln Memorial. Two months later, on behalf of the NAACP, Eleanor Roosevelt officially presented the Spingarn Medal for Freedom to Marian Anderson.

PROGRESS, NOT PERFECTION

Such highly publicized actions of Mrs. Roosevelt, as well as the President's increasingly more egalitarian gestures and rhetoric, had a vital impact on blacks in the 1930s. Although Franklin Roosevelt shied away from any direct challenges to white supremacy, the very fact that he frequently invited blacks to the White House, held conferences with civil rights leaders, and appeared before Afro-American organizations indicated to blacks that they mattered. It was a start. Mindful of political realities, blacks sought progress, not perfection. They understood that no president would act boldly and unyieldingly on black rights until a majority constituency for dramatic change had emerged. Until then, symbolic actions would count, for they played in important role in educating and persuading, in inspiring hope and commitment.

Accordingly, the civil rights leadership and their allies in the 1930s utilized the President's association with the campaigns for antilynching and antipoll tax legislation to mobilize future support. Their public complaints to the contrary, these black rights spokesmen recognized the insurmountable barriers to cloture being voted in the Senate and the necessity for Roosevelt to maintain the backing of the southern leadership in Congress. They knew he would not jeopardize his relief and defense programs for a futile attempt at civil rights legislation. Accordingly, blacks extracted the greatest possible advantages from what the President said and did, however lukewarm and timorous.

On the poll tax, Roosevelt publicly supported the legislative efforts for its abolition. "The right to vote," he declared, "must be open to all our citizens irrespective of race, color, or creed — without tax or artificial restriction of any kind. The sooner we get to that basis of political equality, the better it will be for the country as a whole." In a public letter Roosevelt vigorously endorsed the antipoll tax movement in Arkansas. At a press conference in 1938 he opposed the use of poll taxes: "They are inevitably contrary to the fundamental democracy and its representative form of government in which we believe." No legislator or informed citizen doubted where the President stood on this matter. In part, this helps to explain why the House of Representatives in 1941 voted to pass an antipoll tax bill by a better than three-to-one margin.

Similarly, the President aided the civil rights movement on antilynching, both with public statements to influence mass opinion and private pressures on the Senate to get it to consider legislation, but Roosevelt would neither place the antilynching bills on his list of "must" legislation, nor intervene with the Senate leadership to end the filibusters that doomed the proposals from even coming to a vote. Over a coast-to-coast radio hook-up, early in his administration, Roosevelt denounced lynching as "a vile form of collective murder." Lynch law, he continued, "is murder, a deliberate and definite disobedience of the high command, 'Thou shalt not kill.' We do not excuse those in high places or low who condone lynch law." No president had ever spoken like that before. W.E.B. DuBois, writing immediately afterward in *The Crisis*, observed: "It took war, riot and upheaval to make Wilson say one small word. Nothing ever induced Herbert Hoover to say anything on the subject worth the saying. Even Harding was virtually dumb." Only Roosevelt, DuBois concluded, "has declared frankly that lynching is murder. We all knew it, but it is unusual to have a President of the United States admit it. These things give us hope."

More ambiguously, Roosevelt in 1934 authorized Senators Edward Costigan and Robert Wagner to inform the Majority Leader "that the President will be glad to see the anti-lynching bill pass and wishes it passed." And, in 1935, he requested that the Majority Leader permit the Senate to consider the bill. The half-heartedness of Roosevelt's support did nothing to avert the inevitable southern filibuster that killed the measure in 1935. Meanwhile, Roosevelt's private encouragement of others to keep up the fight led to a protracted and bitter wrangle over antilynching legislation in 1938. A far cry from the charade of 1935 in which both sides went through the motions, the two-month-long talkathon of 1938 smacked of fratricide. The southern senators overwhelmingly blamed the New Deal for provoking the civil rights issues that alienated the South from the Democratic party. They pledged to talk as long as necessary to "preserve the white supremacy of America." And, they held Roosevelt responsible for having the Senate rules enforced "in a technical manner," for holding night sessions in an attempt to break the filibuster, and for trying to invoke cloture twice.

The result in Congress notwithstanding, black leaders gained significantly from the struggle against lynching and from the President's involvement in the cause. Lynchings declined from a high for the decade of twenty-eight in 1933 to eighteen in 1935, six in 1938, and two in 1939. To ward off federal legislation, most southern states made greater efforts to prevent lynching and enacted their own bills to stop the crime. At the end of the decade, Roosevelt, established a special Civil Rights Section of the Justice Department and empowered it to investigate all lynchings that might involve some denial of a federal right. And, in no small part because the public identified the crusade against lynching with the First Family, the campaign for federal legislation attracted new supporters and allies to the black cause who would stay to fight against discrimination in the defense program, segregation in education, and the disfranchisement of Afro-Americans. In this limited regard, the President's pronouncements meant much to blacks. In political language, at least, they were yet another manifestation of Roosevelt's desire to win the allegiance of blacks and to take the steps necessary to retain their loyalty, even at the risk of gradual southern disenchantment with the New Deal.

Roosevelt's overtures in this direction also showed in the series of precedent-shattering "firsts" that he orchestrated in the 1936 campaign. Never before had the Democrats accredited an Afro-American as a convention delegate; in 1936 they accorded thirty blacks that distinction. For the first time, additionally, the national party in 1936 invited black reporters into the regular press box; chose a black minister to offer the convention invocation; selected blacks to deliver the welcome address and one of the speeches seconding Roosevelt's renomination; and placed a black on the delegation to notify the Vice President of his renomination. Yet another significant event at the convention occurred when liberals and New Dealers wiped out the century-old rule, utilized by the South as a political veto, which required the Democratic nominee to win two-thirds of the delegates' votes in order to obtain the nomination. The white South recognized the threat and resented the intrusion. And its fears of a future attempt by the New Deal to alter race relations were heightened when Roosevelt pointedly campaigned before black audiences and promised that in his administration there would be "no forgotten races" as well as no forgotten men. Then in the 1940 presidential race, Roosevelt affirmed his desire to include blacks evenhandedly in defense training and employment, promoted the first black to the rank of Army Brigadier General, and insisted that, for the first time, the Democrats include a specific Negro plank in the party platform, pledging "to strive for complete legislative safeguards against discrimination in government services and benefits."

A NEW DEAL FOR BLACKS:
AN ASSESSMENT

However circumspect this New Deal record seems today, for blacks in the thirties it meant change for the better. The mixture of symbolic and substantive assistance, of rhetoric and recognition, led blacks to cast their ballots overwhelmingly for Roosevelt once the New Deal began. After voting more than 70 percent for Herbert Hoover in 1932, a majority of black voters deserted the Republican party for the first time in history in 1934, about two-thirds of the Afro-Americans registered in 1936 entered the Roosevelt coalition, and nearly 68 percent of all black voters in 1940 went for FDR. This startling shift in the black vote, more pronounced than that of any other ethnic, racial, or religious group, according to the NAACP came not only because of black "concern for immediate relief, either in jobs or direct assistance," but because of "a feeling that Mr. Roosevelt represented a kind of philosophy of government which will mean much to their cause."

Virtually every civil rights spokesman stressed both the value of new government precedents favorable to blacks and the manner in which the New Deal made explicit the federal government's responsibility in the field of civil rights. Editorials in the black press and journals frequently reiterated that the New Deal had ended the "invisibility" of the race problem and had made civil rights a part of the liberal agenda. Perhaps most importantly, blacks in the thirties lauded the manifold ways in which the New Deal reform spirit ushered in a new political climate in which Afro-Americans and their allies could begin to struggle with some expectation of success. They took heart from the expanding authority of the federal government and the changing balance of power in the Democratic party, as well as from the overt sympathy for the underprivileged shown by the Roosevelt Administration; and they made common cause with fellow-sufferers in pressing the New Deal to become even more of an instrument for humane, liberal reform.

These developments did little to change the concrete aspects of life for most blacks in the 1930s. The New Deal failed to end the rampant discrimination against blacks in the North, who were living in ghettos that had turned to slums and who were twice as likely to be unemployed as whites. The Roosevelt Administration also failed to enfranchise black southerners, to eradicate segregation, or to elevate the great mass of blacks who remained a submerged caste of menials, sharecroppers, unskilled laborers, and domestics. These facts cannot be gainsaid. The New Deal record on race is replete with failures and timidity, unfulfilled promises, and insufficient effort. The New Deal did not fundamentally transform the economic, legal, or social status of Afro-Americans.

But for the millions of blacks who hung FDR's picture on their walls, who kept voting for Roosevelt, and naming their children after him, something vital did begin in the New Deal, breaking the crust of quiescence that had long stifled even the dream of equal opportunity and full participation in American life. The New Deal gave blacks hope. A black newspaper called it "the emergence of a new type of faith." The pervasive despondency that had led several generations of Americans, black and white, to regard the racial status quo as immutable gradually gave way to a conviction that racial reform was possible. The dream that would prove indispensable in the continuing struggle for black equality could at last be dreamt. The barely visible flicker of black hope at the start of the New Deal would shine brightly as the United States mobilized for World War II.

SUGGESTED READINGS

This essay is based largely on the research done for Harvard Sitkoff, *A New Deal for Blacks, The Emergence of Civil Rights as a National Issue* (New York, 1978). It also owes much to John B. Kirby, *Black Americans in the Roosevelt Era, Liberalism and Race* (Knoxville, Tenn., 1980), and Raymond Wolters, *Negroes and the Great Depression: The Problem of Economic Recovery* (Westport, Conn., 1970). George B. Tindall, *The Emergence of the New South, 1913–1945* (Baton Rouge, 1976) is indispensable, as is Gunnar Myrdal, *An American Dilemma, The Negro Problem and Modern Democracy* (New York, 1944).

For background on the black experience, see John Hope Franklin, *From Slavery to Freedom: A History of American Negroes* (New York, rev. ed., 1980), and August Meier and Elliot Rudwick, *From Plantation to Ghetto: An Interpretive History of American Negroes* (New York, rev. ed., 1976). Specific New Deal programs and policies are analyzed in Sidney Baldwin, *Poverty and Politics: The Rise and Decline of the Farm Security Administration* (Chapel Hill, N.C., 1968); Donald H.

Grubbs, *Cry from the Cotton, The Southern Tenants Farmers' Union and the New Deal* (Chapel Hill, N.C., 1971); Donald S. Howard, *The WPA and Federal Relief Policy* (New York, 1943); Paul E. Mertz, *New Deal Policy and Southern Rural Poverty* (Baton Rouge, 1978); John A. Salmond, *The Civilian Conservation Corps, 1933–1942: A New Deal Case Study* (Durham, N.C., 1967); and Richard Sterner, *The Negro's Share: A Study of Income, Consumption, Housing and Public Assistance* (New York, 1943).

The role of key individuals is analyzed in Jervis Anderson, *A. Philip Randolph: A Biographical Portrait* (New York, 1973); Andrew Buni, *Robert L. Vann and The Pittsburgh Courier* (Pittsburgh, 1974); Wilma Dykeman and James Stokely, *Seeds of Southern Change: The Life of Will Alexander* (Chicago, 1962); Tamara K. Hareven, *Eleanor Roosevelt: An American Conscience* (Chicago, 1968); Rackham Holt, *Mary McLeod Bethune: A Biography* (New York, 1964); Joseph P. Lash, *Eleanor and Franklin* (New York, 1971); B. Joyce Ross, *J. E. Spingarn and the Rise of the NAACP, 1911–1939* (New York, 1972); and Walter White's autobiography *A Man Called White* (New York, 1948). The following are invaluable for the racial mood of the era and an assessment of the impact of the New Deal: Dan T. Carter, *Scottsboro, A Tragedy of the American South* (New York, 1969); Frank Friedel, *F. D. R. and the South* (Baton Rouge, 1965); Thomas A. Krueger, *And Promises to Keep: The Southern Conference for Human Welfare, 1938–1948* (Nashville, 1967); Rayford W. Logan, ed., *The Attitude of the Southern White Press toward Negro Suffrage, 1932–1940* (Washington, D.C., 1940); Morton Sosna, *In Search of the Silent South: Southern Liberals and the Race Issue* (New York, 1977); Robert L. Zangrando, *The NAACP Crusade Against Lynching, 1909–1950* (Philadelphia, 1980); and especially Ralph J. Bunche, *The Political Status of the Negro in the Age of FDR*, Dewey W. Grantham, ed., (Chicago, 1973).

Women and the New Deal

Susan Ware

The reunion in Washington of old New Dealers was breaking up. They had come together, most of them now in their seventies and eighties, to recall their glory days in Washington in the 1930s. Many had provided poignant and humorous reminiscences of their dealings with President Franklin Delano Roosevelt, but consumer activist Caroline Ware realized that no one had paid tribute to Eleanor Roosevelt for her special contributions to the New Deal. Ware rushed to the microphone as people were beginning to leave and shouted, "We can't go home without mentioning Eleanor." Having said her piece, she then sat down.

This anecdote clearly is applicable to the task at hand: when evaluating the New Deal, we "can't go home" without mentioning women. While conventional accounts rarely cite women's activities in the period, women were a vital part of the New Deal. In fact, the New Deal provided opportunities for women in politics and government that make the 1930s one of the most creative and exciting periods for women in twentieth century political history.

The topic of women in the New Deal has not been totally ignored by historians, but it rarely has been a central concern. Eleanor Roosevelt and Lorena Hickok highlighted women's political and governmental roles in their book, *Ladies of Courage* (1952), as did William Chafe (1972) and Lois Banner (1974) in their surveys of women's public roles. There are biographies of Eleanor Roosevelt by Tamara Hareven and Joseph Lash, among others. Lash's books, *Eleanor and Franklin* (1971) and *Eleanor: The Years Alone* (1972), aroused much popular and scholarly interest. George Martin's biography (1976) of Frances Perkins was one of the few books to analyze an individual woman's impact on the emergence of the New Deal. For the most part, however, standard works on the New Deal completely ignored the contributions of women. In both surveys and monographic studies, women have been practically invisible.

Several factors contributed to this neglect of women in the New Deal literature. Until recently, women were rarely considered topics worthy of attention from serious scholars. Unless a historian was specifically looking for women's contributions, it was far too easy to overlook evidence of women's active roles. In part, this was because women who served in the New Deal did not see feminism as their first priority: they were working to solve the crisis of the Depression. These women often did not hold the most visible top post in an agency or department. Many of these women shunned publicity in order to work quietly (and effectively) behind the scenes. These women felt just as much a part of the New Deal as did their male coworkers, but they rarely received commensurate credit. It was only with the revival of feminism in the 1960s that some of these women looked back on their own experiences in the 1930s from a different perspective.

The contributions of women to the New Deal had also been neglected until recently by scholars interested in the history of American women. Since the study of women's history drew heavily on the methodology of the new social history, attention to political elites (male or female) was a low priority. Another factor that limited attention was the prevailing view that the 1930s was a disastrous decade for women: in the midst of the economic crisis of the Great Depression, women's status declined as they struggled simply to make ends meet. Now this neglect is being supplanted by a burgeoning interest in twentieth-century women's history, especially the postsuffrage period between 1920 and the revival of feminism in the 1960s. This, in turn, has renewed interest in the 1930s, represented by recent work on women in that decade by Lois Scharf, Winifred Wandersee, Susan Becker, Alice Kessler-Harris, and others.

Historians have yet to arrive at a consensus on general trends for American women in the 1930s. Generalizing about women in the New Deal is only slightly more manageable. The most fruitful way to assess the dual questions of women's impact on the New Deal and the New Deal's impact on women is to begin with the realization that the category of "women" is too broad. A three-tiered approach to analyzing women in the New Deal provides a more workable framework. This scheme differentiates among elite women in top policy-making positions, a second level of women holding appointments in New Deal agencies and the federal bureaucracy, and a third level of ordinary women affected by the New Deal relief and welfare programs. Progress varied at each level, and an evaluation of women and the New Deal depends very much on which women are under scrutiny. For some, the record of the New Deal is superlative; for others, only mixed. On the whole, however, the story is a remarkable one.

THE WOMEN'S NETWORK

The level where the most progress undoubtedly occurred was for elite women in the politics and government of the New Deal. This historical moment for women to play vital roles in the planning and administration of New Deal programs resulted from several factors. The chief factor was the Depression itself—a crisis of such overwhelming proportions that it forced the American governmental system to strike out in new directions, which eventually led to the creation of the modern welfare state. Women flourished in this experimental climate. As the majority of social workers, women were often the only ones with the necessary expertise to put large-scale relief and welfare programs into operation. In this case, broad trends of women's entry into professions such as social work intersected with the crisis demands of the Depression, and women moved forward.

Progress for women in the New Deal was also related to the historical circumstances that brought Franklin Roosevelt to the presidency in 1933. Along with Franklin came Eleanor, making the 1932 election one of the greatest two-for-one deals in American political history. Eleanor Roosevelt believed in women's capabilities, and she supported women's causes. She was especially useful to other women administrators in Washington by providing White House access to women who had a program or idea that they wanted brought to the attention of the President. More than once, if a program was stalled, Eleanor Roosevelt offered to hold a conference at the White House, and the resulting publicity soon broke the bureaucratic logjam. Eleanor Roosevelt could also command public attention in her own right through press conferences and her newspaper columns. Women were just one of the several constituencies that Eleanor Roosevelt served, but she served women well. It is practically impossible to imagine so much progress for women in the New Deal without Eleanor Roosevelt in the White House.

While Eleanor Roosevelt was the angel of women in the New Deal, Franklin Roosevelt deserves some credit as well. Without at least his tacit support for increased initiatives for women, even Eleanor would have been powerless. Franklin Roosevelt was a superb politician, and he realized that women could be an asset to the Democrats as they made themselves the dominant political party in the middle third of the twentieth century. He supported the efforts of women's Democratic leader, Molly Dewson, to increase women's access to patronage and to larger substantive and symbolic roles in the Democratic National Committee. In addition, Franklin Roosevelt felt comfortable in entrusting major responsibility to talented professional women like Frances Perkins and Molly Dewson, many of whom he had met through Eleanor. Yet Roosevelt was only willing to go so far: no woman, not even Eleanor, was ever part of his inner circle of advisers. On the whole, however, Franklin Roosevelt was open-minded about women's contributions, a trait not always found in male politicians. Given the experimental climate of the New Deal, his willingness to give women a chance was all that was needed for the flowering of women's talents.

The New Deal's record on opening opportunities for women to serve in major policy-making positions was not matched until the 1960s. The New Deal saw many "firsts" for women: first Cabinet member (Frances Perkins), first woman ambassador (Ruth Bryan Owen), first Assistant Treasurer of the United States (Marion Glass Banister), first Director of the Mint (Nellie Tayloe Ross), and first woman judge on the United States Circuit Court of Appeals (Florence Allen).

Women also held important positions in the new relief agencies, notably Ellen Sullivan Woodward who headed Women's and Professional Projects for the WPA, Hallie Flanagan, head of the Federal Theatre Project, and Hilda Worthington Smith, director of Workers Education for the WPA. In addition, Frances Perkins at the Labor Department gathered a talented group of women administrators, notably Clara Beyer at the Division of Labor Standards, Grace Abbott and Katherine Lenroot at the Children's Bureau, and Mary

Anderson at the Women's Bureau. Josephine Roche was nearby as Assistant Secretary of the Treasury, another first for women. Women active in the consumer and labor field in the National Recovery Administration included Mary Harriman Rumsey, Sue Shelton White, Emily Newell Blair, and Rose Schneiderman; Jane Hoey, Molly Dewson, and Ellen Woodward worked on Social Security. Finally, women found roles in the Democratic party hierarchy: besides Molly Dewson, who served as Director of the Women's Division, Carolyn Wolfe, Dorothy McAllister, Emma Guffey Miller, and Congresswomen Mary T. Norton and Caroline O'Day all played active roles in New Deal Democratic politics.

The women who served in the New Deal were a talented and dedicated group who brought years of experience in politics and social welfare administration to Washington in the 1930s. Strong similarities drew these women together in Washington. They were concentrated in certain areas of the bureaucracy, notably the newer relief agencies and the Labor Department, as well as the Women's Division of the Democratic party. Many of these women had been friends and professional colleagues since the Progressive period; at the least, most had known each other since the 1920s. They shared common ideas about extending the role of the federal government in modern America and about expanding roles for women in public life. From this shared ideology, they developed a network of professional cooperation and personal friendship, which was perhaps the most outstanding characteristic of women's participation in the New Deal.

The women's network comprised almost all the women who held prominent positions in the politics and government of the New Deal. Three women stand out for their contributions. As First Lady, Eleanor Roosevelt represented the most visible public center of this New Deal network. She also served as the network's emotional center, providing a model of public-spirited womanhood that was greatly admired and respected by women in Washington and throughout the nation. A close second to Eleanor Roosevelt in influence was Molly Dewson, who, as director of the Women's Division, was primarily responsible for badgering the men to give women jobs in the early New Deal. More than anyone else, Molly Dewson was the architect of the women's network: her almost daily contact with its members gave focus and shape to its influence. The other member of this triumvirate was Frances Perkins. Perkins has often been described as hostile to women's issues, but in fact she used her position as Secretary of Labor to surround herself with like-minded professional women who worked for the social welfare goals so dear to women in public life in the postsuffrage years. Like Dewson and Roosevelt, Frances Perkins served as an inspiration to women in Washington and in the country as a whole.

One of the few prominent women in the New Deal who was not part of this network is almost the exception that proves the rule. Mary McLeod Bethune, head of the Office of Minority Affairs for the National Youth Administration from 1936 to 1944, held a job as important as many network members, yet she was rarely mentioned as a prominent "woman" in the New Deal. Instead she was seen, and saw herself, as representing the interests of blacks. She served as the unofficial leader of the Black Cabinet, which raised issues of concern to black Americans in ways very similar to the women's network on social reform and feminist issues. Bethune was concerned about the special problems of black women, but for her, race took priority over sex.

Mary McLeod Bethune, Frances Perkins, Molly Dewson, and other women all benefited from the experimental climate of the early New Deal that made this progress for women possible. For the historical record, it is important to identify these women in positions of power and influence, but in the end, what difference did it make that so many women were prominent in the New Deal? In fact, it made quite a lot of difference. Women affected the course of the New Deal, both as individuals assisting in the planning and administration of New Deal programs, and as members of a network where cooperation on common goals enhanced their influence. The women's network had its greatest impact on two areas of the New Deal: Democratic party politics, and the developing social welfare policies of the modern welfare states.

In political circles, women found larger roles in the newly revitalized Democratic party. Molly Dewson was the chief mover here, building the Women's Division into a force of some 60,000 grassroots workers who publicized the accomplishments of the Roosevelt administration through the Reporter Plan. These Democratic women really put the New Deal across in communities throughout the United States. In the 1936 election, for example, Rainbow Fliers—written by the Women's Division—made up 90 percent of the Democratic National Committee's campaign material.

In the field of Democratic politics, Molly Dewson deserves

equal time with other well-known politicians such as James Farley, Stephen Early, or Louis Howe. Yet Molly Dewson cared little about the personalities of politics—she was interested in education and ideas. The social and economic changes of the New Deal supplied the perfect tool for educating women to the need for strong federal action in the areas about which women felt most strongly, especially economic security and social justice. The issue-oriented approach to politics, which Dewson mastered, has characterized women's political participation ever since. These enlarged political roles allowed Dewson to fulfill her second goal: to encourage women to take a more active part in Democratic party affairs. Dewson won increased support for women's activities from the financially strapped Democratic National Committee, and increased women's representation at national conventions and on key party committees. She did not reach her goal of equal numbers of women and men on all party committees, but she did make progress toward that objective.

Women had an even more wide-ranging impact on the social welfare policies of the New Deal. Historians may soon say that women founded the modern welfare state. In 1933, Frances Perkins had presented Franklin Roosevelt with a list of six reforms in the field of social welfare for his endorsement; by 1940, all but health insurance had been enacted. Women in the National Recovery Administration (NRA) drafted provisions setting maximum hours and minimum wages for workers covered by the NRA codes. Women also found scope in the consumer affairs division where they were among those raising protests against the business-oriented thrust of the NRA codes. Frances Perkins and her circle in the Labor Department supplied crucial expertise in the drafting of the 1935 Social Security Act, one of the New Deal's more lasting accomplishments. In addition, provisions for Aid to Dependent Children grew directly out of the collaboration between Grace Abbott and Frances Perkins. And, women in the network helped pass the 1938 Fair Labor Standards Act, which made permanent many of the reforms first enacted under the NRA codes. This 1938 law was the last liberal reform measure won by the Roosevelt administration in the face of opposition from an increasingly conservative Congress.

Women administrators and planners also oversaw the treatment of ordinary women in the relief agencies. When women's relief was lagging in the early days of the New Deal, Eleanor Roosevelt got the ball rolling with a White House Conference on the Emergency

Needs of Unemployed Women. Administrators in the Federal Emergency Relief Administration (FERA) and the Works Progress Administration (WPA) such as Ellen S. Woodward and Hilda Worthington Smith set up separate programs for women and won fairer treatment for women in existing programs. While progress was not uniformly positive, without the efforts of such administrators the needs of women on relief might have been totally forgotten.

The same circumstances that facilitated the contributions of women in New Deal policy-making positions also worked to the benefit of a second tier of women in the New Deal bureaucracy, women just below the level of presidential appointments represented by the women in the network. This second level of women administrators was broader and more extensive than the approximately thirty women who made up the network. Although their salaries and prestige were not as high as those of the women in the network (and probably less than those of comparable male coworkers), the excitement of serving in the New Deal infected this middle level of women bureaucrats just as much as it did Molly Dewson and Frances Perkins.

Historians have noticed that women generally fare better in bureaucracies and organizations when such groups are fairly new because inhibitions about using female talent tend to be weaker. Conversely, when bureaucracies become more entrenched and established, barriers to women's contributions stiffen. In the early years of the New Deal, women at all levels of governmental service benefited from the expansion of government programs; later in the decade, progress slowed. Yet the overall growth was impressive. Women's Bureau studies show that women's percentage of government employees grew from 14.3 percent in 1929 to 18.8 percent in 1939. Furthermore, women's rate of federal employment increased twice as rapidly as men's in the 1930s. Women's jobs were more concentrated in the recently established agencies than in older departments such as War, Navy, Justice, or Commerce. According to Women's Bureau figures for 1939, women's representation in the executive departments was 15.2 percent. This contrasted to women's 34.2 percent share in independent establishments, and their 44.4 percent in the seven newest independent establishments (which included the WPA). Of course, this expansion for women in the federal service did not mean that 175,000 women now had top-level civil service jobs. Then, as now, most of the women working for the federal government were concentrated in the lower ranges of salary and responsibility, especially in the clerical field.

While Women's Bureau studies claimed notable progress for women at all levels of the government bureaucracy, one black mark was Section 213 of the National Economy Act of 1932. A reflection of the tendency to make married women workers into scapegoats for unemployment, Section 213 prohibited both husband and wife from working for the federal government. While sex-neuter in its wording, the law's impact fell far more heavily on women than men, because wives' salaries were invariably less than those of their husbands. In all, some 1,600 married female government employees were forced to resign before the law was rescinded in 1937.

Nevertheless, while popular images portrayed eager young men flocking to staff the New Deal agencies, eager young women flocked to Washington as well. The collective story of this midlevel range of women who served in the New Deal awaits its historian, but several examples suggest the scope of increased opportunities for women in government service. For instance, women found many roles in the arts projects of the WPA known collectively as Federal One. The Federal Writers' Project had fourteen female state directors when it began, and the Federal Art Project provided an especially supportive climate for women artists and art administrators alike. A total of 8,000 women found employment on Federal One before its premature demise in the early 1940s.

Individual women, many at the beginnings of long careers in public life and government service, also found challenging opportunities. Caroline Ware joined the New Deal in 1933–34 as a special assistant to the Consumers' Advisory Board of the NRA, the beginning of her lifelong service to the consumer cause. Elinore Herrick rose to prominence in the National Labor Relations Board as a regional director, a position labor negotiator Anna Rosenberg (who was with the Social Security Board in the 1930s) would later hold. The Social Security Administration employed Maurine Hulliner as technical advisor to the Social Security Board and Lavinia Engle, a top Maryland Democrat, as educational representative. Marion Harron served on the Board of Tax Appeals, and Florence Kerr was a regional supervisor for the WPA before taking over Woodward's job in 1938. Lorena Hickok, one of the many newspaperwomen who flocked to Washington in the 1930s to cover Eleanor Roosevelt and other New Deal activities, signed on as a roving reporter for FERA administrator Harry Hopkins. Eleanor Roosevelt made sure that Lorena Hickok's graphic reports on relief conditions ended up on FDR's bedside table for his nighttime perusal. Dorothea Lange, working for the Farm Security Administration, matched Hickok's words with photographs vividly portraying the human impact of the Depression. This list, while by no means exhaustive, illustrates the important roles played by women throughout the New Deal bureaucracy, both in Washington and out in the field. Recognition of their contribution is long overdue.

THE NEW DEAL'S IMPACT ON WOMEN

In providing opportunities for women at senior and midlevel positions, the New Deal rates a very positive assessment. The New Deal's record on helping ordinary women, however, is more checkered. Both as workers and as members of families disrupted by the Depression, these women were in desperate straits. Since such women often lacked the opportunity to demand fairer treatment from New Deal agencies, their needs were often overlooked or slighted. And yet, the situation of many women was so desperate that any help, no matter how limited, was appreciated. This understanding is central to an evaluation of New Deal relief policies toward women.

The 1933 National Industrial Recovery Act, an attempt at industrial self-regulation through codes of production, was the keystone of the early New Deal recovery program. NRA codes affected more than 4 million women workers. The NRA codes had such a positive effect on women workers that the Women's Bureau concluded that enormous advances had occurred even in the relatively brief span of the law's enforcement. The Women's Bureau specifically cited the stabilization of deteriorating work conditions, which had characterized the early Depression, and the improvement of women's employment through wage and hours provisions mandated by each code. Women's wages were more affected by these minimum provisions than men's; since women earned the lowest wages, they had more to gain, even when the minimum wage was set at 25 cents an hour. Other aspects of the NRA drew vehement protest, especially the provisions in some one-quarter of the codes that mandated a lower minimum wage for women than men in the same jobs. Despite repeated protests from all the major women's organizations, these discriminatory features stood. The other major drawback to the NRA, in fact to all the New Deal welfare legislation, was that many women workers were left outside code protection. Domestic servants were an obvious (and numerous) example.

The Fair Labor Standards Act (FLSA) of 1938 made permanent many of the provisions of the temporary NRA, which had been ruled unconstitutional in 1935. The FLSA followed the precedent of the NRA and set wage and hours standards for both sexes, an important break from the older pattern of providing protection for women workers alone because of their presumed physical inferiority. FLSA wage and hours provisions proved especially beneficial to women workers in the textile and shoe industries, which came under the purview of the law. They offered little, however, to the majority of women workers who did not work in interstate commerce. Major areas of women's employment that were left outside the scope of the law were cannery workers, retail clerks, and domestic servants.

Another law, which made permanent the gains begun under the NRA, was the 1935 National Labor Relations Act, which extended federal support for unions begun under Section 7 (a) of the NRA. This governmental blessing of workers' right to organize encouraged the growth of the labor movement as a major force in American political and economic life, one of the New Deal's most far-reaching changes. Women shared in this progress: by the end of the decade, some 800,000 women belonged to unions, a threefold increase over 1929. Yet this record must be balanced against the large majority of women workers who still remained outside unions. Moreover, women were not exactly welcomed into the labor unions. Few leadership positions were open to them, and unions often collaborated with management in negotiating contracts with unequal pay and work provisions.

The story of women on relief is one of gradual improvement after a very dismal start. When people thought about unemployment, they invariably formed mental images of unemployed male workers—few recognized that more than 2 million women were out of work as well. Only after Eleanor Roosevelt hosted a White House Conference on the Emergency Needs of Women in late November, 1933, did federal relief agencies seriously begin to take the needs of women into account. Still progress was slow. The Civilian Works Administration, designed to get the country through the winter of 1933–1934, gave women only 7 percent of its jobs; the Federal Emergency Relief Administration did little better. A further slap was that the pay on projects where women were concentrated averaged only 30-to-40 cents an hour, while the construction projects in which male workers predominated were guaranteed an hourly wage of $1.

The status of women on relief improved dramatically in 1935 with the establishment of the Works Progress (later, Projects) Administration. Women's percentage of WPA jobs ranged from 12 percent to a high of 19 percent, not too far from women's 24 percent representation in the general work force. On the Federal Art Project, some 41 percent of artists on relief were women. At its peak, 405,000 women were on the WPA, the responsibility of Ellen Woodward and her mainly female staff at the Women's and Professional Projects division. Yet the WPA had its drawbacks for women. Women found it harder to qualify than men, since only one member of a family was eligible. The WPA automatically assumed the man was the primary breadwinner: if a woman had a husband who was able but unwilling to work, the WPA still considered him the head of the household, making her ineligible for work relief. The WPA also continued the pattern of lower pay scales for women, and placed the vast majority of women in sewing rooms and canning projects. This stereotyped women's work demanded few skills and offered no training for more challenging (and remunerative) work when the Depression ended. Finally, the 300,000 to 400,000 women who benefited from WPA employment must be balanced against the several million women who still could not not find work.

Women in government and public life worked hard to increase recognition of ordinary women's needs on relief, but there were limits to what a small group of New Deal administrators and women's organizations could accomplish. The case of camps for unemployed women showed this dramatically. The Civilian Conservation Corps (CCC), one of the New Deal's most popular programs, sent 2.5 million young men off to the woods to live in camps and do reforestation work. The CCC was the only New Deal program limited by statute to men, which led critics to ask, where was the "she-she-she"? It was only due to the efforts of the WPA administrator, Hilda Worthington Smith, and Eleanor Roosevelt's timely offer to host yet another White House conference that a similar program for women won any support. It was a pathetically meager program compared to the men's: only 45 camps for 8,500 women were set up throughout the country. The program was abruptly terminated in 1937. It is hard to disagree with Hilda Worthington Smith's plaintive assessment: "As so often the case, the boys get the breaks, the girls are neglected."

The Social Security Act of 1935 did not so much neglect women as penalize them. In the general excitement over the passage of Social Security, several discriminatory features were written into the law. While the Act provided maternal and pediatric programs and aid to mothers with dependent children, it slighted women who did not work for pay outside the home, the great majority of American women. Until the 1939 revisions, which shifted the emphasis from the individual worker to the worker's family, a wife was not even entitled to widow's benefits if her husband died. After 1939, the widow received only half her husband's benefits. Moreover, there were no widower's benefits if the wife died, even if she had been contributing Social Security taxes at the same rate as a working man. The operative assumption for Social Security was that men were the primary breadwinners and heads of household; women were secondary earners, who were less entitled to protection. In addition to those discriminatory aspects, many groups of women, such as agricultural workers and domestic servants, were excluded from coverage entirely.

Few would have argued against the enactment of Social Security because of these discriminatory features: as with the relief policies, the overwhelming need for immediate federal action outweighed the limitations of specific laws. Historian Lois Scharf captured this response well: "Women protected by a discriminatory wage standard, who had never had a floor under their wages before, cared little for the sexist implications. For desperate women on relief, the sewing room represented survival rather than a sex-segregated handout." The same held true for Social Security.

When coming to a general assessment of New Deal relief policies as they affected women, one cannot escape the fact that many women (and men) were left outside New Deal protection. Nothing can change the discriminatory and indeed sexist assumptions behind many relief and recovery programs. Yet benefits and limitations must be weighed: is it more important that one-quarter of the

NRA codes discriminated against women or that three-quarters did not? Do we applaud the threefold increase in women in labor unions or bemoan the fact that so many women were still outside union protection? Whether one cheers the advances or harps on the drawbacks in large part comes down to an individual's ideological stance toward the New Deal itself. This in turn raises the perennial question of whether the New Deal could have made more sweeping reforms than it did, or whether it pragmatically accomplished all that it could within the context of America in the 1930s. For many historians, the New Deal provides more to praise than to condemn, and that judgment applies to women's treatment in the New Deal as well.

AN ASSESSMENT

The year 1936 marked the peak of women's participation in the New Deal. In the second term, progress was stalemated. The social and welfare programs, in which women administrators were concentrated, and which benefited ordinary women on relief, were cut back by an increasingly conservative Congress. Once women lined up in the Democratic camp in the 1936 election, they found themselves taken more for granted politically. Eleanor Roosevelt shifted her attention away from women's issues in the second term, and the network leadership was weakened by the retirement of Molly Dewson. Finally, as the political dialogue shifted from Depression to war in the late 1930s, women's contributions were in less demand. The unique congruence of factors that had set up progress for women in the early New Deal was already on the wane.

While some of the progress for women in the New Deal was temporary, women's collective stories still have much to add to historians' understanding of the New Deal, as well as to the contours of twentieth-century political history and women's history. The New Deal is perhaps the most studied period in American political history, and yet until recently women's roles in the period received hardly any notice at all. That an actively functioning network of women could have escaped the attention of historians who had scrutinized practically every nook and cranny of the New Deal suggests that women may have been a more active force in political life than previously suspected. If women played such large roles in government and politics as far back as the 1930s, then perhaps women have made contributions to public life in other periods as well. And, since politics has traditionally been one of the areas least hospitable to women's talents, this progress is even more remarkable.

The story of women in the 1930s also adds to our understanding of New Deal historiography. One clear area of overlap is chronology. Many New Deal monographs start with the excitement of the first 100 days, move into the administrative accomplishments of the first term, and then describe stalemate, retrenchment, and decline after 1937. This pattern was perhaps best analyzed in James Patterson's influential study of congressional conservatism in the New Deal. The experiences of women follow a nearly parallel trail. The first term was a period of exciting new innovations for women in government and politics — they shared in the experimental climate of the early New Deal. Women's participation peaked in 1936 when the network was at its height and women played large roles in the successful election campaign. After 1936, women's progress stalled, in part because of attrition in the network but mainly because the New Deal was stalemated. Since women were concentrated in the very social welfare areas of the New Deal under the most severe attack, they were especially hard hit by the changing New Deal.

The story of women in the New Deal parallels broader New Deal historiography in other ways. Many historians have interpreted the New Deal as the epitome of the liberal broker state, a stark contrast to the single-interest, business-dominated government of the 1920s. One of the New Deal's most lasting contributions was to open up the political process to previously excluded groups of interests or voters. As such, historians often speak of a New Deal for blacks, or labor, or various ethnic groups. Equally, there was a New Deal for women. This is not just because a group of high-powered women took jobs in the Roosevelt Administration. These women advocated and represented the interests of women in a direct and self-conscious manner. Molly Dewson's efforts in politics, for example, strongly fostered such an awareness. The 1930s emerges as one of the few times to date when women have been seen as a specific group whose needs must be addressed in order to win their support.

There are especially strong parallels between the experiences of women and of blacks in the New Deal. Both groups experienced raised expectations and increased recognition during the decade.

Both groups found it necessary and efficient to develop informal networks in Washington to keep in touch with each other, and to advance the needs of sex or race at every possible opportunity. Actually, the Black Cabinet and the women's network shared more than just tactics: both were dependent on the support and help of Eleanor Roosevelt, without whom either group would have made far less remarkable progress. Both groups received somewhat more grudging support from Franklin Roosevelt, who responded to their requests in proportion to their increasing roles in the Democratic party and the New Deal coalition. Yet Franklin Roosevelt never gave either women or blacks anywhere near what they were asking for, or what, in fairness, they deserved. Both groups suffered from societal hostility toward their goals that contrasted sharply with the more supportive atmosphere they found in the New Deal. One final parallel might be that the activities of blacks and women in the 1930s were part of an historical process that culminated in the struggles of the civil rights and women's movements of the 1960s and 1970s.

There might be some who would say that the New Deal for women, either on the level of the network or the treatment of ordinary women by relief agencies, has very little to do with American feminism. The lack of a broad-based women's movement in the 1930s meant few voices were raised in protest against the unequal treatment of women in New Deal programs or in American society as a whole. The gains of elite women in the New Deal bureaucracy were the product of a propitious historical moment rather than the long-term development of feminism in the United States. Partial proof lies in the network's failure to institutionalize its gains. Another indication is the network's reluctance to address the contradiction between its belief in a democratic system based on merit and the obvious limits placed on women's advancement in American society. These women erroneously believed that if they did their jobs well, future barriers for women would tumble—a naive faith that offered little challenge to fundamental patterns of discrimination in American life. In this view, the story of women in the New Deal was one of a missed feminist opportunity.

While there is much to support such a negative interpretation of women's experiences in the New Deal, it remains unsatisfying. Women New Dealers were admittedly ambivalent about the priorities they assigned to issues specifically affecting women and those pertaining to broader social reform. For many women in public life in the 1930s, general reform concerns won out. Women's issues were squarely on their agenda, however, and they were willing to back up their convictions with action. Journalist Ruby Black captured this well when she said of Eleanor Roosevelt, "She talks like a social worker and acts like a Feminist." Women in the New Deal worked to promote more opportunities for women in public life and looked out for the interests of ordinary women hard hit by the Depression. This consciousness of women's interests shows one direction that feminism took in the postsuffrage years and places activities in the New Deal within a broader historical continuum that stretches from the suffrage movement to the revival of feminism in the 1960s. Feminism did not die after 1920. One of the areas in which it took root, however tentatively, was in the politics and government of the New Deal.

The impact of the New Deal on women in general, beyond those exceptional women who served in the New Deal administration, remains mixed. The treatment of women by relief agencies and New Deal policies parallels a pattern applicable to most aspects of the New Deal: those whom it helped never forgot the aid they received from the federal government, but many received little or nothing at all. This applied to both men and women, but women had to struggle even harder to get their due.

Yet women as a group did benefit from the policies of the New Deal: from Social Security, the NRA codes, the Fair Labor Standards Act, Aid to Dependent Children, and the WPA relief projects. For the most part, however, this progress for women came about not because of specific attempts to single out women for treatment, but as part of a broader effort to improve the conditions and economic security of all Americans. In the current metaphor, a rising tide lifts all ships equally. Women benefited not so much because they were women but because the federal government guaranteed the basic social security of all American citizens in response to the economic crisis of the Depression. While discriminatory features occasionally penalized women's interests, for the most part women shared in the salutory effect of this new legislation.

In the end, any evaluation of women and the New Deal must grapple with the irony that the New Deal's social welfare programs became institutionalized as the modern welfare state, while the positive gains for women were not. The federal government now has a controlling role in planning and managing the economy; it now guarantees, at least in theory, the basic economic and social security of all Americans from birth to death. The political process permanently includes such interest groups as labor, blacks, and minorities. Progress for women has proven more illusory. Unlike the popular support for the New Deal, there was no widespread interest in changing women's roles in the 1930s. Lacking a popular base to force recognition of women's concerns, women largely remained dependent on whatever benefits might trickle their way. For all the activities of the network on behalf of women and reform, the most long-lasting legacy of the New Deal for women may be the founding of the modern welfare state, which has improved women's lives along with men's.

The message that the New Deal experience offers to women is a contradictory one: organize as women in order to make your special needs known, but also work for broad-based reforms that will help all citizens. Eleanor Roosevelt addressed the same paradox in an April 1940 article on women in politics commissioned by *Good Housekeeping*: "Women must become more conscious of themselves as women and of their ability to function as a group. At the same time they must try to wipe from men's consciousness the need to consider them as a group or as women in their everyday activities, especially as workers in industry or the professions." Eleanor Roosevelt realized that it was not enough to let general social progress sweep women along with the tide: women must unite on issues of fundamental concern to them as women although women's interests were increasingly difficult to separate from men's. Whether women should organize independently from men to advance their cause or stress the similarities between the two sexes has been the crucial question of feminism in the postsuffrage age. The contradictions of women's experiences in the New Deal show how hard a question this is to resolve.

It is wrong to end on such an ambiguous note. Even if women in the New Deal did not solve all the problems of access to politics and government, even if New Deal programs sometimes slighted the needs of women, the 1930s still remains a period of important breakthroughs for women. The New Deal's experimental climate, which opened up opportunities for other previously excluded groups, did the same for women. Into the void stepped a group of women who showed conclusively and with great style how much women had to offer to public life. The social programs of the New Deal might not have have succeeded to the extent they did without the contributions of this spirited and well-trained corps of women. The New Deal certainly would have been a far less humane undertaking without their collective presence. Historians of the New Deal have much to learn from the experiences of American women in the of the 1930s.

SUGGESTED READINGS

Most of the material in this essay is drawn from Susan Ware, *Beyond Suffrage: Women in the New Deal* (Cambridge, Mass., 1981) and Ware, *Holding Their Own: American Women in the 1930s* (Boston, 1982). Other major sources on women in the 1930s include Alice Kessler-Harris, *Out to Work: A History of Wage-Earning Women in the United States* (New York, 1982); Lois Scharf, *To Work and to Wed: Female Employment, Feminism and the Great Depression* (Westport, Conn., 1980); Winifred Wandersee, *Women's Work and Family Values, 1920–1940* (Cambridge, Mass., 1981); and Susan D. Becker, *The Origins of the Equal Rights Amendment: American Feminism Between the Wars* (Westport, Conn., 1981). Useful introductions to women's history in twentieth-century America include William H. Chafe, *The American Woman, 1920–1970* (New York, 1972), and Lois W. Banner, *Women in Modern America: A Brief History* (New York, 1974). Lorena Hickok and Eleanor Roosevelt, *Ladies of Courage* (New York, 1954) provides a good overview of women's political roles in the New Deal and biographical vignettes of many of the prominent women New Dealers.

For specific women in the New Deal, the biographies collected in *Notable American Women* (Cambridge, Mass., 1971) and *Notable American Women: The Modern Period* (Cambridge, Mass., 1980) provide an excellent starting point. Eleanor Roosevelt has received the most biographical treatment: see Tamara Hareven, *Eleanor Roosevelt: An American Conscience* (New York, 1968); Joseph P. Lash, *Eleanor and Franklin* (New York, 1971) and *Eleanor: The Years Alone* (New York, 1972). Lash's books contain a wealth of information about the broad spectrum of women's activities in the New Deal as they coalesced around Eleanor Roosevelt. For Frances Perkins, see George Martin, *Madame Secretary* (Boston, 1976). Susan Ware is currently writing a biography of Molly Dewson. Eleanor Roosevelt, Frances Perkins, Mary Anderson, Rose Schneiderman, Hallie

Flanagan, and Florence Jaffray Harriman are among the New Deal women who published autobiographies describing their years in Washington. For Hickok's unsurpassed reportage on the impact of the Depression on ordinary Americans, see *One Third of a Nation: Lorena Hickok Reports on the Great Depression* (Urbana, Ill., 1981), edited by Richard Lowitt and Marine Beasley.

The New Deal
and the Cities

Charles H. Trout

From the inception of the Republic, anti-urban themes have permeated American intellectual and cultural life, and it is no novelty to observe that bias against the city has been a part of the nation's political oratory as well. "Ah, my friends," said William Jennings Bryan in his "Cross of Gold" speech, "we say not one word against those who live upon the Atlantic coast, but the hardy pioneers who have braved all the dangers of the wilderness, who have made the desert to blossom as the rose—the pioneers away out there [pointing to the West], who rear their children near to Nature's heart, where they can mingle their voices with the voices of the birds[,] . . . [i]t is for these that we speak." Bryan's agrocentric, physiocratic view of the universe led him to argue that "great cities rest upon our broad and fertile plains." "Burn down your cities and leave our farms, and your cities will spring up again as if by magic; but destroy our farms and the grass will grow in the streets of every city in the country."

Franklin Delano Roosevelt has been linked to this anti-urban tradition not because he, like Bryan, was concerned about "the plain people" who toiled on prairie farms but because he, as a Dutchess County aristocrat, had made as the "focus of his secure world" his "carefully managed estate at Hyde Park, with its planted and tended forests, sleek herds of cattle, and carefully cultivated fields." So writes historian Paul Conkin, who claims that Roosevelt's passion for the conservation of natural resources, his "near-romantic love of trees," and his interest in agricultural problems were "deep commitments always colored by happy memories" derived from childhood. These commitments, Conkin and others have argued, meant that an aristocratic Roosevelt was incapable of charting a coherent program for urban America. According to this view, Roosevelt's answer to the plight of cities was to siphon off a source of urban discontent by sending young men into the nation's forests with the Civilian Conservation Corps and to resettle the urban unemployed on subsistence homesteads. To Conkin, Roosevelt's favorite color was green — not the green of big-city Irish bosses, for whom he had contempt, but the green of parks, greenbelt cities, and a movement back to the land. At best, Roosevelt's contribution to the well-being of cities, as if by accident, flowed from legislation that lacked an explicitly urban purpose. Lost in a world of aristocratic conventionalities, or so the story goes, Roosevelt remained in Rexford Tugwell's words "a child of the country," a President who believed to the end that cities were nothing more than "a perhaps necessary nuisance."

If, for the sake of argument, it is momentarily conceded that Roosevelt harbored deep-seated reservations about cities, this is not to say that among the nation's political leaders he was in any way unusual: nothing in the administration of his predecessor, Herbert Hoover, suggested a pro-urban vision. Confronted by lengthening bread lines, shrinking payrolls, and bankrupt cities, Hoover, after considerable urging, advocated an economic recovery program based on the assumption that a government lending agency, authorized to issue tax-exempt bonds and empowered to extend credit, would stimulate the economy. On February 2, 1932, the Reconstruction Finance Corporation (RFC) was formally established. After six months, the RFC had made some 5,000 loans to banks, insurance companies, and agricultural credit corporations, but the agency might just as well have hung up a sign that read, "Municipalities need not apply." Of the first $1.5 billion made available by Congress in July 1932 for public works, less than 1 percent went to cities. Faced with the requirement that works projects be self-liquidating (that is, they had to pay for themselves, such as toll bridges or public housing), the nation's mayors declined to approach the federal government. Moreover, Hoover exhibited a small businessman's conception of urban decay. Drawing a distinction between homes and housing, he expressed preference for the former and contempt for the latter. Addressing a private organization called "Better Homes in America," the President revealed his preference for single-family units. Home ownership, he argues, provided a bulwark against threats to democracy. "There is," he observed, "a wide distinction between homes and mere housing."

Those immortal ballads "Home, Sweet Home," "My Old Kentucky Home," and "Little Gray Home in the West" were not written about tenements or apartments. They are the expressions of racial longing which find outlet in the living poetry and songs of our people. . . . To own one's own house is a physical expression of individualism, of enterprise, or independence, and of the freedom of spirit.

Hoover and his Republican high command, even more than the leadership of the Democratic party, failed to recognize the realities of urban life in the midst of the Great Depression. As Mark Gelfond has pointed out in A Nation of Cities, it was "the thin ranks of social workers and city planners," not major-party leadership, who tried "to articulate the problems of poverty, poor housing, and inadequate transportation."

THE DARK REALITIES OF THE MOMENT

Franklin Delano Roosevelt welcomed a number of these urban progressives into his Administration, and their presence served to move the New Deal toward policies of substantial benefit to cities. Harry Hopkins, Harold Ickes, John Ihlder, Frances Perkins, and a number of others had forged careers in the crucible of urban America. Then, too, Roosevelt himself possessed the requisite sensitivity to respond to urban suffering. His travels during the 1932 campaign and in the period between the election and the inauguration exposed him to grim reminders of the Great Depression. As his train wheeled into sidings, he saw hoboes warming themselves by fires and transients riding in boxcars. On any number of occasions, he saw the jerrybuilt Hoovervilles that had begun to blight the landscape of urban America.

A month before his inauguration, Roosevelt visited Miami, Florida, where he conversed with Anton Cermak, the Mayor of "Cashless Chicago." Cermak acquainted Roosevelt with the realities of big cities in the Great Depression—the efforts to help the jobless at Christmas, the creation of a special milk fund set up to supplement the diets of destitute Chicagoans, the provisions of the Chicago City Council to appoint "competent persons who need employment in the place of . . . married women," the effort to reduce street railway fares for children of families receiving aid from the Illinois Relief Commission. Moments later, a crazed gunman opened fire. Cermak died, Roosevelt was mercifully spared, and what the President-elect would call in his Inaugural Address "the dark realities of the moment" were, in a flash, all too apparent.

For the nation's cities, those "realities" were bleak indeed. Franklin Murphy, the Mayor of Detroit, roamed Wall Street in a fruitless quest for loans; the jobless of New Orleans peddled oranges obtained at discount prices from City Hall. Municipally financed construction had all but come to a standstill: only half of all city engineers employed in the late 1920s still held their jobs at the time of Roosevelt's inauguration. In the peak year of 1928, cities had spent $170 million for sanitation facilities. Four years later, the outlay had dipped below $50 million. Teachers were lopped from payrolls, thousands of municipal workers were paid in scrip, and systems of barter, not unlike those in the isolated coal camps of Appalachia, sprang up in Dayton, Seattle, and Los Angeles. Real property assessments plummeted, tax delinquencies soared, and welfare costs in city after city imposed impossible burdens on cash-starved treasuries. In Boston, men with self-inflicted wounds entered hospitals and jails to escape the cold, and in New York City a couple moved into a cave in Central Park.

In such a setting, the nation's mayors were not calling for something that today would pass for sophisticated, comprehensive urban policy: to saddle Roosevelt and the New Deal with a 1980's basis for judgment would be unfair. What then passed for an urban lobby — journals like *The National Municipal Review* and *The American City*, organizations such as the United States Conference of Mayors and the National Municipal League — focused upon joblessness and the need for public works. The February 1933 edition of *The American City*, for instance, placed Abraham Lincoln on its cover. "If the Great Emancipator were alive today," what would he do? His answer would have been "to solve the problem [of enforced idleness] by peaceful means — by putting the powers of the Government to work through a gigantic program of public works — national, state and local — to substitute jobs for doles and prosperity for poverty." A month later, the editors listed three primary tasks for the new administration: Roosevelt must "overcome the absurd idea that stopping public works is a desirable economy, and that tax reduction is more urgent than business expansion." Second, he must eliminate the self-liquidating requirements of the Reconstruction Finance Commission and facilitate not only public works but public housing. Third, he must construct a municipal-state-federal partnership to provide "socially useful, self-respecting work for the involuntarily unemployed." Noting with approval that Rexford Tugwell, a member of Roosevelt's Brain Trust, in a January 1933 interview with the Scripps-Howard newspapers, had advocated a $5-billion public works program, coupled with funds for direct relief, and the "intense stimulation of semi-public works projects, such as slum clearance, through the Reconstruction Finance Corporation," *The American City* looked to the New Deal for deliverance.

THE FEDERAL GOVERNMENT STEPS IN

Municipal leaders did not have to wait long for signals that the federal government intended to intervene. On April 10, 1933, Roosevelt called upon the nation's mayors to devise plans in anticipation of a massive infusion of federal money for relief and public works. The President's message, a sharp break from the venerable notion that urban crises were for localities to solve, represented the opening thrust toward a pronounced change in municipal-federal relations. Two months later, Roosevelt signed into law the National Industrial Recovery Act (NIRA), a statute which, for all its limitations, was to affect profoundly the traditional autonomy of American cities.

Through Title II of the NIRA, New Dealers created the Public Works Administration (PWA). Supported by the unprecedented appropriation of $3.3 billion and placed under the cautious guidance of Harold Ickes, the PWA was designed to generate construction projects costing in excess of $25,000. State Emergency Finance Boards were set up to receive proposals from cities, but funding depended upon a 30 percent federal-70 percent city match. Projects were to be "socially desirable in the sense of contributing something of value to the equipment of the community . . . ." In looking askance at proposals that were "isolated and unrelated," the PWA contributed substantially to the growth of urban planning in America by urging cities to integrate a series of designs into a coherent whole. "Our National Treasury is waiting to be drawn upon," Ickes told the U.S. Conference of Mayors, and cities lined up to avail themselves of the promised bounty.

Simultaneously, the NIRA allowed New Dealers to initiate the first federal venture into the field of public housing. Through Section 202(d) of the NIRA, a PWA Housing Division was established. Just as PWA guidelines for construction compelled states to create emergency relief organizations and provided incentives for cities to establish planning boards, the new housing program stimulated the formation of local housing authorities. In city after city, the New Deal was forcing governmental bodies to experiment with new, more sophisticated structures. The Cleveland Metropolitan Housing Authority, the Boston Housing Authority, and countless similar organizations originated in this period. Indeed, every bit as much as the dollars themselves, the critical legacy of the PWA experiment may well have been the lasting changes it fashioned in the structure and conduct of municipal government. To staff these new agencies, experts were invited in and political hacks were displaced.

The PWA's rescue mission moved slowly, but this did not mean the agency did not move at all. From Pahokee, Florida, to Newcastle, Wyoming, cities matched federal dollars to construct municipal waterworks. In the summer of 1933, Washington, D.C. received nearly $2 million for a sewerage system. In New York City the Triborough Bridge Authority garnered a loan-grant package in excess of $44 million, and the Port of New York Authority captured $37.5 million to build the Lincoln Tunnel. Planners began to chart urban highways: PWA money was used not only to resurface existing roads but to construct bypasses around central business districts in places such as Ogden, Provo, and Salt Lake City, Utah. With the PWA insisting that at least 25 percent of highway funds allocated to the states be spent within city limits, municipal officials spotted opportunities to modernize transportation routes. Even in the first six months of PWA, a number of cities were able to eliminate hazardous grade crossing, get rid of footpaths, and build bridges that had been deferred for several years. School and hospital construction, the clearing of recreation sites, and municipal power projects were all part of the early PWA activities. Within four months after its creation, the PWA Housing Division had approved seventeen projects in locales from Brooklyn and Queens to Hutchinson, Kansas. Models of municipal-state-federal cooperation abounded, and Harold Ickes drove home the point that in the competition for federal dollars, cities with planning boards—Los Angeles and Sacramento, Detroit and St. Louis, Pittsburgh, and Richmond, for example—fared better than those with none.

LOCAL OBSTACLES TO CHANGE

Despite the PWA's early achievements, however, the agency encountered any number of difficulties and soon had a reputation for excessive red tape and delay. Six months after Roosevelt affixed his signature to the public works bill, for instance, the City of Boston still had not put a single man to work on a PWA project, and it was not until 1935 that the city treasurer recorded the first dollars from this source. By February 1934, applications had almost doubled the $3.3 billion congressional appropriation, but only a small fraction of that sum had been spent.

While it has been fashionable to place much of the blame for the PWA's start-up difficulties upon Harold Ickes and "the semi-colon boys" in Washington, a good many of the agency's troubles can be traced to local inertia. Time and again, the PWA rescinded projects that had been awarded federal grants because municipalities failed to execute contracts with the construction firms that would be doing the work. Innumerable cities had trouble in coming up with their 70 percent share of project costs—either because city councils or boards of aldermen were composed of fiscal conservatives who were unwilling to embrace the doctrine of deficit spending, or because a number of municipal governments had lost their historic fight for home rule and were under the sway of state legislatures controlled by suburban and agrarian interests. The State of Indiana, for example, had imposed severe tax-limitation laws upon its cities, and East Chicago lost a $145,000 federal grant because it lacked the power to pass along the costs to property owners. To combat Irish control of Boston, the Massachusetts legislature had imposed a debt limit that severely limited Boston's capacity to enter into loan-grant arrangements with the PWA. Moreover, state emergency relief boards, which had to approve municipal projects, were often packed with political foes of big-city mayors: the conflict between Governor Huey Long and New Orleans' T. Semmes Walmsley, and the acrimony between Ohio's troglodytic Governor, Martin Davey, and the principal cities in the state were only two of a number of destructive relationships that New Dealers could not have been expected to have solved—nor did they. To put it another way, cities entered the New Deal period with attributes that did not always mesh easily with what the New Deal was trying to accomplish.

In particular, the federal experiment in public housing repeatedly ran up against entrenched interests that were difficult to overcome.

In 1933 when Chicago accepted PWA funds to launch what at that point was the largest slum clearance project in the nation's history, officials viewed with dismay the task of assembling 160 acres of land in the central city. To put the parcels together, federal officials had to file 26 condemnation suits involving some 10,000 defendants. While the Chicago effort eventually succeeded, condemnation proceedings foundered in other locales. Slumlords, land speculators, mortgage-banking interests and, in some cases, slumdwellers who did not wish to be displaced were able to block land-takings for considerable periods of time. For example, a Circuit Court ruling in 1935 that the government was not entitled to exercise the right of eminent domain in the City of Louisville brought federal land-takings to a halt for more than a year.

To circumvent difficulties of this sort, compromises had to be made: twenty-four of the fifty-one PWA housing projects that were eventually completed rested on terrain that had never seen a slum because it was easier to assign open, city-owned land to the federal projects than to clear privately owned, blighted neighborhoods. In this sense, it is questionable whether the term "federal project" had much meaning: so-called "federal" housing was often transmuted by local circumstances, even including rental levels and tenant lists. While rent was in every case pegged below city medians, averaging $5.37 per room per month, there was considerable variation from city to city. As one dismayed City Council member put it, Boston's Old Harbor Village was less a "happy hunting ground for the poor" than a refuge for the middle class. Frequently, control over tenant lists fell into the hands either of urban congressmen or local politicians. When this occurred, fealty to the Democratic party or affiliation with a particular ethnic group became a more important consideration than a family's need. While some cities ruled that only those with jobs in the private sector were eligible to occupy PWA housing units, others welcomed families whose source of income depended upon federal work relief. Variations of this sort, in turn, suggest that several of the New Deal's shortcomings in the field of public housing are traceable to local circumstances. The reverse side of this contention is, of course, that Roosevelt, Ickes, and New Dealers in Congress declined to establish dictatorial control over urban housing policy: they declined but they were, after all, moving into uncharted waters. That the PWA ultimately provided housing for 25,000 urbanites and broke a number of important precedents in doing so is, in the end, more important than the agency's alleged timidity.

To suggest that Roosevelt should have waved his magic wand, thus eradicating local obstacles to change, is not only unrealistic but seriously underestimates local resistance to New Deal programs. The PWA was plagued by litigation not only in its public housing ventures but in many of its other endeavors as well. By 1937, for instance, some 52 lawsuits, most of them brought by private utilities companies (who opposed the idea of municipal ownership of utilities), were holding up more than $52 million of public works money that had been earmarked for municipally owned power plants, electrical distribution systems, and water works. Roosevelt instructed the Department of Justice to fight back, thus tacitly giving recognition to one of the most cherished goals of municipal socialists like Mayor Daniel Hoan of Milwaukee. On another but related front, Roosevelt fought private utilities companies in their efforts to thwart the Tennessee Valley Authority's sale of power to such cities as Louisville, Nashville, Lexington, and Memphis. In this instance, the battle was carried all the way into the 1940 election when the Republican party nominated Wendell Willkie, the former president of the Commonwealth and Southern Corporation and an archfoe of federal assistance to cities. Although there were many issues involved in Willkie's campaign, his candidacy, at least in part, serves as a reminder of the extent to which powerful interest groups arrayed themselves against the New Deal in the cities.

THE PWA'S ACHIEVEMENTS

Despite the many setbacks the PWA encountered along the way, the agency in several respects changed the face of urban centers. By the time the PWA had closed its doors in 1939, its dams and reservoirs had impounded enough water for the nation's cities to float 1 million ships the size of the *Queen Mary*, or to reduce the world's ocean level by one-quarter of an inch, or to cover the whole State of Pennsylvania with 2 feet of water. Residents of Oklahoma City took pride in a civic center development that included a courthouse, a new city hall, an 8,000-seat auditorium, new police headquarters, and a jail. Like many of the better PWA projects, the one in Oklahoma City derived from a comprehensive plan for center-city redevelopment. The planning mechanisms themselves, enduring long beyond the life of the PWA, were perhaps more important to the future than the civic center project. "[A] builder to rival Cheops," as William Leuchtenburg has called him, Harold Ickes and the PWA were responsible for constructing nearly three-fourths of the new school buildings erected during the Depression; 65 percent of the nation's courthouses, city halls, and sewerage plants; and roughly one-third of its hospitals and health facilities. From a rose garden and a golf course in Fort Worth to major repair of the Statue of Liberty, the PWA gave American cities a significant face-lifting.

In addition, the PWA shifted the gaze of municipal leaders away from state capitals and toward Washington, D.C. By 1934, the PWA required localities to put up 55 percent of project costs, not 70 percent, and applications for loan-grant arrangments became noticeably more popular. To the extent that ideological reservations had initially restrained municipal leaders from seeking the federal government's assistance, by mid-decade that restraint had all but vanished. Mayors who were able to deal with Washington came to be valued, while those who could not were frequently turned out of office. Sidelined until Roosevelt came to power, municipal engineers, draftsmen, architects, and social planners assumed an important role in designing projects that would attract Washington's favor. In a number of cities, and again with an eye toward currying favor with Washington, moves were made to centralize purchasing, modernize accounting departments, and upgrade planning operations. Although not enormously glamorous, these developments, in part a response to the New Deal, were of permanent consequence for the better management of cities.

There is little to no evidence that Franklin Delano Roosevelt directly sought these changes or that he was particularly interested in any of them. In pointing to the President's lack of enthusiasm for low-cost federal housing "as a permanent government activity," William Leuchtenburg has reminded us once again that Roosevelt was "[a] man with small love for the city. . . ." Need we demand that Roosevelt declare his affection for the metropolis? Probably not. Instead, Roosevelt's impact upon the city needs to be judged by assessing the extent to which he responded to the agenda proposed by urban lobbyists of the 1930s. More than anything else, the municipal leaders of America wanted the new administration to take people off relief rosters and put them to work. Roosevelt responded through the Federal Emergency Relief Administration (FERA), the Civil Works Administration (CWA), and the Works Progress Administration (WPA). Time and again, city councils passed resolutions, almost always unanimous, thanking Roosevelt for what a Chicago alderman called his "earnest and unremitting efforts . . . to alleviate the want and suffering" of urban dwellers. His efforts, continued the alderman, had shown "how great the man is and how compassionate is his heart for all who look to him for guidance and help." Throughout the Great Depression, Roosevelt's appearances in the nation's urban centers were greeted with unparalleled outbursts of enthusiasm from record-setting crowds. For a President allegedly enamored of rural America, he had either hoodwinked millions of urbanites or, as is more likely, he had come forward with programs that contributed to the well-being of those who lived in cities. As Mark Gelfand has shrewdly observed, Roosevelt may not have cared for the city as a place in which to live but he cared enormously about the people who resided therein.

WORK RELIEF AND THE CITIES

Robert Bremner has already addressed the question of New Deal welfare policies and has found them in some ways wanting (see pp. 69–92). It is important nevertheless to consider work relief in its urban context. When that record is unveiled, a mixed picture emerges. On balance, however, the federal government's intervention in what had previously been viewed as a local problem had profound and lasting consequences. Moreover, the ways in which federal work-relief programs were tailored to municipal needs suggests that anti-urbanism was assuredly not a New Deal trait.

In May 1933 the Federal Emergency Relief Administration (FERA), backed by a $500-million appropriation, came into being. In the nation's thirteen cities with populations of 500,000 people or more, the unemployment rate hovered in the vicinity of 30 percent, and the FERA, for all its shortcomings, seemed heaven-sent. FERA employees, most of them taken from municipal welfare rolls, fanned out through the cities to work for Uncle Sam at $15 a week.

Women on federal sewing projects made garments for the poor; men removed old hulks and pilings from harbors; public buildings were sand-blasted; public parks were weeded; shelters were set up for transients; and FERA employees staffed recreation projects for urban youngsters. Meanwhile, the Federal Surplus Relief Corporation distributed canned beef and veal, butter and evaporated milk, and fruit and vegetables to those in need.

To tide the nation over the winter of 1933–34, Congress established the Civil Works Administration (CWA). Even more urban-oriented than the FERA, the CWA displayed adroitness in devising projects that were helpful not only to the jobless but to the well-being of the physical city as well. Summoned to Washington on November 15, 1933, hundreds of the nation's mayors, joined by governors and other state officials, listened to Harry Hopkins in disbelief as he announced that they would have three weeks to put 4 million men and women to work. Despite start-up delays in some localities, cities were generally equal to the task. With each city receiving aid in proportion to its share of state population, mayors scurried to draw up proposals for one of more of the eighty types of municipal projects eligible for funding.

Many of the projects recognized the extent to which urban services had deteriorated during the Depression, and CWA crews were sent out to clean up rubbish and tear down "useless and insanitary structures" as part of a fire-prevention program. By the time the CWA was phased out in the early spring of 1934, to be replaced by another round of FERA, the agency had built athletic fields and golf courses, installed electric transmission lines and built heating plants, labored on jails and retaining walls, schools and streets, stadiums and swimming pools, water mains and sewers. In several cities, the CWA offered nursery school services, as well as adult and vocational education programs. Cities with populations above 25,000 put the unemployed to work on community traffic surveys, and in 60 cities some 11,000 men and women were assigned the task of drawing up the CWA's "Real Property Inventory," the first systematic attempt in the nation's history to survey the condition of its urban housing stock. Like many of the PWA projects, both the community traffic surveys and the property inventory inspired long-range planning and were therefore of special importance. Subsequent public works projects, in fact, were frequently designed to implement the recommendations that emanated from these surveys.

From the spring of 1934 into the summer of 1935, a second version of the FERA continued many of these projects until the Works Progress Administration was established. The WPA, brought into being by the $4.88-billion Emergency Relief Act of 1935, also exhibited a distinctly urban favor. By sponsoring projects of the FERA-CWA type, the WPA made it possible for cities to forge ahead with construction projects that would otherwise have been unthinkable. Critics accused the WPA of being merely a ditch-digging agency, but there was nothing "mere" about the millions of linear feet the WPA carved out of the ground for water mains and sewers. In its first two years, the WPA constructed 73 new municipal buildings in Kansas; the streets of Montgomery, Alabama, made of cobblestone brought as ballast for slave ships, were repaved with granite; Cleveland boasted a new, lakefront boulevard; in New Orleans during a single, twelve-hour work day, the old wooden slabs of Exchange Alley were torn up and replaced by asphalt. Within the first 24 months of the WPA, in fact, some 100,000 blocks of city streets were either improved or newly constructed.

Once again, the WPA proved a catalyst for urban planning. Several cities, for instance, used federal workers to devise topographical maps far more sophisticated than they had ever known before: Denver's metropolitan survey, for example, tracked 800 square miles at a cost of $350,000. Teams of WPA workers devised new tax collection methods and introduced improved property-assessment systems, while WPA engineers undertook feasibility studies for additional projects. By again making clear that integrated projects ran a better chance of being funded than one that stood in isolation, Harry Hopkins delivered a blow on behalf of those committed to comprehensive urban design.

In addition to attending to the physical plight of cities, the WPA also looked after the more spiritual side of urban life. Although the Federal Art Project had its rural dimension, the majority of the writers, musicians, actors, and artists who received paychecks from Washington flourished in urban settings. Cities of antiquity had functioned as seats of culture. In the New Deal years, this attribute was both recognized and promoted. WPA civic orchestras, sometimes led by celebrity conductors such as Arthur Fiedler, WPA choruses, and WPA vaudeville troupes not only benefited the participants but lifted the spirits of eager audiences as well. When WPA "opera on the dole," as a *Globe* reviewer called it, "made its bow in Boston," the potentialities of government-supported music were revealed. An art form with a previously limited clientele had been made available to the masses:

> Footlights illuminating the W.P.A. production of Humperdinck's "Hansel and Gretel" flashed to the diamond horseshoe of the 400 and reflected to the orchestra circle the sheen of a celluloid collar on an Elevated motorman. . . . It was opera for the 4,000,000, and the sign on the door warning "Drivers, Chauffeurs, Footmen not allowed to stand in the vestibule," might just as well have been draped, for the drivers, chauffeurs, and footmen were occupying seats of the master and the madame at 83 cents per chair.

Meanwhile, federal writers put together guidebooks that included extensive portraits of cities, and federal actors drew S.R.O. audiences from New York to San Francisco.

URBAN WORK RELIEF: THE BALANCE SHEET

There were, of course, any number of inadequacies in federal work relief programs. For every jobless urbanite who received a federal paycheck, three to four were excluded. Funding was often spasmodic, and from week to week the size of the workforce oscillated—sometimes wildly. Not every project was socially useful; not every city succeeded in forming a grand design that pieced together the components parts of work relief into a coherent whole. As Harvard Sitkoff reminds us, racial discimination flourished more often than should have been the case (see pp. 93–112). The same thing was true of ethnic biases. In a city such as Pittsburgh, a weak Democratic party became overwhelmingly powerful when it was able to capture control of work relief and dispense jobs on the basis of political loyalties. On occasion, regulations dictated from the mountain tops of Washington were ludicrous. Federal opera managers, for example, were faced with a decree that allowed no solos. Instead, so-called "solos" had to be sung by groups of at least ten otherwise jobless musicians. Thus in "La Traviata," the death of Violetta, occupying the whole of the final act, may well have been the most clamorous in operatic history.

Much like the difficulties encountered by the PWA, many of the deficiencies of urban work relief were linked not to Roosevelt and his aides but to local impediments. City councils were required to appropriate money for tools and building materials but city councils were not always forthcoming with the requisite funds. Although the FERA, the CWA, and the WPA were "federal" programs, they were manned by locals with various degrees of competency. There were instances when weekly WPA payrolls were lost — not in Washington but in cities where ineptitude prevailed. When audition boards excluded members of a particular ethnic group from joining a "federal" chorus or orchestra, those boards were comprised of city dwellers with discriminatory proclivities. New Deal discrimination against blacks is perhaps best-remembered in descriptions of the ways in which local Agricultural Adjustment Administration boards drove Negro tenant farmers off the land. Urban counterparts existed in the South and the North: almost nowhere did blacks receive federal work relief in proportion to their unemployment rates. While Congressman Martin Dies of Texas is invariably associated with successful, anti-Communist fulminations that led to the termination of the Federal Art Projects, it should not be forgotten that residents of Massachusetts burned federal guidebooks on the Boston Common, or that members of the New York City Council swooped down on "Revolt of the Beavers," a children's play in which the bad beaver king was overthrown: the evil monarch was succeeded by a collectivist regime that parceled out ice-cream cones to eager children. Local solons objected while New Dealers in Washington cringed. In Baltimore and San Francisco, cadres of work-relief employees organized into unions to protest various aspects of the FERA and the WPA. As Robert Bremner has pointed out, New Deal work-relief was not over-generous, but a number of the difficulties cited by dissident workers were attributable not to pecksniffean attitudes in Washington but to state Emergency Relief Boards and their politically motivated efforts to divert funds from cities to suburbs and rural areas.

Uneven distribution of New Deal benefits to cities is well-exemplified in the case of Wisconsin, a state far less politically troubled than, say, Texas, North Dakota, or Ohio. The only state with an unemployment insurance plan at the time of the stock market collapse of 1929, with a public-welfare history extending back to Robert La Follette and turn-of-the-century progressivism,

Wisconsin nevertheless exhibited patterns of aid ascribable not to the vagaries of New Dealers but to the predilections of officials in Madison. Despite roughly the same unemployment rates, Milwaukee was able to parcel out federal benefits to only 16.4 percent of its population while Kenosha boasted that 23 percent of its residents profited from work-relief and Social Security programs. In Wisconsin's northern, rural counties, as many as 39.7 percent of all residents received federal assistance. While the Wisconsin Department of Public Welfare could boast of "the diminution of social stigma formerly attached to the acceptance of public aid," the "stigma" diminished less in Racine and Sheboygan than it did in the sparsely populated regions to the North.

None of this is to say that Franklin Roosevelt and the New Deal should be exempted from criticism to the effect that they stopped short of a grand design for cities. The New Deal's urban efforts tended to be piecemeal, not systematic, and that portion of expenditures destined for cities from March 1933 into 1937, when the New Deal had largely run its course, totaled little more than $3 billion, a paltry figure compared to the outlays it would take to fight World War II. Moreover, the decision in 1935 to turn over all transients and the chronically unemployable to local agencies, rather than absorb them in the WPA, was little short of callous. At no point did the New Deal impose uniform standards upon local welfare departments. Left to their own devices, urban welfare operations in general were less reform-minded after 1935 than before. Meanwhile, Roosevelt and his advisers shied away from placing a moratorium upon municipal debt, and proposals for a Land Bank that would have allowed cities to borrow against property they had acquired for non-payment of taxes were all but ignored. The Federal Municipal Debt Adjustment Act of 1934 rated high on piety but low on content: instead of allowing federal courts to declare a moratorium of up to ten years on interest payments, as Mayor Murphy of Detroit was urging, Congress enacted a law that simply allowed cities and their bond-holders to renegotiate the terms under which municipal debt would have to be paid. Roosevelt had no interest in generating plans for an urban renaissance, nor was he ever given to outpourings of affection for cities. Regarding urban bosses like Ed Kelly of Chicago and Frank Hague of Jersey City as, at best, a necessary nuisance, he never developed ardor for cities. No president ever has.

THE NEW DEAL'S URBAN LEGACY

By the standards of the era, and even applying tests that might be used in the Ronald Reagan years, however, Roosevelt and his cohorts come out well. Intergovernmental relationships underwent pronounced shifts, and the parade of mayors that cluttered the President's weekly calendar was unprecedented. In 1929, postal workers and customs insectors had drawn federal paychecks. From 1933 to 1940, fully half the population of Philadelphia had at one time or another cashed payments from Uncle Sam. Although physically and spiritually battered by the ravages of the Great Depression, the nation's cities would have looked very different by 1940 had Roosevelt and the New Deal not intervened. Even as the Washington, D.C. Alley Authority eliminated more than 200 unsightly, unlivable byways, other cities made superb use of federal money to arrest physical decay. Housing authorities and planning agencies were summoned into being by the New Deal. Cities like Philadelphia, which had no public welfare systems at all on March 4, 1933, replaced private charity with a structure that depended upon cooperation with Washington. By the standards of what passed as an urban lobby, 1930s style, the New Deal earned high marks. Indeed, Roosevelt had not only instituted massive public works and put millions of urban jobless on payrolls but his agency heads, Hopkins and Ickes in particular, had tailored federal programs to meet municipal needs.

Even as the New Deal sputtered, the 1933 commitment to public housing did not wane. Through the Wagner-Steagall Housing Act of 1937, which created the United States Housing Authority (USHA), the initial efforts of the PWA markedly enlarged. This time, the federal share of project costs reached a whopping 90 percent, cities could take up to 60 years to repay federal loans, and interest costs dipped to 3 percent, a full point below the controversial 4 percent the PWA Housing Division had required. As a consequence, cities lined up for federal funds with a zeal they had not always exhibited in 1933. Although the federal government's commitment of $800 million fell billions of dollars short of what it would have taken to have eliminated the nation's slums, and even though Roosevelt instructed his hand-picked USHA Chairman, Nathan Straus, to make certain that small cities would receive a substantial slice of the pie, the housing program of the late 1930s reenforced the shift in intergovernmental relationships that had been taking place since Roosevelt's inauguration.

In many of the best-run USHA projects, the federal government was involved not only in underwriting construction costs but in teaming with municipal agencies to foster a spirit of community among the tenants. Before congressional conservatives hatcheted the Federal Art Project, it was not unusual for big-city housing projects to have their own choruses, and even their own orchestras. WPA workers ran adult education projects, National Youth Administration employees supervised playrooms for children, and Federal Writers' Project personnel helped tenants to produce their own newspapers. Simultaneously, local housing authorities, in combination with social workers supplied by others municipal agencies or by private groups, organized arts and crafts projects, softball teams, and bowling leagues, whist parties, dances, and film programs. Municipal health departments helped tenants form organizations to care for the ill. A number of cities dispatched fiscal experts to help tenants set up credit unions or to extend other kinds of financial advice. Police departments loaned officers to run crime-prevention programs. Although creative federal-municipal partnerships of this sort were quickly disrupted by end-of-decade congressional cutbacks and by the new priorities of a nation preparing for war, they provided a model of what imaginative social engineering could accomplish in the city.

Given the intense opposition to public housing that existed in almost every city, it is remarkable not that the New Deal failed to make more sizeable inroads upon a major national problem, as critics on the left have complained, but that it bequeathed any legacy at all. City officials worried about the removal of private property from municipal tax lists, and negotiations with the USHA frequently bogged down when city councils insisted that the federal government make substantial payments in lieu of taxes for garbage removal, fire protection, and police protection. Although urban liberals pointed out that the solvency of cities did not depend upon the taxes yielded by the hovels of the poor, and even though it was demonstrably the case that slums cost cities more in services and in depressed land values than they yielded in revenue, real estate interests created a very different impression. Slumlords, supported by mortgage bankers, battled federal land-takings and insisted upon a "fair market price" for property that was nearly valueless. According to this view, federal intrusion was "only one step removed from socialism." Poor housing might be an evil, but as one lawyer put it in a suit against the USHA, it did not follow that the government should attempt to remedy the situation either by taking private property or by spending public money seized from the rich to help the poor. "The doctrine is a dangerous one that everyone is entitled to be well-fed, well-clothed, and well-housed, and if one by reason of misfortune, incompetence or sloth cannot achieve that end by his own efforts, the public will pay the bill." Armed with arguments of this sort, aldermen from middle-class wards blocked appropriations for badly needed USHA projects or, at the very least, managed to keep USHA projects out of their districts. Clearly, the New Deal did not operate in a vacuum. Especially because the Wagner-Steagall Act had to be implemented precisely at a time when conservative assaults upon the New Deal were virtually unrestrained, the USHA's achievements, instead of being denounced for their inadequacy, might better be viewed as little short of extraordinary.

Far from adopting a Bryanesque vision of America, Roosevelt and his Brain Trust recognized that the city occupied a vital place in shaping the nation's destiny. Two-thirds of America's population and wealth were lodged in urban centers, and the cities could not be ignored. Accordingly, in the summer of 1933, Harold Ickes established the National Planning Board, soon renamed the National Resources Board (NRB), and appointed the President's uncle, Frederic A. Delano, to head it. As the agency most concerned with urban affairs, the NRB studied cities in virtually every aspect and functioned as a kind of pro-urban lobby within the federal government. Convinced of the need for nationwide urban planning, the NRB also issued constant reminders of the city's "insistent demand for a just participation in the gains of our civilization." The agency acknowledged that "There is fertility and creation in the rich soil of the broad countryside, but there is also fertility and creativeness in forms of industry, art, personality, emerging even from the city streets and reaching toward the sky."

In 1937, the NRB's Urbanism Committee issued an eighty-eight page report entitled "Our Cities — Their Role in the National Economy," and the committee's policy recommendations left no doubt that New Dealers had established an agenda for cities. The federal government was urged to continue its programs of broad public assistance. Public housing initiatives should be expanded: indeed, there should be a national policy to abolish slums and rehouse the poor. Instead of standing aloof, the federal government should play an active role in devising a national transportation policy, should enter the field of crime prevention, and should help cities find ways to achieve greater home rule. Drives toward the creation of metropolitan districts needed federal encouragement. To assure continuity in national urban planning, the committee advocated the formation of a cabinet-level Bureau of Urban Affairs. Although the political realities of the late 1930s prevented implementation of all aspects of the report, there could be no doubt that New Dealers had noticed the American city.

If Franklin Delano Roosevelt was "a child of the country" when he assumed office in 1933, his origins did not prevent him from becoming a patron of the metropolis as well. Interested in the concept of an "ever-normal granary" for the nation's farms, he simultaneously concerned himself with a parallel reserve for cities, a reserve consisting of public credit, public works, public relief, public housing and, not least, public recognition. "[I]f the city fails," the National Resources Board concluded, "American fails." The record tells us that Roosevelt heartily concurred.

SUGGESTED READINGS

The New Deal's urban activities must inevitably lead the serious student to the National Archives where records of the WPA, the FERA, the CWA, the PWA, and the CCC are lodged. Other primary sources of substantial value include the Lorena Hickok, Harry Hopkins, and John Ihlder Mss. at the Franklin D. Roosevelt Library. Scattered correspondence between F.D.R. and key big-city mayors can be found in both the President's Personal File and his Official File at Hyde Park.

Several magazines of the 1930s are an important source for an examination of the New Deal's urban impact. The most important are *The American City, Survey Graphic,* and *The National Municipal Review*.

Unpublished doctoral dissertations that provide insights into the New Deal's impact upon particular cities include John F. Bauman, "The City, the Depression, and Relief: The Philadelphia Experience, 1929-1939" (Rutgers, 1969); Leonard Leader, "Los Angeles and the

Great Depression" (U.C.L.A., 1972); and JoAnn Argersinger, "Baltimore: The Depression Years" (George Washington University, 1979).

Municipal and state publications are also revealing about cities in the 1930s: *Proceedings of the City Council, Chicago, Proceedings of the City Council of Boston,* and the *Wisconsin Public Welfare Review* were of special usefulness to the author of this essay.

Morton and Lucia White's *The Intellectual Versus the City* (Cambridge, Mass., 1962) provides a stimulating framework for considering a set of traditions with which the New Deal had to contend, while Paul K. Conkin's *The New Deal* (New York, 1967) places F.D.R. in this anti-urban context. An essential urban overview of the period is provided in Mark I. Gelfand, *A Nation of Cities: The Federal Government and Urban America, 1933–1965* (New York, 1975), and any student of Roosevelt will profit from William E. Leuchtenburg's *Franklin D. Roosevelt and the New Deal* (New York, 1963). Other books of particular usefulness include Paul K. Conkin, *Tomorrow a New World* (Ithaca, N.Y., 1959); Charles H. Trout, *Boston, the Great Depression, and the New Deal* (New York, 1977); Sidney Fine, *Frank Murphy: The Detroit Years* (Ann Arbor, Mich., 1975); Bruce Stave, *The New Deal and the Last Hurrah: Pittsburgh Machine Politics* (Pittsburgh, 1970); and Rexford Tugwell, *The Democratic Roosevelt* (Garden City, N.Y., 1957), as well as Tugwell's *The Brain Trust* (New York, 1968).

The Cultural Legacy of the New Deal

Alan Lawson

While the study of culture in the United States has had much to say about the 1930s and its legacy, it has not included much mention of the New Deal which commanded that era. Partly that is because politics has generally been considered a reflection of culture, rather than a source of it, and so seems rather incidental, except to show how customs and values have been translated into action. In the case of the New Deal, there is the additional reason that Roosevelt and his associates were pointedly averse to anything that smacked of ideology or dogma.

Recently, however, appraisals of New Deal relief programs for artists have begun to see an affinity between the New Deal as a conceptual force and all that is denoted by the term "culture." As Jane DeHart Matthews has felicitously put it in her study of the arts programs, the New Deal pursued its recovery efforts within a larger "quest for a cultural democracy."

The issue of involvement in such a quest reflects the special intensity of the time when the New Deal appeared. The Great Crash forced all leaders and critics to think seriously about the nation's cultural fate. Although the New Deal was shunned by many artists and intellectuals, it was necessarily bound up in the mainstream of cultural transformation that developed.

Roosevelt, true to his progressive political experience and the noblesse oblige benevolence in which he was raised, welcomed the unifying tide. His New Deal aimed toward the fusion of all segments of society into a cooperative commonwealth, using national planning to consolidate the country's resources.

To promote such radical change, Roosevelt made use of his gift for enveloping others in expansive good cheer. For all the truth there is to arguments that Hoover built prototypes of the New Deal recovery mechanism, the difference between Hoover's grudging attitude and Roosevelt's zest is a difference whose cultural, as well as practical, impact was of vast significance. Hoover chilled the instinct to reform—meeting with him, as one dispirited consultant recalled, was like being bathed in ink. Roosevelt radiated hope and inspired collective action. As T. V. Smith put it in his pioneering discussion of "The New Deal as a Cultural Phenomenon," Roosevelt "was enormously successful in *politicizing* the whole of American life." When asked where he stood ideologically, Roosevelt made the famous, perhaps ingenuous, response that he was merely "a Christian and a Democrat." To appeal thus to the unifying rootedness of Americans in religion and the democratic sense of community was, calculatedly or not, the most promising way of drawing the nation together.

Roosevelt's mastery of vague but inspirational generalities makes it possible to accept the opposite of Smith's point—that is, the New Deal took on the character of a cultural movement rather than politicizing the culture. Roosevelt's all-embracing strategy was to appear as the patron of the average American, commanding attention not merely because he was the nation's leader, blessed with a benignly superior, cultivated background, but also by suggesting that he could help define the true average.

In the course of developing his unusual political persona, Roosevelt learned as much as he could about geography and devised an organizational chart of Democratic politicians that gave him a superb grasp of the details of how the country operated on the local level. To that base, Roosevelt added whatever lore came his way. He was blessed, as a member of the Brain Trust, Rexford Tugwell, noted, with a "fly-paper mind," which enabled him to amaze listeners with his factual range, even though he remained cavalier about any coherency the multitude of facts might have. The effect was to identify Roosevelt with everyplace and everyone in his constituency. But, in part, the knowing mode was also defensive since it enabled Roosevelt to build a perimeter of facts and anecdotes that could ward off inconvenient issues.

Roosevelt used his peculiar blend of personal remoteness and vaguely general attunement to advance a case that the New Deal spoke for "common man"—the phrase so frequently heard in those days of common subjection to hardship. In his fireside chats, Roosevelt conveyed that image with the widest success. The innovation of nationwide broadcasts was perfectly suited to his duality, combining as it did personal remoteness with a skillfully contrived sense of the nation being drawn to the presidential hearth for warmth and advice.

For all its stress on the plain and simple, however, the common man approach was necessarily abstract and idealized. Its references were not to the depressed present but to an ideal of what once was and the attainment of what should be. Through this calculation of past glories and future hopes, the common man ethos generated a highly emotional aura within which major New Deal programs expressed Roosevelt's vision of a cooperative commonwealth with romantic elan, best exemplified, perhaps, by the Tennessee Valley Administration (TVA). Not only did the TVA seek to transform an area of abject poverty into a beautiful land of communal prosperity, it would do so through a decentralized plan of "grassroots democracy" that would attach the uplifted common men of the region to a benevolent federal government. To head the project, engineer Arthur Morgan was drawn from Antioch College in full knowledge that he was a devotee of Edward Bellamy's utopian conception of the cooperative commonwealth. The National Recovery Administration, under the leadership of Hugh Johnson, hoped to play a similar role for business and labor. And, to complete the round, the Agricultural Adjustment Administration sought to extend the benefits of idealized democracy to farmers under the guidance of yet another visionary—indeed the most conspicuous publicist of the idea that the New Deal had ushered in the "Age of the Common Man"—Henry Wallace.

That these grand conceptions either fizzled or were transformed into something less exalted than monuments to the comomon man was an accident of circumstances that altered neither Roosevelt's convictions nor the nature of the ideal. What makes the import of those convictions and the ideal difficult to assess is the paradox that, although the common man concept was highly susceptible to criticism, even debunking, it succeeded in drawing adulation and power to the New Deal. And, the success has been spectacularly enduring. Polls taken in 1982, the centennial year of Roosevelt's birth, showed that he stood higher in the estimation of his countrymen than any president other than Lincoln.

SPOKESMEN OF THE NEW DEAL

No one was ever able exactly to formulate the New Deal appeal, or, when they tried, to capture public loyalty the way Roosevelt did. But the three persons who came closest to being the official spokesman for New Deal governing concepts at least pointed toward the essence of the New Deal balancing act between the practical and the ideal. Two of them were members of the Brain Trust—Adolf Berle and Rexford Tugwell—and the other, Thurman Arnold, was a Yale Law School professor who made his mark in the later New Deal as head of the Antitrust Division of the Justice Department.

Berle's main contribution, drawing on his pathbreaking study with Gardiner Means, *The Modern Corporation and Private Property* (1932), was the concept that American economic life had "matured." The frontier was gone and with it the dream of endlessly expanding natural resources and opportunity. Instead, control over the crystallizing economy had gravitated into the hands of some 200 corporations, run by professional managers rather than their owners. Berle's counsel, most importantly broadcast in Roosevelt's 1932 campaign speech to the Commonwealth Club of San Francisco, was that Americans should recognize the need to pool diminished resources by careful planning and greater equalization of wealth. Berle, the loyal son of a social gospel minister,* saw a measure of hope in the consolidating pattern. As managerial control over the economy solidified, the main outlet for ambition was apt to shift from the material to more intellectual and spiritual areas of creativity and service. Social reform, the environment, and the arts could well preoccupy the most able Americans far more than was possible in the days of the great entrepreneurs that had ended with the Crash.

To that creative and humane prospect, Tugwell added his concept of a "concert of interests" to guide the socially responsible planning he hoped the New Deal would make a central feature of the federal government. Tugwell urged Roosevelt to concentrate on "disciplining" all factions of society in a cooperative effort to raise the level of American life ethically and aesthetically, as well as materially.

Thurman Arnold, the third major articulator of New Deal thought, made recovery of that reach for common cultural ideals

---

* Social gospel ministers were those who believed that religion should serve the cause of progressive social reform.

difficult by wrapping New Deal reform aims in tough, pragmatic language, which he believed more likely to gain leverage in a period when hard-boiled realism was in vogue. Beneath Arnold's sardonic manner, however, was an emotional dreamer from Wyoming who was very much in tune with the common man ideal and its praise for the shrewd and hearty frontier spirit. In his books, *The Symbols of Government* (1935) and *The Folklore of Capitalism* (1937), Arnold ridiculed the reluctance of conventional wisdom to accept interference with free enterprise as a species of superstition that catered to the interests of the powerful few while hoodwinking the common folk into thinking that it also served their best interests, or, in any event, was required by natural law and justice. He advised New Dealers to recognize that superstition is best countered by the provision of a more appealing superstition because people require myths and use reason mostly to justify them. But, although Arnold won acclaim for a witty case that made him seem the only New Dealer with a definite philosophic outlook, he pressed his cynically manipulative view to the point where it lost its ethical bearings and revealed that the common man strategy entailed practices that might not be entirely moral or rational.

The vast political and cultural adventuring of the New Deal was spared the full consequences of Arnold's looseness, however, by the fact that the majority of social critics at the time were in favor of some sort of collectivism. There, in the midst of crisis, liberals dropped their reluctance to compromise individual freedom and integrity and instead turned their attention to finding ways of reconciling a reasonable degree of individualism with the need for collective action.

IDEOLOGIES FOR THE NEW DEAL

The concept on which the most significant agreement was reached was formulated by America's most eminent philosopher, John Dewey, especially in his books, *Individualism, Old and New* (1929) and *Liberalism and Social Action* (1935). Dewey argued that persons most fully realized their individuality in association with others. A society in which persons, acting together, are "continuously planning," rather than submitting to a planned dogma, and in which the primary decision-making unit is the local, "face-to-face" community, would best ensure both the general welfare and the fullest develop-ment of individual character and talent. To show the cultural conse-quences of that collectivist view, Dewey wrote *Art and Experience* (1934) in which he argued that art is both the highest expression of individuality and most beautifully derived from social experience. This balance of individual and group, local community and national whole, squared very well with the common man doctrine of balance; but it is important to recall that Dewey was never satisfied with the New Deal, preferring a more explicitly designed socialism to the vague expediencies of Roosevelt and the tricky manipulations of Thurman Arnold. Arnold revealed the inability, or unwillingness, of the New Deal to tighten its activities into a more self-aware pattern and face up to certain ethical and intellectual issues; Dewey sug-gested ways in which those issues might be met. By his aloofness, Dewey indicated that the solutions were not forthcoming from an administration averse to thought as systematic as his own.

Such an inchoate situation meant that to make liberal cultural concepts fit comfortably with the New Deal, they had to be more vague and ethically relaxed than Dewey's. The social critics and theorists associated with the prominent cultural relativist school of thought were more obliging than Dewey. Mobilized earlier in the century to combat discrimination against immigrants and non-whites, cultural relativism led to the view that nations, as primary cultural groups, had separate and distinct characters, just as did the various subgroups within them. The concept of a culturally unified nation of distinctive local groups was a close analogue to the cooper-ative commonwealth that the New Deal sought. The concept was endorsed in Ruth Benedict's *Patterns of Culture* (1934), one of the most widely read anthropology books ever written. Benedict argued that the integration of cultures follows "the same process by which a style in art comes into being and persists." Directly defending the New Deal-Deweyan concept of the balance between individual and group, Benedict went on to declare that "there is no proper antagon-ism between the role of society and that of the individual." Benedict acknowledged that "the vast proportion of all individuals who are born into any society always and whatever the idiosyncracies of its institutions, assume . . . the behavior dictated by that society." But the cultural relativist avoids the mistake of thinking that those norms are in place because they represent universal truth and, thus, condemn the nonconformist. Each separate culture in the sea of relativity is whole, Benedict insisted, and so, by definition, has a place for every distinct person within it. Whoever does not fit the status quo of the moment is best regarded as one for whom the culture has not evolved a rightful place. Unfortunately, Benedict added, "Dewey has pointed out how possible and yet drastic such social engineering would be." This was exactly the point, of course, that held Dewey aloof from the temporizing New Deal. Dewey urged formation of a third political party, devoted to planning society toward the drastic ideal. Benedict and the cultural relativists avoided radical measures by stressing the apolitical needs for tolerance, which aligned them vaguely with the pluralist sympathies of the New Deal.

Such social scientific support for the ineffable New Deal style was matched on the side of creative culture by the writings of an admiring acquaintance of Ruth Benedict, the literary critic and historian Constance Rourke. Just before Roosevelt's attempt to draw the American people together, Rourke provided a base for the New Deal cultural position with her celebrated book, *American Humor* (1931). At first glance a compendium of folklore and customs, Rourke's study was really a polemical attempt to establish a case for American culture as a unique entity that grew from folk roots.

Devoted to her midwestern past and to progressive reform, Rourke strove to rebut the intellectual cynicism toward the frontier and Puritan New England that arose after World War I. Such a view, Rourke believed, led the cynical into a trap. If they accepted the idea that the wellsprings of artistic and intellectual fineness lay in Europe, they must then either aspire to their own version of that fineness, and thus be alienated from the crude materialist mainstream of America, or else become fully at home by entering into that native materialist chase, at the cost of art and intellect. For Rourke there was no such Hobson's choice and thus no temptation to become estranged from America. A close look would show that in trying to understand themselves, Americans have always been thrown back upon their past: "the distant, the retrospective, the legendary have prevailed even in the new period."

Since Americans, compared with their European forebears, have had to form their character swiftly, certain traits have naturally crowded to the fore. A strategy of nimble experimentation and innovation, sometimes slapdash but shrewdly attuned to the need to act quickly to capture novelty, has been central. Aware that although such a strategy worked, it was flawed by an apparent disrespect for craftsmanship and finesse, Americans developed certain protective shields. Most intriguing to Rourke was the way Americans had befuddled strangers—especially Europeans—with humor of a sort that caused the visitor to feel superior, in an irritated way, while the American naif was left laughing up his sleeve and often holding all the high cards.

The major benefit of this strategy of evasion has been the preservation of a private, inward territory that gave rise to a rhapsodic, even mystical, turn to the American character. Within that subjective realm, Americans have been free to conjure up potent images and emotions that have enabled them to take full possession of their culture and, in turn, made the culture powerful enough to take full possession of them.

The affinity of Rourke's concept to Benedict's lay both in their intuitiveness and inclusiveness. Taken together, those qualities enabled Rourke to posit depth behind Americans' prosaic surface and to declare that foreign elements could enter only as subordinate parts of the whole native culture rather than as guiding influences. Not only foreigners but expatriates were gathered thus into the fold. Those who flee have claimed alienation but, Rourke countered, their flight mainly signified acute sensitivity to the American fate. Approvingly, she quoted the dictum of T. S. Eliot that the writer must know "the mind of his own country—a mind which he learns in time to be much more important than his own private mind." To do that in as yet not fully formed America, Rourke concluded, requires a great critical undertaking of national cultural discovery. Later, in the wake of the critics' labors, "the artist will steep himself in the gathered light." The artist will enjoy the personal fulfillment that comes of immersion in the whole, which was the crux of Benedict's and Dewey's balance of individualism and collectivism. "The single writer—the single production—will no longer stand solitary or aggressive but within a natural sequence."

Rourke's cultural thesis conformed beautifully with the spirit of common cause, aimed at a communal future, which Roosevelt would soon try to instill in the electorate. Its reliance on a "natural sequence"—on organic process, rather than rational system-building—helped also to explain why, in the midst of an age often characterized as ideological, so little ideology actually took hold at the center of American affairs. The appeal of Rourke and Roosevelt focused on more fluid, emotional qualities — on communal hope and sympathy and memory. Indeed, Roosevelt could stand as Rourke's representative American, with his reticence, his humorous strategy of evasion, his fealty to old values, his simple optimism overlaying fathomless complexity. The other major New Dealers — among them, Berle, Tugwell, Arnold, and Wallace — also fit the Rourkean mold of practical dreamers.

NEW DEAL CULTURAL PROJECTS

The most direct occasion for employing what we might call the New Deal cultural synthesis was in response to the desperate plight of artists and writers. By bringing thousands of destitute writers and artists onto the relief rolls of the WPA and allowing them wide latitude to decide what they would create, the New Deal offered the greatest opportunity for artistic freedom and collective collaboration that American artists had ever enjoyed. The volume of works turned out in the few years of the program's existence was truly staggering; comparably impressive was the number of those relief recipients who eventually became among the most important of America's artists and writers. According to the final report of the Federal Art Project, its workers had produced 1,566 murals, 17,744 pieces of sculpture, 108,099 paintings, and 240,000 copies of original designs in various media. In addition, as part of its intent to infuse art into the nation's daily life, the Federal Art Project in 160 locations taught more than 2 million students in all phases of art. The Federal Theatre Project staged over 1,000 plays, of which 77 were written specifically for the FTP. But probably the most astonishing item appeared in the final report of artistic director of the Music Project, Nikolai Sokoloff, who noted that his musicians had performed the compositions of 14,000 American composers. The outpouring of creative expression indicated that the New Deal support and concern for linking artists, free to draw upon their own genius and origins, with the national purpose had tapped some great wellspring. In the background echoed Rourke's prophecy in "Traditions for Young People" (1937), as the projects were getting underway: "If we could open our past to young people in genuine abundance, with its poetry and homeliness, its occasional strange sparseness, its cruelties and dark failures, we might have a great literature and music and art upon us before we know it. We might even be able to devise equable ways of living."

The Federal Writers' Project and parallel efforts to record images of the countryside and its people by the Farm Security Administration's battalion of photographers, and a crew of film makers under the direction of Pare Lorentz, played a supporting role. In its American Guide Series to states and localities, and allied oral histories and regional studies, the Writers' Project provided the first comprehensive description of the nation since the limited and outdated Baedeker's guide of the 1890s. At the same time the Writers' Project offered desperately poor novices, among them such future notables as Edward Dahlberg, Ralph Ellison, Richard Wright, Saul Bellow, and Eudora Welty, the chance to prepare for professional careers.

In sum, the artists and writers projects played a major role in rechanneling the nation's cultural energies. The distinctive results were closely in tune with the Rourke-Benedict concept of art as the expression of common experience and values, and so a combination of the objective and the subjective. Indeed, Rourke herself found a place within the Art Project as the director of *The Index of American Design*, where her sensitivity to the blend of folk realism and abstractness helped the Index win praise from some cultural critics as the most successful of all the New Deal projects.

CULTURAL TRENDS OF THE THIRTIES

The power of the New Deal cultural synthesis became increasingly apparent as the decade wore on. When Roosevelt won his smashing reelection victory in 1936, the hopes of rival political parties on the left and right evaporated. Coincidentally, the Soviet Comintern announced that those devoted to the Communist cause should align themselves with noncommunists who favored building a progressive society. Since the new directive changed the status of the New Deal from enemy to fellow progressive, the Popular Front of leftist reform included support of New Deal programs. Accordingly, as Richard Pells has told us in his study of American culture during the thirties, the left "internalized many of the values of the New Deal." A bridge was fashioned, but it proved to be essentially one way. Left intellectuals found that the Popular Front causes they were championing (antifascism, social reform, and free expression) had already been incorporated within the common man consensus.

At the same time, Constance Rourke was preparing to climax her work with a vast survey of American culture. The work was unfinished at the time of her death in 1942, but the finished portions were put together into a book entitled *The Roots of American Culture*. Too fragmentary to stand as a demonstration of the full complexity and uniqueness that Rourke intended, *Roots* nonetheless refined her earlier argument and pointed the way forward for the New Deal cultural synthesis. In the concluding chapter on "American Art: A Possible Future," Rourke expressed values honed by her time on the Federal Arts Project in which she showed remarkable prescience about the subsequent development of modernist trends.

> The American painter might gain assurance in a contemporary mode if he knew by heart the spare abstract as this appears in many phases of our folk-expression. . . . Woven into all our folklore is an acute observation of the external world which any artist could afford to know well, and this tends to be poetic rather than naturalistic. It is typically in key with the abstract. . . . [the American artist] cannot escape his fate all at once, as an American with a partially illegible and syncopated history behind him, or as a citizen of a world that now seems to face many economic, social, and cultural crossroads. Yet recognition of the peculiar elements which form American culture would seem fundamental for both the artist and the critic, whether or not they wholly like what they find.

But at just that moment of resolve, World War II put an end to the cultural experimentation. By 1943 the WPA Arts and Writers' project had disappeared and the documentary film and photography projects had been transformed into propaganda for the military cause. The common man had swiftly been lifted out of the ruck of poverty and rushed into combat or war production in the revived factories. A sense of momentous change was widespread, and many participants were prepared to agree with cultural critic Lewis Mumford that "a thousand years separate 1940 from 1930. . . ."

Others might say that span was as nothing compared with the gulf between 1940 and 1945. In conflicting moods of relief and shock Americans moved toward a new destiny. For some, the carnage of war, culminating in the Holocaust and the atomic bombs dropped on Japan, corroborated their worst fears about innate human depravity. Yet, of course, the war was won. Right had triumphed over evil, and it seemed reasonable to expect that an era of social fulfillment would dawn, provided that the heirs of the New Deal managed to keep the Depression from recurring.

POSTWAR REFLECTIONS ON THE NEW DEAL

The return of peace had great significance for the New Deal cultural synthesis. Wartime prosperity, which had so rapidly ended the Depression, confounded the majority of experts and persisted after demobilization. For many the era of the common man, proclaimed by Vice President Henry Wallace in 1942, meant transformation from working-class to middle-class status. Returning servicemen in droves broke the pattern of their deprived past by taking advantage of the G.I. Bill and becoming the first in their families to attend college. Others who took up jobs in the revived economy enjoyed economic returns that also lifted them out of the old ways and made it possible to move into the mushrooming suburbs.

A cluster of intellectuals joined in the enthusiasm by flocking back to Greenwich Village and other city centers to revive the bohemian spirit. The existentialist philosopher William Barrett remembered how his return from the war soon brought him into the presence of the poet Delmore Schwartz. Schwartz, who was always surrounded by a certain electric excitement, glowed especially brightly as he exclaimed, "1919! 1919! It's 1919 over again." Listening to that evocation of an earlier postwar era of creative greatness, Barrett "felt a new world was opening up before one.... It was a feeling I was sharing with millions of other Americans."

But there was a somber side to the war's end that cast an everlengthening shadow as the initial euphoria subsided. To the trauma of Holocaust and atomic bombs, creative writers added their own special bad news about the experience of war. From their combat experience, James Jones and Norman Mailer dominated fictional accounts with descriptions of cruelty and violence that added up to an argument that war was the creation of those who reveled in it and victimized the rest. Idealism of the sort the New Deal cultural synthesis mustered against fascism had a scant role to play in their accounts, and that mostly as a cover for baser motives.

Mailer and Jones reflected a bleak mood among postwar American writers, which John Aldridge gained the greatest credit for explaining in his *After the Lost Generation* (1951). In terms that showed how fully the collective, folk-rooted spirit of the thirties had departed from critical consciousness, Aldridge contrasted the youth who entered World War I, suffused in Victorian moral values, with the hard-bitten generation that survived World War II. The latter had been harried into cynical weariness:

> Their lives, as far back as they could remember, had been spent in a world continually at war with itself, in an economic order that fluctuated from dizzy prosperity to the most abject depression. . . . There was for them no warm world of childhood to which they could return when things went badly. . . . Childhood now was other memories: the failure of a business, a bank door locked shut with the family savings inside, a milk truck overturned on a Nebraska highway by farmers carrying clubs, and long lines of men waiting in front of courthouses through Arkansas and Tennessee.

Aldridge's view expressed a growing inclination to reject the ferment of the thirties as a futile attempt to get around the fact that "the basic social changes brought about by the rise of modern America in the first three decades of the century have been largely completed." So firmly entrenched had "the Babbitt class" become that "the problems which concerned the writers of the 1930s might just as well have never existed." For those who, like Aldridge, served in the war, the lesson was especially sharp:

> The war years gave many of the new writers an opportunity to leave the country, stay away for a time, and come back again. . . . If what they found at home had offered them a new contact with experience, they might have been afforded . . . the sense of criticism and of valuation needed for fresh writing. But the country they returned to was much the same . . . country which had been responsible for the vehement exile of the Lost Generation. . . . The ingredients for another all-out war of artistic secession were there, but the will to revolt was not. The most aborting truth was that it had all been done before.

In other words, Delmore Schwartz had been both right and wrong; it was 1919 all over again. But that was cause for despair, not exhilaration—despair that all the pains of rebellion and suffering during the intervening years had been for naught.

The only hope Aldridge offered to a receptive readership was repudiation of the common man theme — an artifact to join all the rest of the thirties on the junk heap. Aldridge urged the artist to go it alone — to generate from within "a dogmatic belief in his supreme power as an individual and a complete contempt for everything which stands in the way of its exercise."

Schwartz's and Aldridge's outcries struck at the foundations of the New Deal cultural synthesis. Their differing interpretations of the cultural situation denied the consensus the New Deal had sought. Both men also rejected the concept of the common man and the view that collectivism would enhance individual fulfill-ment. Schwartz foresaw the imminent revival of the twenties with its irresponsibility, which had been so deplored by the New Deal. Aldridge, disowning the recent past altogether, anticipated a darker future of fiercely independent creators. Gradually, in the face of these heralded changes, the New Deal wore away, the victim of shifting values and of social analysis whose tests the common man proposition could not meet.

The fortunes of the New Deal synthesis, which had been dealt an early blow by Constance Rourke's death, were further jarred by the passing of Ruth Benedict in 1948. But for some time before her death Benedict helped to keep the cultural ideal alive. Under her aegis, and with the special goal of understanding the nature of the world's people caught in war, the work of examining national character proceded resolutely. Between 1942 and 1953 some dozen notable books on the collective character of several nations ap-peared. Under a grant from the Office of Naval Research, Benedict organized the Columbia University Research in Contemporary Cultures program and then published the most brilliant of the ensu-ing studies, *The Chrysanthemum and the Sword: Patterns of Japanese Culture* (1946). Interest in national character became a ma-jor preoccupation of government officials and scholars alike, and the holistic emphasis on national culture propounded by the com-mon man theme of the thirties seemed about to embark on a crucial chapter.

The legacy of New Deal culture was also reflected in postwar in-terest in the study of material culture — an appreciation of "things" that was in line with the concreteness of the appeal to experience and with the cultural yearning of the thirties for restoration of a life of plenty. In his *Made in America* (1948), John Kouwenhoven endorsed Rourke's folk roots view against elitist tendencies such as Aldridge was soon to proclaim. "Civilization in America," Kouwenhoven declared, "insofar as it can be identified with the vernacular influences this book has sought to define, *has* sprung from the people." Like Rourke, Kouwenhoven called for a cosmopolitan fusion, with American root forms predominating, to explain and advance culture. Although "forms inherited from an older tradition still must play an important role if we are not to be esthetically starved ... "—in the end the vernacular is the crux. In Kouwenhoven's view, "The important thing about the vernacular is that it possesses inherent qualities of vitality and adaptability, of organic as opposed to static form, of energy rather than repose, that are particularly appropriate to the civilization which, during the brief life span of the United States, has transformed the world. ...."

It was at this point of apparent readiness to carry the mission of national culture to fulfillment that the fragility of the New Deal synthesis and the changes in social and intellectual climate became evident. In the increasingly sober and specialized way of the postwar era, analysts of culture fell prey to disagreement and by the end of the fifties had either ceased believing that there was a coherent national character or else acknowledged that understanding was far out of reach. The remaining impetus fragmented into competing angles of vision. Deprived of the spirit of higher unity in the New Deal cultural synthesis, postwar assessments of American character differed strikingly, in their variously anxious ways, from the assertive optimism of the New Deal synthesis. Certainly, there was nothing to suggest that a comic spirit could be at the root of the human condition in America. Rather, the new interpretations stressed loneliness, authoritarian personality, adolescent identity crises, and material acquisition.

By 1960 the field of anthropology, which had been the primary professional area of study seeking to define national character, had largely abandoned the effort. The *American Anthropologist* no longer published articles on the subject; and, except for Jules Henry's *Culture Against Man* (1963), books on national character from the anthropological perspective ceased appearing. Indeed, Henry was something of a grave-digger. His book was so far from Rourkean affirmation as to convince readers that the culture Rourke celebrated had been buried beneath corrupt commercial ways—beyond the grasp of those who might like to follow Rourke's optimistic lead. Anthropologists returned to their first love, the study of remote, usually premodern, cultures and, in some cases, even went on to explain human behavior in terms of basic animal instinct.

The turn away from a stress on psychic refinement and social integration was part of a disturbing coincidence between the onset of material abundance and the deflation of idealism. In many ways the attainment of prosperity tested the speculation during the Depression that some happy relationship obtained between economic security and values. David Potter's A *People of Plenty* (1954) placed the matter in historical perspective by explaining how Americans had always defined themselves in terms of material prosperity. The legacy of the thirties thus seemed clear. Because during that cruel decade so much emphasis had been put upon poverty as the source of misery, the onset of affluence beyond anything ever experienced before naturally led to a belief that the basis for full happiness had come around the corner. The cultural synthesis set out by Rourke and Benedict did not, in its emphasis on simple folk roots, make quite that connection. But many of the forms of cultural expression and measurement allied with the New Deal cultural synthesis leaned in that direction. Documentary photography, social science inventories, and naturalistic writing concentrated on the "things" present or absent in people's lives, as John Aldridge did in retrospect. How those people regarded themselves, what they aspired to, what sort of stimuli toward thought and emotion they encountered, and what sort of influences they could bring to bear on their families — all these measures of life seemed contingent upon material objects, and mirrored by them. Even the great, poetic testimony to the nobility of those in poverty, James Agee's and Walker Evans' *Let Us Now Praise Famous Men* (1941), conveyed that sense through the affecting photographs and descriptions of the simple objects that were part of the lives of southern sharecroppers.

The equation between possessions and fulfillment never worked very well, however, as the creators of the New Deal cultural synthesis realized. To see deprivation as a barrier to happiness and greatness of soul was plausible enough; to believe that abundance, after removing the barriers, would lead to a realization of those dreams was quite another proposition that was not susceptible to testing. In 1946, as part of the Maximum Employment Act designed to provide general job security, a system of economic indicators was established by the federal government. Much progress was hoped for from the use of those indicators. But, in the 1960s, after confessions by those who sponsored the indicators that prosperity and human misery often went together, a new set of measurements, called social indicators, were devised to gauge the disposition of the general public toward a wide range of noneconomic issues. Several years and a number of social reports later, the usefulness of the social indicators remains unclear. Social science, ever more subject to the rigors of empirical precision, has not shown an ability to reach successfully into the realms of feeling and value.

The uncertain grapplings of social scientists with cultural issues at least provided grist for writers and artists, who had been mainly skeptical of the New Deal from the start. Though writers as a social group benefited from the New Deal and shared certain common man precepts, they had never been much inspired by it. Not even sympathy for humane reforms could alter the fact that a mammoth bureaucratic attempt to revive the economy was far from the usual stuff of literary imagination—"about as exciting as near beer," one writer put it. Moreover, the artist's habitual sympathy for the outsider inclined writers away from the Establishment and so toward discounting the New Deal as just another compromising power faction. Instead, as Malcolm Cowley has explained, writers held a "dream of the golden mountains," where the ideals of social justice and free imagination would meet in the army of the disaffected and the dispossessed. The dream was utopian, even apocalyptic, and dismissed New Deal politics and culture for not being radical enough.

When disillusion set in after the war, writers moved past the New Deal toward the other extreme. They gravitated from the poles toward common dismissal, not only of the leftist and rightist gods that failed, but of all reform idealism. The convergence was concretely shown by the founding of the Kenyon School of English in 1948. Its sponsors were John Crowe Ransom, leader of the conservative Southern Agrarians in the thirties, and Lionel Trilling, a member of the New York intellectual group which had formed the influential left-radical journal of literary criticism, *Partisan Review*, Their common ground, aptly located in a rural midwestern retreat, was a place of recoil. Ransom, having given up on agrarianism as a viable social and political platform, promoted the notion, soon to dominate in critical circles, that literary texts should be judged on artistic terms distinct from their social milieu. The "New Criticism" had much in common with Trilling's recoil from radicalism into espousal of a new literature of ideas that would draw upon Matthew Arnold's concept of culture as the product of the finest minds in need of protection from the philistines. Ransom rusticated gently in the Midwest as tutor of the finest minds; Trilling remained in New York where the consequences of recoil were more poignant. Despite an intention to knit literature and life into a new form of American vocation, Trilling and his followers felt increasing alienation, punctuated by references to Kierkegaard and Kafka and laments about the loss of mass man's sincerity and authenticity. The roots of American culture became more and more remote from their concerns, and the life in the streets around them increasingly strange and even sinister.

The increasing reliance of the literary coalition on European models and categories whipsawed the remnants of the New Deal cultural synthesis. Critics variously portrayed the common man as a dupe of the "red menace," a slave of commerce, a philistine destroyer of his cultural heritage, and an anti-intellectual bigot. Any hopes that were once invested in a folk-rooted, diverse, democratically whole culture now seemed naive echoes of a legendary past that had been valuable for mustering reformers and easing pain so long as certain harsh realities could be kept at a distance. War and the Holocaust had closed in on the "dream of the golden mountains." Not gold but iron was the yield, and irony became the dominant postwar style. Ransom, Trilling, and their colleagues used irony to reject the holistic legacy of the New Deal cultural synthesis and then, irony of ironies, were forced into living with their inability to construct any other workable synthesis. They fell into the trap Rourke had warned against by trying to find a place for themselves in American culture through reliance on imported concepts which stressed the absurd and depraved side of life. After fruitlessly trying to amalgamate European pessimism and traditional forms of authority with modernist free expression, the critics in Rourke's trap became predictably alienated and, in their frustration, sought to blame the contradictions in which they had caught themselves on the vulgarities of American society and, in the larger sense, what political theorist Hannah Arendt lamented in her influential book as *The Human Condition* (1958).

Artists had a happier transition to the postwar world than writers but eventually foundered in confusions of the same sort, far from the New Deal cultural synthesis. Those who had been rescued by the Federal Art Project were inspirited by the greatest degree of creative freedom ever granted to a group of artists in America. In part, that freedom was used to advance the common-man reform message; but in more significantly long-range measure, the freedom gave opportunity for artists to look inward. In corroboration of such American seers as Emerson and Whitman, and comparable seekers after roots, like Rourke, the most prominent trend in painting to follow the Federal Art Project was intensely personal abstract expressionalism — personal but not isolationist. The intention of abstractness was to communicate feeling; and that, as its most articulate spokesman on the Federal Art Project, left activist Stuart Davis understood, rested on a faith that people within a common culture have a rapport that does not depend on outward representational forms.

By turning to abstract expressionism, then, artists entered the forties in a way that maintained continuity with the New Deal cultural synthesis. They formed an avant-garde that established, in critic Harold Rosenberg's apt phrase, a "tradition of the new," linking new expression with the spirit and some of the forms of the great innovators earlier in the century. It dovetailed with the view John Dewey expressed in *Art as Experience* (1934), which served as the bible of Federal Art Project director Holger Cahill, that direct experience, even the most commonplace, is the stuff of fully realized art. And, the practice confirmed the prediction of Constance Rourke, also a follower of Dewey, that American art, left to its own tendency, would combine modern techniques with traditional folk inclinations toward abstractness.

Despite the spectacular success of abstract expressionists in capturing critical acclaim and making New York the art capital of the world, the root of it in the patronage of the New Deal cultural synthesis was not a welcome fact. As was the case with the Writers' Project for many years after the New Deal ended, the Federal Art Project was regarded as an embarrassment. The most conspicuous social realism seemed so dated, once the crisis had passed — a case of bleeding hearts worn awkwardly on the sleeve and "garish cartoons on public buildings." The callous way the project was closed out was indicative. No provisions were made to take care of the art that had been produced, and many works — even by artists destined for fame — were consigned to junk shops, stored haphazardly, or simply lost. Disapproval of the art produced was another problem. Sometimes artists had flaunted their radicalism or unconventionality and then suffered the ignominy of having their work denounced or, as was the case with some public murals, erased. In the cold war atmosphere of later years many veterans of the Art Project found it prudent to play down their participation.

Literary critics of art encouraged the false distancing of postwar modernism from the New Deal cultural synthesis by contending that the artists who had made New York preeminent did so by successfully adapting to the modernism that had first arisen in Europe before World War I. The arrival of significant numbers of refugee European artists in the thirties, it was argued, was instrumental in setting the new course. Seldom was it noted that almost all the new wave of artists began their development on the Federal Art Project. Nor was there any apparent conjecture that the raw energy so characteristic of these "action painters" may have resulted from their involvement within the exciting world of joint projects, artists' unions, and an unprecedented creative freedom that gave zest and self-respect to their socially conscious undertakings. In retrospect one notices how, once severed from the world of the project days, the avant-garde artists lost energy. A new community in Greenwich Village and other bohemias failed to materialize, and, amidst growing wealth for many former relief recipients, isolation increased and with it a loss, weary with angst, of the sense of a serious common message to impart. Improvisation, whimsy, designs to delight the linoleum makers, and spoofs to provoke the philistines marked the passage from avant-garde modernism to post-modernist eclecticism.

In the artistic, as well as literary realm, the momentum of social activism slowed, and the urge to consolidate increased. With satisfaction Clement Greenberg, the leading defender of abstract art, declared in a 1948 *Partisan Review* symposium that "stabilization of the avant-garde, accompanied by its growing acceptance by official and comercial culture," had become the most pervasive art trend.

Four years later, in another *Partisan Review* symposium on "Our Country and Our Culture," the disturbing implications of that consolidation appeared. Clearly, to be fixed within an avant-garde meant, by definition, to be at odds with the cultural mainstream.

Thus, the editor lamented, "the artist and intellectual . . . is faced with a mass culture which makes him feel that he is still outside looking in." So sharp was the pain of exclusion that the editors invoked the authority of Ortega y Gasset, whose fearful tract *The Revolt of the Masses* (1932) warned against cultural democracy at the very time the New Deal appeared with a mission to advance it. Ortega, the editors nodded in agreement, explained that mass man is the "kind of man to be found today in all social classes, who consequently represents our age" and who "acts to crush everything that is excellent, individual, qualified and select." And yet, the editors also acknowledged, political democracy "seems to coexist with the domination of the 'masses.'" Therefore, "whatever the cultural consequences may be, the democratic values which America either embodies or promises are desirable in purely human terms." It was a "paradox," creating "many difficulties for American writers and intellectuals who are trying to realize themselves in relation to their country and its cultural life."

As the fifties wore on, the paradox was not resolved. Instead, partisans gathered on each side. Most professional critics joined in a campaign against the pseudoculture of the "middle-brows," as Dwight Macdonald tagged the growing numbers of middle-class readers and gallery and concertgoers. But the "masses" who had risen out of the New Deal experience, inspirited by newfound respect for the arts and for their commonness, were not to be headed off by disdain. A great expansion of popular arts and amusements ensued to the point where, as Daniel Boorstin has observed, America witnessed the first mass-produced folk culture in history. At the same time Americans crowded into the realms of higher culture, thus vindicating the hope of the New Deal that providing "art for the millions" would release untapped reservoirs of imaginativeness and discernment. The old museums, theaters, and concert halls swelled while new ones appeared in the provinces. In addition, students entering the conservatories and art and drama schools in great numbers gave promise that the inferior artistic relation of America to Europe would at last be ended.

The reaction against common man aspirations was powerful, however. Literary critics, as we have seen, sided with disillusioned writers to remove literature from much immediate involvement with the social milieu. Artists also recoiled from public affairs. And the centers of credentialing—the universities and professional schools—remained in the hands of a self-perpetuating elite that accepted sociologist Daniel Bell's prescription for a "meritocracy"—a society run by "men who are best in their field, as judged by their peers." There was to be little truck with common man democracy; instead, Bell promised, "a well-tempered meritocracy can be a society, not of equals but of the just." The flaw in the proposition was, of course, that the meritocratic principle did not provide clear standards of how the "just" would select their "peers." As a result, widespread acceptance of meritocracy enabled centers of unaccountable privilege to entrench themselves against opportunities for newcomers and the full appraisal of diverse cultural roots and resources that the New Deal had sought. Around the process was wrapped a layer of snobbish resentment that a rabble, "in hot pursuit of affluence," as critic Marya Mannes put it in 1960, had invaded places that had formerly been sanctuaries for beauty. Appalled by those from the lower orders who had caught a glimpse of that beauty, she concluded in words echoed frequently that "easy money, easy vice, a profound cynicism, an encompassing nihilism—all these are the dark companions of affluence."

Artists themselves seemed threatened. To protect them Harold Rosenberg, the witty opponent of mass culture, urged that art be removed from the sort of leisure activity most people enjoyed. "People don't need works of art any more for entertainment," Rosenberg declared. "There are too many commodities more directly designed for that purpose." In direct opposition to the New Deal cultural synthesis, Rosenberg insisted that "if art becomes an extension of daily life it loses itself; it becomes a commodity among commodities, kitsch." As for true art, it "will continue its maneuverings of retreat. . . . More and more the condition of art turns into its own affair and resistant to the generalizations of those who would fit it into their system of functions."

ECHOES OF THE NEW DEAL IN THE SIXTIES

The postwar situation of anxiety and alienation that thus arose proved highly resistant to any revival of the New Deal cultural synthesis. Still, the common man ideal persisted as part of continued public allegiance to the New Deal political coalition. When John Kennedy took over from the Eisenhower Administration—that "mausoleum of the human heart," as poet Robert Lowell termed it—flurries of hope arose that the old reformist zest could be rekindled in culture, as well as politics. Kennedy called for intellectuals to commit themselves once again to the national cause and shrewdly mated his sophisticated style with the populist term "New Frontier" to describe his brand of reform activism. Unlike Franklin Roosevelt, the activist with whom Kennedy was most often compared, Kennedy did not face a clearly defined crisis. The problem was more subjective, a matter of malaise, of slackness and complacency covering a loss of confidence. Kennedy's ironic poise, firmly secured by wealth and the graces of an Ivy League education, which he displayed like an F. Scott Fitzgerald hero, was beautifully suited to the occasion. Kennedy's athletic trimness was a rebuke to sloth, as he quickly projected through the President's Physical Fitness program. His jaunty willingness to persevere, despite recognition that life was unfair, appealed to intellectuals imbued with respect for disillusioned courage. And yet his earnest call for commitment and excellence also inspired idealists looking for a cause after years spent throwing off the yoke of McCarthyism and the milder stays of Eisenhower's presidency.

In response to Kennedy's plea for national renewal a wave of earnest reformers entered the Peace Corps, the civil rights movement, and kindred reform efforts. Shocked by the revelations of suffering and poverty in Michael Harrington's *The Other America* (1962), the activists moved toward the conclusion that another new deal for the common man was needed. But the conviction never reached the level of identification with the common man that had been the staple of New Deal reform and cultural expression. The New Frontier occurred during a period of general affluence, rather than depression. Prosperity meant that Kennedy activists were essentially part of the great middle class, entering social action less for survival than from a desire to justify their existence and to find exciting outlets for their energies and education. Moreover, the "cool" mystique of skepticism toward human nature and a growing preference for European culture over American diminished empathy. For all the concern about poverty in Appalachia and the inner cities, the poor were for most of those involved just as Harrington described them—the "other America," not "us."

The cultural style of the New Frontier also showed more detachment from the common life than had the New Deal, although here, as in social reform, comparison with the New Deal seemed appropriate. The establishment of the President's Advisory Council on the Arts in 1963 set in motion the first revival of federal support for the arts since the demise of the WPA projects. In accord with the New Frontier ideal of raising the quality of American life, August Heckscher, the chairman of the Advisory Council, stressed in his report to Kennedy how patronage of the arts fitted the ideal of civic responsibility. In contrast to the concern for a common style in the thirties, however, Heckscher and the administration that welcomed his words stressed the distance between the average man and a great artist who "has seen more deeply . . . into the existing state of things . . . [and] what is destined to come." There was no talk of federal *relief* for destitute artists; rather, the aim was a kind of corporate partnership for the improvement of taste and enrichment of culture. Allowing for efforts by some officials to retain the thirties model of the federal government as purveyor of "arts for the millions," the National Endowment for the Arts mostly awarded funds to well-established applicants and, accordingly, supported specialized projects rather than those with broad communal impact.

The exigencies of the times only briefly closed the cultural gap between the centers of cultural expression and the common, or in postwar parlance, mass man. Kennedy's assassination opened the way for Lyndon Johnson to express his allegiance to the New Deal through his Great Society programs. Soon, however, the Vietnam War aroused antiwar protest that transformed the desire for reform into a vehement contest over the true nature and destiny of the nation's basic institutions. As racial ghettos were torched by those forced to live within them and students protesting war-related research and indifference to social ills invaded university sanctuaries, artists and writers once again spoke of solidarity with the people and the need to construct a radical new society. Out of the fervor came, not only a New Left to take the place of the old, but also renewed interest in the lost style and content of the New Deal cultural synthesis. A number of excellent accounts of WPA artists and writers projects appeared in the early seventies, along with extensive recovery of the art works and documentary photography long since repudiated or forgotten. Against the stultifying elitism of the postwar period, against its cold war tremors and its doubts about the worth of human nature, the thirties offered a culture of militant compassion well suited to the resurgence of hopeful social action.

But the reprise of the thirties was not a return to the New Deal cultural synthesis in any deeply committed way. To be sure, there were groups far removed from the cultural mainstream that were stirred by the call of the times for social justice to reassert their folk roots and the right to a fairer share of society's rewards. Such was the case with the black, Chicano, and native American minorities and with non-Anglo-Saxon whites who undertook the revolt of the ethnics. Still, while the interests of various disadvantaged groups were advanced, there was no coherent cultural focus created for the whole society. Most of those who drew up thirties forms did not share the optimism of their predecessors but continued to thrive on the *Weltschmerz* of alienation that was so deeply ingrained in the experience of the fifties and sixties. Solidarity with select subgroups helped alleviate lonely helplessness, but such solidarity was often defined in terms of its antagonism to the majority norms of society and tended thus to increase alienation toward any concept of a shared culture. So, too, the new interest in folkways, which was part of popular response to the alarums of the time, led to revival of folk music, some experiments in going back to the land, and concern for preserving remnants of the past; but the movement was mostly furthered by the well-assimilated and college educated who had no intention of making very extensive use of folk origins. Rediscovery of thirties culture was essentially the work of researchers who were interested in what could be learned about it, not lived. The upheavals of the late sixties had both fomented and legitimated interest in the thirties culture, but they did not lead to much incorporation of it.

For one thing, there was not enough time. As the Vietnam War grew larger and more deadly, the activism of the era became harsher and the radical spirit strained toward the extreme and soon burned itself out. From its peak, passion swiftly subsided, partly from a surfeit of emotion, partly because of the turn of events. When the threat of a military draft and war ended, concern about resisting an oppressive state eased. And, when the prosperity that had risen steadily since the end of World War II dipped in the early seventies, attention shifted toward job and status prospects. Hard times brought an end to the desire to replay the era of Hard Times and restored dominant position to a now less economically complacent middle-class society that had taken shape after World War II.

In the period of retrenchment that followed the radical sixties, the distance between intellectuals and the common life became wider than ever. The failure to enact revolutionary change left most of those who had advocated it prey to bitterness about the nation's democratic institutions and "The People" who had refused to seize their historic due. Those who had opposed the movement, on the other hand, saw it as evidence that America suffered from self-destructive permissiveness. The darkening tone of criticism that ensued stands in revealing contrast to the fifties when critics worried about middle-class *angst*—about ending up, that is, as "sad hearts at the supermarket," in poet Randall Jarrell's memorable phrase. After being annealed in the fires of the sixties, intellectuals tended toward the apocalyptic. The masses now seemed less lonely and foolish than sinister, their affluent delights bearing the mark of narcissistic mental disorder. Clearly, the issue for American life was no longer absurd alienation but the destruction of civilization itself.

As creative writers and artists increasingly indulged in what Warren Wagar has called "Terminal Visions," critics sought to head off apocalypse by a recapture of past virtues. Nobody quite urged repeal of the social and economic gains made by the New Deal, but there was considerable nostalgia for the threadbare simplicity that preceded it. Critics harked back to early days when the civic spirit of small communities and the solidity of the traditional family were a hedge against anarchy and despair.

But what of the common man himself? In recent years, no major voice has been heard on behalf of the New Deal cultural synthesis—indeed, cultural criticism has made hardly any reference to the New Deal at all. And yet, measurements of public opinion since 1940 have indicated that, although the tides of cultural concerns have moved away from folk roots, the general public has retained the cultural aspirations to which Roosevelt made such successful appeal and on which his current status as a folk hero rests. As some New Dealers surmised, spiritual concerns were of very high importance to allegedly materialistic Americans. When asked, the public consistently showed that although its anxieties are about material things, its aims are modestly nonmaterialistic. From the first, peace of mind, family contentment, and good health have been most valued; a lack of education most regretted. Even making allowance for the tendency of people to give the "respectable" answer to questions of values, the polling results are too uniform over a long period to allow for cynical disregard of their findings. Roosevelt, even before public opinion could be systematically tapped, had understood his constituency's heart of hearts when he stressed economic security and personal liberty, the former being the passport to unassuming use of the latter.

The New Deal cultural synthesis sought to root those simple aspirations within a cultural heritage. Fifty years later hardly a memory of that cultural conception is left; and no other cultural focus has succeeded in taking its place. Neither revolutionary anger nor calls for retreat into a restoration of decentralized authority have answered the public yearning for community. In the face of continued popular fealty to the common man standard and Roosevelt's high personal stature, there are strong grounds for reassessing the cultural synthesis of the New Deal. With shrewd attention to what experience has shown about naïveté and wickedness—along with a certain Rooseveltian flair for inspiring confidence—that reassessment could allay fear of apocalypse and of the masses, while reviving the constructive quest of the thirties for ways of making American culture whole.

SUGGESTED READINGS

Despite the vast literature on every phase of the New Deal, the inner workings of Roosevelt's mind and the relationship of the New Deal to the social and intellectual currents around it remain obscure. This is true in spite of a pioneer essay by T. V. Smith, "The New Deal as a Cultural Phenomenon," in F. S. C. Northup, ed., *Ideological Differences and World Order* (New Haven, 1949), which argued intelligently that the New Deal enveloped the whole of American culture in its welfare state web. Howard Zinn, writing later and from a strongly activist position within the New Left, provided an excellent collection of readings on *New Deal Thought* (Indianapolis, 1966) that showed the broad outreach of the New Deal, which was judged short of the range of radical influence Zinn and others on the left favored. Writing in sympathy with the desire expressed by John Dewey in the thirties for a drastic overhaul of the nation's institutions from the standpoint of pragmatic moral intelligence, Paul Conkin in *The New Deal* (New York, 1967) expressed comparable disappointment that the New Deal was too timid to engage in true social experimentation. Soon afterward Arthur A. Ekirch, Jr., in *Ideologies and*

Utopias: The Impact of the New Deal on American Thought (Chicago, 1969), echoed the broad claims T. V. Smith had made twenty years earlier by declaring that the New Deal ushered in a revolutionary new era in thought; but Ekirch's general résumé of New Deal policies does not go deep enough into cultural life to support his thesis.

In the next decade, Theodore Rosenof in *Dogma, Depression and the New Deal* (Port Washington, N.Y., 1975) and Steven Kesselman in *The Modernization of American Reform: Structures and Perceptions* (New York, 1979) concentrated on relating New Deal policies to their ideological milieu. Rosenof argued that the New Deal urge toward radical action was thwarted by free enterprise dogma. Kesselman dealt informatively with the way the chief advisers, Tugwell and Arnold, sought to redirect earlier pragmatic and utopian thought. These works, along with numerous others that touch glancingly on the cultural implications of the New Deal, are tentative introductions to the role of the New Deal in culture. To carry the story further, there are two main avenues to follow. The first travels through the specific history of New Deal sponsorship of cultural projects, mainly in the form of relief for unemployed artists and writers. The second avenue is one of inference, drawing from the cultural ferment of the thirties and the literature that has sprung up to explain it. The following are among the most useful sources for each approach.

New Deal Cultural Projects

William Francis McDonald, *Federal Relief Administration and the Arts* (Columbus, Ohio, 1969).

Richard McKinzie, *The New Deal for Artists* (Princeton, 1973).

Jerre G. Mangione, *The Dream and the Deal: The Federal Writers' Project, 1935–1943* (Boston, 1972).

Karal Ann Marling, *Wall-to-Wall America: A Cultural History of Post-Office Murals in the Great Depression* (Minneapolis, 1982). Marling's work takes the story of the Federal Art Project beyond the essentially administrative focus of earlier works to concern for the quality and meaning of the art itself. Her achievement is a significant breakthrough into the history of aesthetic culture.

Jane DeHart Matthews, "Arts and the People: The New Deal Quest for a Cultural Democracy," *Journal of American History* 62 (September, 1975): 316–337.

———, *The Federal Theatre, 1935–1939: Plays, Relief and Politics* (Princeton, 1967).

Francis V. O'Connor, *Art for the Millions: Essays from the 1930s by Artists and Administrators of the WPA Federal Art Project* (New York, 1973).

_____, *Federal Support for the Visual Arts: The New Deal and Now* (New York, 1969).

Monty Noam Penkower, *The Federal Writers' Project; A Study in Government Patronage of the Arts* (Urbana, Ill., 1977).

Film and Photography

F. Jack Hurley, *Portrait of a Decade: Roy Stryker and the Development of Documentary Photography in the Thirties* (Baton Rouge, 1972).

Richard Dyer McCann, *The People's Films: A Political History of U.S. Government Motion Pictures* (New York, 1973).

Robert L. Snyder, *Pare Lorentz and the Documentary Film* (Norman, Okla., 1968).

Roy Stryker, *In This Proud Land: America, 1935–1943, As Seen in the FSA Photographs* (New York, 1973).

Cultural Trends of the Thirties

General Works

James Agee and Walker Evans, *Let Us Now Praise Famous Men* (Boston, 1941). The classic work of firsthand literary and photographic reportage on the spirit and substance of the "common" people.

Alfred Haworth Jones, "The Search for a Usable American Past in the New Deal Era," *American Quarterly* 23 (December 1971): 710–724.

Richard H. Pells, *Radical Visions and American Dreams: Culture and Social Thought in the Depression Years* (New York, 1973).

Warren Susman, "The Thirties." In Stanley Cohen and Lorman Ratner, eds., *The Development of an American Culture* (Englewood Cliffs, N.J., 1970), 179–218.

The Study of Culture

Ruth Benedict, *Patterns of Culture* (Boston, 1934).

Thomas L. Hartshorne, *The Distorted Image: Changing Conceptions of the American Character Since Turner* (Cleveland, 1968).

Charles R. Hearn, *The American Dream in the Great Depression* (Westport, Conn., 1977).

Clyde Kluckhohn, *Mirror for Man* (New York, 1944).

Robert S. Lynd, *Knowledge for What? The Place of Social Science in American Culture* (Princeton, 1939).

Constance Rourke, *American Humor: A Study of the National Character* (New York, 1931).

_____, *The Roots of American Culture and Other Essays* (New York, 1942).

Joan Shelley Rubin, *Constance Rourke and American Culture* (Chapel Hill, N.C., 1980).

Among the most useful books in the first group are those by William McDonald, Richard McKinzie, Jerre Mangione, and William Stott; in the second group they are the books by Charles Hearn and Richard Pells.

Postwar Reflections

General Trends

William Barrett, *The Truants: Adventures Among the Intellectuals* (New York, 1982).

Daniel Boorstin, *Democracy and Its Discontents: Reflections on Everyday America* (New York, 1974).

Henry Fairlie, *The Spoiled Child of the Western World: The Miscarriage of the American Idea in Our Time* (Garden City, N.Y., 1976).

Jeffrey Hart, *When the Going Was Good: American Life in the Fifties* (New York, 1982).

Max Lerner, *America as a Civilization: Life and Thought in the United States* (New York, 1957).

Theodore J. Lowi, *The End of Liberalism: Ideology, Policy, and the Crisis of Public Authority* (New York, 1969).

Dwight Macdonald, *Against the American Grain* (New York, 1962).

Douglas T. Miller and Marion Nowak, *The Fifties: The Way We Really Were* (New York, 1977).

Geoffrey Perrett, *A Dream of Greatness: The American People, 1945–1963* (New York, 1979).

Bernard Rosenberg and David M. Whited, eds., *Mass Culture* (New York, 1957).

Harold Rosenberg, *The Tradition of the New* (New York, 1959).

The Arts

Dore Ashton, *American Art Since 1945* (New York, 1982).

John A. Kouwenhoven, *The Arts in Modern Civilization* (New York, 1948).

Jane DeHart Matthews, "Art and Politics in Cold War America," *The American Historical Review* 81 (October 1976): 762–787.

Michael Mooney, *The Ministry of Culture: Connections Among Art, Money, and Politics* (New York, 1980).

Dick Netzer, *The Subsidized Muse: Public Support and the Arts in the United States* (New York, 1978).

Irving Sandler, *The Triumph of American Painting: A History of Abstract Expressionion* (New York, 1978).

Alvin Toffler, *The Culture Consumers: A Study of Art and Affluence in America* (New York, 1964).

Literature

John W. Aldridge, *After the Lost Generation: A Critical Study of the Writers of Two Wars* (New York, 1951).

Richard Chase, *Democratic Vista* (New York, 1958).

Malcolm Cowley, *The Literary Situation* (New York, 1954).

Leslie Fiedler, *What Was Literature? Class, Culture, and Mass Society* (New York, 1982).

Irving Howe, *A Margin of Hope: An Intellectual Autobiography* (New York, 1982).

Lionel Trilling, *The Liberal Imagination* (New York, 1953).

Grant Webster, *The Republic of Letters: A History of Postwar American Literary Opinion* (Baltimore, 1979).

Social Science

T. W. Adorno et al., *The Authoritarian Personality* (New York, 1949).

Reuel Denney, "How Americans See Themselves: Studies of American National Character," *Annals of the American Academy of Political and Social Sciences* 295 (September 1954): 12–20.

Erik H. Erikson, *Children and Society* (New York, 1950).

Hazel Erskine, "The Polls: Hopes, Fears, and Regrets," *Public Opinion Quarterly* 37 (Spring 1973): 132–145.

Clifford Geertz, *The Interpretation of Cultures* (New York, 1973).

David Potter, *People of Plenty* (Chicago, 1954).

David Riesman, with Reuel Denney and Nathan Glazer, *The Lonely Crowd* (New Haven, 1950).

William H. Whyte, *The Organization Man* (New York, 1956).

Post-Vietnam Reevaluations

Daniel Bell, *Cultural Contradictions of Capitalism* (New York, 1976).

Marvin Harris, *America Now: The Anthropology of a Changing Culture* (New York, 1981).

Jim Hougan, *Decadence: Radical Nostalgia, Narcissism, and Decline in the Seventies* (New York, 1975).

Christopher Lasch, *The Culture of Narcissism: American Life in an Age of Diminishing Expectations* (New York, 1979).

Robert Nisbet, *Twilight of Authority* (New York, 1975).

Richard Sennett, *The Fall of Public Man* (New York, 1977).

W. Warren Wagar, *Terminal Visions: The Literature of Last Things* (Bloomington, Ind., 1982).

Appeasement and Aggression: The New Deal and the Origins of the Second World War

Arnold A. Offner

President Franklin D. Roosevelt's first inaugural address dedicated the New Deal foremost to dealing with the domestic consequences of the Great Depression, but his administration soon confronted escalating crises in Europe and Asia. Within six years Adolf Hitler's saber-rattling diplomacy overturned the balance of power in Europe and then German armies overran Poland and western Europe in 1939–1940, and invaded the Soviet Union in 1941. Japan meanwhile had completed its conquest of Manchuria (thereafter Manchukuo) by early 1933, dominated northern China and then began undeclared war there in 1937, proclaimed a New Order in Asia in 1938, and signed a Tripartite Pact with Germany and Italy in 1940. The next year the Japanese occupied French Indochina and began their final drive to subdue China, ultimately attacking American, British, and Dutch possessions in the Pacific and Southeast Asia on December 7, 1941; four days later Germany and Italy declared war on the United States, bringing the United States into the Second World War.

Historians have fiercely debated the origins of the New Deal's rendezvous with global war. Revisionist historians first argued that the administration turned deceptively from nonintervention — or "isolation"—after 1937, became belligerent toward Germany during 1939–1941 by aiding the British and Russians, and then maneuvered the United States to war through rigid diplomacy toward Japan over China. Roosevelt's defenders responded that isolationism and domestic crises restrained the internationalist administration until 1938–1939, but that thereafter the President grasped the necessities of history and national security and made Great Britain and China America's line of defense against the combined forces of aggression. More recently, neorevisionist, or New Left, historians have argued that the United States has chiefly sought "Open Doors" for American capital to dominate markets and raw materials, and opted for war when another nation challenged its economic primacy in a crucial region.

These views have not measured sufficiently the dynamics of German or Japanese foreign policy, nor the way in which American diplomats viewed the current world political order, the major nations upon the diplomatic stage, and the role the United States should play—and the means it should use—to resolve the world's diplomatic problems. Nor have they stressed that in the 1930s appeasement did not connote diplomats bending supinely before dictators, but meant accommodation, conciliation, and rectification of legitimate grievances. Close analysis of these factors leads to the conclusion that from 1933 until March 1940 the Roosevelt Administration pursued a logical but flawed policy of appeasement of Germany and Japan, and from then until the spring of 1941 sought to lend all possible aid to those who resisted aggression, hoping that this might foster a settlement and keep America at peace. Thereafter the Roosevelt Administration determined to stretch its aid and executive authority to the legal limit and beyond, and to maintain a firm but proper policy toward Japan even if this meant being "pushed," as the President said, into the hostilities in Europe and Asia that were generally perceived to be a single world conflict that menaced American—and Western—civilization.

AMERICA AND THE EUROPEAN CRISIS: 1933–1941

To look first at Europe—Roosevelt's primary concern—most American diplomats believed that instability there resulted from Germany's efforts to throw off the Treaty of Versailles and from the 1919 Paris Peace Conference treaty structure that had created out of the former Austro-Hungarian Empire independent but rivalrous nations in east-central Europe that were also subject to great power pressure. Senior officials such as Roosevelt's closest diplomatic adviser, Under Secretary of State Sumner Welles, and Assistant Secretary of State Adolf A. Berle argued consistently that the World War I settlements had created a "vicious circle" of political and economic injustices. The prohibition of German-Austrian unity created economic and political instability in landlocked Austria and, as Berle said in 1938, if it were not for Hitler's cruelty, German plans to absorb "some, if not all" of Czechoslovakia would be regarded as merely "reconstituting the old system, undoing the unsound work of Versailles." American officials also viewed German predominance in Eastern Europe as inevitable, and preferable to Soviet domination.

This does not deny, as economically oriented historians in the United States and Germany have argued, that Americans opposed the way Germany enhanced its trade and investment, especially in Eastern Europe and Latin America, through severe restrictions on the convertibility and transferability of its currency, rigid import-export quotas, and bilateral treaties to guarantee Germany a favorable balance of trade. But while American officials subscribed to traditional liberal economics (convertible currency, repatriation of profits made abroad, and multilateral agreements lowering trade barriers and providing equal opportunity to markets, resources, and investments), they accommodated German realities. The State Department permitted American importers and exporters to "barter" American cotton, copper, and petroleum for German goods, and American corporations that could not bring home their profits reinvested them in Germany to build globally useful transportation and storage facilities. Hence, while recovery of German-American trade lagged behind world trade recovery in the 1930s, the United States ranked first in value of exports to Germany in 1933, 1934, 1938, and Germany had constant access to critical American materials (petroleum, copper, iron, scrap steel, uranium) and grains through 1938. Among the corporations that maintained secret, restrictive agreements (some through 1941) with German firms on the production of rubber, chemicals, and aviation fuel, and facilitated Germany's stockpiling of strategic materials were Standard Oil of New Jersey, General Motors, and DuPont. Not until Germany invaded Poland in 1939 did the Roosevelt Administration invoke real trade war measures: freezing German assets and putting permanently high import duties on its goods, using licenses and subsidies to force American firms to break their ties with German firms in the Balkans and Latin America, and taking over vital transportation and communications routes.

Americans were of two minds about Germany—or thought there were two Germanies. During the 1920s the United States had fostered the reintegration of Weimar Germany into the Western political and economic community, and in the 1930s there persisted respect for traditional German (as distinct from Nazi) culture. In 1933 Roosevelt hoped to see a return to that "German sanity of the old type" and, as late as October 1939, he wrote approvingly of German "upbringing," "independence of family life," and property-holding traditions—which he contrasted to "the Russian form of brutality." At the same time Nazi brutality horrified Americans, and from 1933 diplomats reported that the "nation which loves to be led, is again marching," that the Nazis sought to dominate Europe, and that war was inevitable shortly. The crucial dilemma therefore was how to readjust the post-1919 Versailles order so that a prosperous and content Germany could play its proper role in Europe.

Finally, it must be recalled that Americans took a dim view of their former World War I associates. New Deal officials perceived the British to be old-fashioned Tories or imperial Victorians mainly determined to preserve their Empire. Roosevelt denigrated the "Bank of England crowd," and especially Neville Chamberlain, powerful Chancellor of the Exchequer in 1933–1937 and Prime Minister in 1937–1940. The President complained that the British took 80 percent of every deal and sought to make America "a tail to the British kite," and that they needed to show a "little more unselfish spine," abandon their "muddle through" attitude, and take "a good stiff grog" to awaken to their responsibility to deal with Hitler. Americans also thought that French politicians lacked "moral or intellectual honesty" and that successive French governments had shown themselves incapable of ruling at home or abroad and had shut the door "to any possible appeasement with Germany."

The United States therefore followed a deliberate "hands off" policy when Germany quit the Geneva Disarmament Conference and League of Nations in 1933, announced rearmament in March 1935, and remilitarized the Rhineland in March 1936. "Versailles is dead," the American military attaché in Berlin wrote with typical ambivalence in March 1936. "There may possibly be a German catastrophe and a new Versailles, but it will not be the Versailles which has hung like a dark cloud over Europe since 1920."

President Roosevelt and his aides nonetheless feared that Germany's unilateral renunciation of treaties might trigger war and embroil the United States, and they sought to foster political appeasement through arms reduction and economic appeasement. From mid-1936 Roosevelt made numerous overtures about a heads of state meeting to draft arms reduction and economic procedures that might, as the State Department noted in 1937, precipitate "comprehensive" political and economic settlements that would preclude Germany's need to "explode" down the Danube. But Hitler evinced no interest and the British denigrated the proposals as "dangerous drivel."

Finally, in October 1937, Under Secretary Welles persuaded Roosevelt to summon a world conference on Armistice Day to establish universal codes for international relations, trade practices, neutral rights, and — most significantly — peaceful revision of treaties. Whether such a convocation might have succeeded is moot. But the President was dissuaded from trying first by his exceedingly cautious and suspicious Secretary of State, Cordell Hull, and then again in early 1938 both by Prime Minister Chamberlain's cold response and ominous German developments, including Hitler's purge of leading conservative military and diplomatic officials and then his annexation of Austria on March 13, 1938.

No one contested the Anschluss, although all deplored Hitler's use of Austrian Nazis to provoke a crisis and then to summon German troops to restore order. Diplomats feared a repeat performance in Czechoslovakia, where Nazi-led Sudeten Germans first demanded autonomous rule and then that the Sudetenland revert to Germany. Roosevelt remained of divided mind, angrily charging that the British and French would abandon Czechoslovakia "and wash the Judas Iscariot blood from their hands" — and only embolden Hitler to greater demands — but the President also listened to diplomats assail the Treaty of Versailles and the failure to reconstitute the Austro-Hungarian Empire in some form. Roosevelt feared encouraging the Czechs to "vain resistance," and on September 20 he encouraged the British to avert war but blockade Germany, and said that he would attend a conference to reorganize all unsatisfactory frontiers. Then, on September 26–27, he cabled the various heads of state to continue negotiations and consider parallel political and economic appeasement conferences. Word the next day that Chamberlain had accepted Hitler's last-minute invitation to Munich led Adolph Berle to declare "The 'break'! Thank God," while Roosevelt wired Chamberlain: "Good man."

The results of the Munich Conference of September 29–30, 1938, were foreordained and surprised no one. Czechoslovakia had to cede one-third of its territory and population to Germany and to Poland and Hungary. Some American diplomats deplored the "rape of the Czechs," and the "darkest hour" for Britain and France. But Roosevelt convinced himself that he was "not a bit upset over the results," and Welles announced on national radio that there was more opportunity than at any time since 1919 to reestablish a just and lawful world order.

Roosevelt's annual message in January 1939, however, proposed "methods short of war" to resist global aggression: sharply increased defense expenditures, and revision of the neutrality legislation of 1935–1937 to permit "cash-and-carry" arms sales to nations under attack. Roosevelt also told the Senate Military Affairs Committee that Germany—and Italy and Japan—sought "world domination" and that America's first line of defense had to be the "continued, independent existence" of eighteen nations from the Baltic to the Balkans to Turkey and Persia. Germany's occupation of rump Czecho-Slovakia in March 1939 and Italy's invasion of Albania in April convinced even the appeasement-oriented Berle that the "German Napoleonic machine" would seek unlimited expansion, and Hull warned congressmen that the coming struggle would not be "another goddamn piddling dispute over a boundary line" but a global contest against "barbarism."

German pressure on Poland over Danzig and the Polish Corridor convinced State Department officials that the Germans were "beginning to beat the tom-toms for war" and that an unchecked German-Italian combination threatened the Atlantic and Latin America. The stunning Nazi-Soviet Nonaggression Pact of August 23, 1939—with its widely known "secret" provision to divide Poland in event of war—led American diplomats to conclude that the "combined Soviet-Nazi allies now have all Europe," and to fear that the British might "sell out" in Europe and Asia. After Germany attacked

Poland on September 1 and precipitated war with Great Britain and France, Roosevelt insisted that America could not be neutral in thought or conscience, and Congress shortly agreed to permit the "cash-and-carry" sale of war goods, which Roosevelt said would sustain England as a citadel of civilization and — he half-believed — keep America out of war.

The Roosevelt Administration was most disconcerted in autumn 1939, however, by the Soviet Union's mid-September attack upon Poland, which was promptly partitioned between Germany and the USSR, and then the Soviets' November 30 "dreadful rape" — as Roosevelt said — of Finland. By the year's end Roosevelt was fearfully uncertain whether ultimately Germany and Russia would assault one another or divide Europe, Africa, and Asia Minor between them — and jeopardize American civilization. At the same time many diplomatic and public spokesmen urged the President to mediate peace in Europe. Consequently, he sent Under Secretary of State Welles to Europe during February 26–March 19, 1940, on an ambiguous mission: at best to achieve a negotiated settlement; perhaps to delay Germany's spring offensives; at worst to demonstrate that no peace was possible and thereby rouse the American people. Appropriately, Welles believed firmly in revising the Versailles order and was also properly antagonistic toward the British, hostile toward the Russians but mindful of their historical and security-oriented territorial claims, and amenable to recognizing Italy's 1935–1936 conquest of Ethiopia, if Mussolini furthered peace with Germany.

In Berlin, however, Hitler dismissed Welles' overtures with tirades against the Versailles system and insisted that Germany alone would determine its security and its economic and colonial needs. Welles next pressed his ideas in France, where he was surprised by French resistance, and then in London, where Chamberlain and others derided Roosevelt's election-year grandstanding and argued with "white-hot" anger that peace was not possible "until Hitlerism has been overthrown." The British finally agreed to negotiate if by some "miracle" Hitler first guaranteed independent but smaller Polish and Czech states and began troop withdrawals. Welles then encouraged Mussolini to initiate negotiations, but the Italian dictator demanded that Roosevelt guarantee the political settlement, which the President deemed too risky. Thus, Mussolini met Hitler at the Brenner Pass and pledged that Italy would join Germany "at the decisive hour."

Welles now reported that Mussolini's "obsession" was to re-create the Roman Empire, and that he would follow Hitler into war, while the German people were living on "another planet" where "lies have become truth; evil, good; and aggression, self-defense." As the young diplomat George F. Kennan, who had joined the Welles mission, then wrote, peace was impossible because "the Nazi system is built on the assumption that war, not peace, represents the normal condition of mankind."

The Welles mission—like American appeasement—had only angered the British and French, who resented the American failure to assume political-territorial responsibilities while advocating universal codes for international behavior; probably roused Soviet suspicions about Western efforts to turn Hitler eastward; and caused Hitler to strengthen his ties with Mussolini. Both Welles and Roosevelt still retained slight belief in a negotiated settlement, or hoped to restrain Mussolini. But peace talks became unthinkable after Germany occupied Norway and Denmark on April 9 and then launched its offensive on May 10 against Belgium and Holland and then France.

Americans now believed, as Roosevelt said on April 15, that "old dreams of universal empire are again rampant." Thereafter the administration never spoke of Germany but only of a "totalitarian" Nazi state bent on global conquest. On June 10 Roosevelt denounced Italy's attack on France—"the hand that held the dagger has struck it into the back of its neighbor"—but more significantly pledged to extend American resources to the nations battling the "gods of force and hate" and to upgrade American military forces for "hemispheric defense." Roosevelt never deviated from this dual diplomacy, which he hoped might preclude American military intervention yet prepare the nation psychologically and realistically for the war he deemed likely or necessary. The consequence was presidential leadership and diplomacy that was often as clear and forceful as its legitimate purposes, and sometimes too indirect or misleading for the national good.

Beginning in May 1940 Roosevelt successfully pressed Congress for dramatic increases in defense spending and the nation's first peacetime draft, while he brought into his Cabinet two Republican spokesmen for preparedness and intervention: former Secretary of State Henry L. Stimson as Secretary of War, and Frank L. Knox, publisher of the Chicago *Daily News*, as Secretary of the Navy.

When in May 1940 the new British Prime Minister, Winston Churchill, unashamedly asked for all aid short of troops, even if the British could not pay, Roosevelt gingerly sold him $37 million in "surplus" planes and guns. But the President withheld ships to convoy purchases until the recently formed Committee to Defend America by Aiding the Allies, led by Republican journalist William Allen White, established the public mood and legal basis for the ship sales and got the Republican presidential candidate, Wendell Willkie, to acquiesce. Finally, on September 2, 1940, Roosevelt announced his executive agreement *fait accompli*: exchange of fifty "overage" destroyers for eight British bases stretching from Newfoundland to Bermuda, and in the Bahamas, and British Guiana.

The destroyer deal was unneutral and violated the spirit, if not the letter, of Congress' June 28, 1940 restrictions on the sale of defense materials. Roosevelt also strained the fair use of executive authority, although he probably spared Congress a controversial election-year roll-call. However, the destroyer deal also precipitated formation of the America First Committee, which sharply criticized Roosevelt's policies and insisted that aid to Britain would pull America into a European power struggle.

Germany, Italy, and Japan shortly signed their September 27, 1940, Tripartite Pact, which pledged a New Order in Europe and Asia and mutual aid in event of an attack by a nation not then at war, but exempted the Soviet Union. As stated by the chief German proponent of this pact, Foreign Minister Joachim von Ribbentrop, the alliance was "exclusively directed against the American warmongers," and sought to intimidate the United States into inaction in the Atlantic and the Pacific. Ironically, as Secretary Stimson noted, substantively the pact merely meant "making a bad face at us," but it produced a "clamor" for an alliance with Great Britain and gave Roosevelt occasion on Octorber 12 to denounce the "totalitarian powers" and warn that "no combination of dictator countries" would halt American aid to the "last free people now fighting to hold them at bay." Nonetheless, when Willkie switched from his presidential campaign charge that Roosevelt had "appeased the democratic world into destruction" to allege that the President's reelection would mean that American boys were "almost on transports," Roosevelt declared on Octorber 30 that "I will say it again and again: Your boys are not going to be sent into any foreign wars," and shortly insisted that "the country is not going to go to war." Roosevelt later told critics he meant that American boys would not fight except in case of attack — as the Democratic platform stated — but even granting this and Willkie's opportunism, an unsettled President had bowed to expediency and given misleading assurances.

Safely reelected, however, Roosevelt consistently urged in December 1940 that "the best defense of Great Britain is the best defense of the United States," which should therefore manufacture British war goods and "lease . . . or sell" them with no more concern for payment than that of a neighbor who lends another a garden hose to fight a fire and expects only return of the hose. He then denounced the "new order" of Axis powers as an "unholy alliance," insisted that "no nation can appease the Nazis," who sought to "enslave" Europe and then "the world." Americans had to meet their gravest crisis in history by providing the British with everything they needed in the fight "for their liberty and our security," and the United States had to become "the great arsenal of democracy."

Beginning in January 1941 the administration shepherded through Congress its Lend Lease bill — H.R. 1776 — which authorized the President to sell, lend, or lease war materials to any nation he deemed vital to American security and to determine repayment. Congress quickly appropriated the first $7 billion of an ultimate $50 billion commitment, and on March 15 Roosevelt proclaimed: "Let not the dictators of Europe or Asia doubt our unanimity now." Democracy moved slowly, he said, "but the world is no longer left in doubt."

Simultaneously, secret Anglo-American military talks during January 29–March 27, 1941, provided that if the United States became involved in war with Germany or Japan, or both, the battle to defeat Germany would come first. Roosevelt withheld formal approval of this ABC-1 Staff Agreement, which was not a commitment — or conspiracy — to enter the war. But the unprecedented exchange of technical information and plans for America to take over Britain's primary role in the Atlantic approximated, as an admirer of Roosevelt's judged, a "common-law alliance," with the United States as senior partner.

More significant at the time was Hitler's effort to choke British supply lines by extending the war zone for German submarines westward to Greenland. Roosevelt used the rubric of "hemispheric defense" to forestall German naval bases there by announcing on April 9 a secretly negotiated agreement with the Danish minister in

Washington to protect Greenland. The President then ordered the Navy to "patrol" to the mid-Atlantic, while Stimson, who was anxious for war, thought Roosevelt should be "honest with himself" and admit his "hostile act to Germany." But characteristically, when in mid-May Secretary of the Treasury Henry Morgenthau, Jr., urged war, Roosevelt replied, "I am waiting to be pushed into this situation." However, German advances in Greece and North Africa, and the sinking of the American freighter *Robin Moor*, led Roosevelt to declare a national emergency on May 27 and to allege that the Nazis planned to conquer Latin America and "strangle" the United States and Canada. He then stretched "hemispheric defense" to take over Britain's military occupation of Iceland—at that government's request—when the Germans extended their blockade there, but did not send troops until Germany invaded the Soviet Union on June 22, 1941.

Roosevelt now moved deftly to aid Russia. At first he provided only the few assets legally available, but within a few months, reassured about Russian ability to resist and congressional appropriations, he facilitated massive Lend-Lease supplies. Roosevelt had deep misgivings about the Soviets, especially because of their reannexation in the summer of 1940 of their former Baltic provinces of Estonia, Latvia, and Lithuania, and then their recent war against Finland. But just as Churchill had said that the British would aid any nation fighting "Nazidom," so Under Secretary Welles stated the guiding principle of American military diplomacy on June 23, 1941: "Hitler's armies are today the chief danger." As Roosevelt persisted in September, nothing was more important to humanity (or the military balance) than to defeat the Nazi dictatorship, and "to cross this bridge I would hold hands with the Devil."

Roosevelt also inclined toward war. He had met secretly during August 9–12 with Churchill at Argentia Bay in Newfoundland, where they agreed—and disagreed—about political, economic, and military principles. Roosevelt shied away from British diplomatic advice to precipitate war, but when on September 4 the President heard that a German submarine had fired two torpedoes at the U.S. destroyer *Greer* 175 miles southwest of Iceland, he rushed to call the attack deliberate. Then, despite having learned that the *Greer* had been tracking the submarine for an attacking British plane before the submarine fired, Roosevelt on September 11 publicly branded the German action "piracy," proof of their intent to create "a permanent world system based on force, on terror, and on murder." He ordered American ships to convoy and to assume "active defense" in the Atlantic—a virtual "shoot on sight" policy. As Admiral Harold Stark, Chief of Naval Operations, said of this Atlantic war, "We are all but, if not actually, in it."

Roosevelt's rhetoric, and occasionally disingenuous tactics, heated with the Atlantic conflict. In a rousing Navy Day speech on October 27, he purported to have a "secret" map and documents showing Nazi intentions to carve Central and South America into vassal states, to liquidate religion and the clergy, and to replace the "God of Love and Mercy" with the "God of Blood and Iron." And, he insisted, Americans were ready to do their duty. But Congress remained more cautious, and it was not until the Germans sank the destroyer *Reuben James* 600 miles west of Iceland on October 31 that the administration could secure final revision of the neutrality law to permit American merchant ships to be armed and to enter war zones.

The Roosevelt Administration had reached its limits in deed and rhetoric, and the law of the land reflected its policy of all aid to Great Britain and the Soviet Union and undeclared naval war against Germany. Roosevelt resisted Cabinet and military pressure to declare war because he believed that the American people would assent only if war were thrust upon them. The German admiralty would have done this, for throughout the spring and summer of 1941 they urged attack on all American ships. But Hitler ordered limited sinkings because he wanted no diversions from his consuming war against the Russians. Nevertheless, as Hitler told Japan's ambassador in July 1941, their two countries had to "annihilate" the United States, although in December his primary tactic was still to encourage Japan's expansion in the Far East, where war would come upon the Americans.

AMERICAN FOREIGN POLICY IN THE FAR EAST: 1933–1940

American policy in the Far East from 1933 until 1940 remained as cautious and appeasement-oriented as it was in Europe. Diplomats sought to avoid involvement in China's myriad domestic and foreign problems because there was little aid that China might be usefully afforded, and because the Japanese might regard such aid as having hostile intent toward them. Americans were not prepared to use force to preserve their traditional economic—or Open Door—rights in the Far East, and recognized that despite decades of talk about the "China market," the Japanese were far superior trading partners who took 8.5 percent of American exports annually while the Chinese never exceeded 3 percent. Further, American officials believed that because the British, French, and Russians had far greater interests at stake, they bore primary responsibility for preserving order in the Far East. And, as Roosevelt reiterated privately, the United States would not be "pushed out front" or be made a "tail to the British kite."

American officials took a dim view of Generalissimo Chiang Kaishek's Kuomintang (Nationalist) government, which had established its rule in 1927 but thereafter primarily enhanced the fortunes of its elite banking, commercial, and landed constituents; ignored the plight of China's peasantry, 90 percent of the population; and warred almost exclusively against Chinese Communists while waiting for the Western powers to restrain Japan. As Nelson Johnson, the conservative U.S. Minister to China from 1929 to1941, reported from late 1932 onwards, China presented a "pathetic and humiliating" spectacle. While Chiang governed as a "dictator," the Kuomintang did nothing to establish effective central authority and permitted its regional governors and military commanders to indulge their thirst for territory and revenues rather that resist foreign aggression. The people had lost faith in the government and the entire state of affairs "would be funny if it were not so tragic." Similarly the feisty American military attaché, Colonel Joseph Stilwell, reported in 1935–1936 that the Chinese government was corrupt beyond redemption, and that despite Chiang's spending 80 percent of his revenue on his military, he did nothing and was "utterly ignorant" of how to prepare to fight a "first class power." Roosevelt meanwhile firmly believed that nothing any Western society did "can ever affect the people of China very deeply," since they had to solve their problems themselves.

At the same time New Deal officials were hopeful about relations with Japan. Joseph C. Grew, Ambassador in Tokyo from 1931 to1941, insisted in 1933 that American-Japanese economic conflict was unlikely because their different manufactures and raw materials did not compete directly. At first he believed that Japan's 1931–1933 assault on Manchuria might bring order to the region and restrain the Russians, and when Japan's "war psychology" distressed him in 1934, he argued that neither moral, nor military, nor economic sanctions would deter the Japanese. Similarly, Stanley K. Hornbeck, who was Chief of the State Department's Division of Far Eastern Affairs and often hostile toward Japan, argued that although the Japanese had made war an instrument of national policy, the United States "had nothing to gain by aiding China and playing Santa Claus in Asia." Eventually, he contended, Japan's invasion would ebb against rising Chinese nationalism and logistical difficulties.

Hence while President Roosevelt in early 1933 endorsed the doctrine of nonrecognition of Japan's conquest of Manchukuo which both the Hoover Administration and the League of Nations had adopted, the United States did not resist Japan's increasing political and economic domination of northern China during the next four years. Meanwhile the Japanese government, increasingly dominated by its military, in August 1936 began to assess a set of "Fundamental Principles of National Policy" that called for increasing military and economic integration of Japan, Manchukuo, and North China, and peaceful penetration of Southeast Asia to build a self-sufficient economy and a navy powerful enough "to secure command of the western Pacific."

Then came Japan's "undeclared war" against China, originating in a clash on July 7, 1937, between Chinese and Japanese troops outside of Peking. Both anxious governments rushed reinforcements, and the Japanese then determined to win a quick, overpowering victory to force agreement over Manchukuo and North China. Nevertheless, virtually every American diplomat agreed with Grew that the United States should remain aloof from the "Far Eastern mess," avoid "pulling the British chestnuts out of the fire," and remain "Japan's fair-haired boy . . . . What a change since 1931 and 1932!" The State Department turned aside three British inquiries about joint mediation, and on July 16 Hull merely reiterated publicly America's commitment to international law.

Roosevelt was distressed by what he perceived to be an "amazingly successful" German-Italian-Japanese combination — "bluff, power, accomplishment, or whatever" — and equally by a "peace at any price mentality." Thus on October 5, 1937, he called for a "quarantine" to halt the "epidemic of world lawlessness," but immediately declared that sanctions were "out of the window," and confided that a "quarantine" was the "Christian" way — as opposed to war — to deal with Japan. Roosevelt did become enraged when the Japanese began their December assault upon Chiang's seat of government in Nanking by sinking the American gunboat *Panay* and damaging several other American and British ships on the Yangtze River. The President quickly accepted Japan's apology, then grew angry to the point of talking about an oil and cotton embargo and an Anglo-American blockade of the Japanese when he learned that they had sunk the *Panay* deliberately, and then promptly accepted an indemnity. By 1938 the United States had virtually abandoned its interest in China. The Japanese, meanwhile, escalated their political, economic, and military advances in northern and central China, and then launched a major offensive in the South upon Hankow and Canton. By the end of 1938 the Japanese had driven the Kuomintang into a fortress-like retreat in Chungking in southwest China, cut off from all supply routes except the 650-mile Burma Road. The Japanese, partly to justify their unanticipated vast military and economic expenditures, then proclaimed their New Order in Asia, which envisioned political and economic coordination of Japan, Manchukuo, and China; established a puppet regime in Nanking to rival Chiang's government; and stated that the Open Door in China could not be guaranteed.

Diplomats—such as Johnson and Grew—now wrote with as much anxiety as conviction that the United States would soon have to "stand at Armageddon" to confront international "gangsterdom" and the "totalitarian states . . . rapidly lining up in battle array." In late 1938, however, the administration only quietly refused to recognize Japan's New Order, and provided China with a small $25 million commodities credit. Not until March 1940 did they give further aid—$20 million—by which time the Russians had given China over $500 million in support, more than the combined total provided by all other nations.

Germany's conquest of Western Europe in the spring of 1940, however, led the Japanese into new opportunity—or temptation. First they pressed the beleaguered Dutch for increased access to the East Indies trade. Next they sought to shut off supplies to the Kuomintang in Chungking by sending troops to the borders of Indochina and ships to the Gulf of Tonkin, and insisting that the French shut the routes in Indochina and that the British close the Burma Road. Then Japanese troops entered northern Indochina.

The Roosevelt Administration responded with admonitions and half-measures. After the U.S. fleet based in California held maneuvers near Hawaii in April 1940, Roosevelt ordered that the fleet remain at Pearl Harbor, in part to deter Japanese pressure on the East Indies but equally because "when I don't know how to move, I stay put." Similarly, State Department officials urged against any diplomatic or military maneuver and told the French — on the verge of surrender to Germany — that they had to yield to Japan's pressures on Indochina. That led the British to insist that they could not fight alone in Europe and Asia, and that the United States either must force Japan to respect the status quo or "wean Japan from aggression by a concrete offer" — to which the British would contribute materially. The Americans, however, insisted that they saw "no virtues in appeasement in Europe in 1938 and in Asia in 1940," but that they had taken all measures short of military hostilities to stabilize Japan. In late July, Roosevelt yielded to Stimson and Morgenthau to embargo iron, scrap steel, and oil products to Japan, but the President immediately restricted the embargo to aviation fuel and the highest grades of iron and scrap steel.

By the summer of 1940 even Ambassador Grew insisted that the German victories were "strong wine" for the Japanese, who were now "hell bent toward the Axis and establishment of the New Order in East Asia." In mid-September he proffered his famous "Green Light" cable, insisting that Japan and the "predatory powers" threatened the "way of life" of the English-speaking peoples, and until the war in Europe was either won or lost the United States had to preserve the British Empire and the status quo in the Pacific, even if this meant the use of force to achieve an equitable settlement. Japan's signature of the Tripartite Pact two weeks later further convinced Grew that "in the Far East we should profit by Mr. Chamberlain's bitter experience in Europe," and caused Roosevelt to extend the embargo to include all scrap materials. But in November the President insisted that an oil embargo would compel Japan to attack the East Indies and spread war in the Far East.

Roosevelt was certain by January 1941 that the hostilities in Europe, Africa, and Asia "are all part of a single world conflict" which menaced American interests in Europe and Asia, and that the American strategy of "self-defense" had to be "global." But he and his senior advisers were firm that Europe came first, or as General Marshall said in autum 1940, "If we lose in the Atlantic we lose everywhere." And both the Anglo-American ABC-1 agreement of March 1941 and the report of the Joint Board of the Army and Navy in November 1941 stressed that Germany was the primary, and most dangerous, enemy, and that conflict in the Pacific would seriously diminish capabilities in the Atlantic. In April 1941, therefore, at the time Japan secured its northern flank with a neutrality pact with the Soviet Union, Secretary Hull began intense negotiations with Ambassador Kichisaburo Nomura.

The Hull-Nomura talks of April-December 1941 did suffer from diplomatic misunderstandings. In mid-April Hull stipulated Four Points for negotiations: respect for every nation's sovereignty; noninterference in their internal affairs; equal commercial opportunity; and no use of force to alter the status quo. Unfortunately, Normura delayed conveying these points to Tokyo, where the government did not grasp Hull's seriousness until September. But great powers often spoke — and violated — these principles, and adherence was always subject to interpretation. Successful negotiations depended far less on agreement on principles than on substantive issues, and on Japan's diplomatic-military framework and timetables. The Roosevelt Administration sought an accord, while Ambassador Grew, who had reversed his harsh outlook, said that many Tokyo officials also sought agreement.

Two essential issues, the Tripartite Pact and Japan's unrecognized conquest of Manchukuo, were virtually resolved when the Japanese conceded that their "defensive" alliance was "normal" and Manchukuo was exempted from Hull's principles and left for "amicable negotiation" after a general settlement. Then the Japanese proposed in May that the United States resume normal trade relations and induce the Chinese to negotiate peace with prior acceptance of Japan's political and economic leadership of the New Order in Asia and staged withdrawal of Japan's troops from China. If the Chinese refused, American aid would end. On June 21 Hull countered with an "exploratory" proposal: that Japan remove the bulk of its troops from China as soon as possible and discuss terms for those to remain. But before the Japanese negotiators could respond, Germany's invasion that day of the Soviet Union led the Japanese government at an Imperial Conference on July 2 to decide to establish its Greater East Asia Co-Prosperity Sphere and to settle the China Incident by southward advance, even at risk of war with the United States and Great Britain.

The Americans knew the gist of these decisions because they were able to decipher Japan's diplomatic codes. Roosevelt thus sought to deter Japan, yet avoid war, because "every little episode in the Pacific means fewer ships in the Atlantic." He ruled out an oil embargo because that might precipitate a Japanese attack on the Dutch East Indies. But after Japanese troops occupied all of Indochina, Roosevelt on July 26 froze Japanese assets and required licenses for exports to Japan. The President did not seek to strangle Japan, a Cabinet official noted, but to put a noose around its neck and "give it a jerk every now and then." Strong-willed State Department officers, however, blocked Japanese oil licenses, and by the time Roosevelt discovered this in September, he concluded that reversal of this de facto oil embargo—which the public approved—would be misinterpreted as retreat. The issue was now joined: the Japanese had determined to achieve their goals even at risk of war in China. The Japanese thus concluded that they had to act definitively—or not at all—by December. The United States, Japan's major supplier of oil, meanwhile decided that it had to appear firm by continuing the embargo at risk of angering Japan, or reverse itself and appear—at home and abroad—willing to fuel the Japanese war machine. Moreover, American ability to force the Chinese to the negotiating table, even by cutting off aid, remained doubtful.

Prime Minister Konoye sought to resolve the dilemma by meeting with Roosevelt, while the Japanese government in early September reaffirmed its "minimum" demands: the right to conclude the China Incident with guaranteed access to resources, and afterwards to retain Manchukuo, maintain troops in Inner Mongolia and North China for "a necessary period," and manage its Greater East Asia Co-Prosperity Sphere. If these demands were not met, war would ensue.

Roosevelt found a summit meeting appealing, but his diplomats, except for Grew, had grave reservations because of Japan's "minimum" demands, refusal to give prior guarantees, for example, about troop withdrawals, and doubts that Konoye could restrain his military. The Americans also feared the adverse impact of a "Pacific Munich" on British and Russian resistance to Germany and the American public's support for methods short of war. The President thus declined the invitation in early October. Two weeks later the powerful War Minister, General Hideki Tojo, became Prime Minister with an Imperial "clean slate" for eleventh-hour negotiations but with two major constraints: a diplomatic deadline of November 29 and Supreme Command operational preparations for an "inevitable" war against the Americans, British, and Dutch by early December.

The Japanese first presented their long-term "Plan A," which provided no substantive change in position, and Hull and Roosevelt declined it in the days between November 10 and 20. Then Japan's "Plan B" proposed that the United States suspend aid to China and resume trade (including oil) with Japan, which would seek to negotiate with China and not move further south. Roosevelt wanted to give Japan "some oil and rice now and more later," if only to delay its southward thrust, and Secretary Morgenthau urged a more complex proposal—wholly unlikely to gain Japanese acceptance—intended, as he noted, chiefly to free American forces to ensure Germany's defeat. The American quest for a temporary accord thus continued despite interception of a Japanese cable of November 22, which stated that after November 29 "things are automatically going to happen," and Roosevelt's opinion on November 25 that an attack was imminent and Stimson's belief that the issue seemed to be how to "maneuver" the Japanese "into firing the first shot without allowing too much danger to ourselves." But just as Roosevelt approved a stop-gap modus vivendi—a 90-day truce and resumed, but monitored trade with Japan in return for troop withdrawals from southern Indochina—word of massive Japanese troop movements southward by land and sea caused the President to back off.

The Americans then presented the Japanese with the Ten Point Note of November 26, which insisted that they withdraw their forces from all of China (including Manchuria) and Indochina, recognize Chiang's government, and sign a multilateral nonagression pact for the Pacific in exchange for trade and other concessions. This was not an ultimatum, for there were no deadlines nor threatened action and Japan could have ignored the proposal. But the American reiteration at this late hour of its maximal position, which anticipated a return to the pre-1931 status quo, foreclosed negotiation. Indeed, the administration sent war warnings to its military installations in the Pacific on November 24, 27, and 28, while the British sought assurances in case Japan attacked only their possessions. On December 1 Roosevelt said that if Japan attacked only British and Dutch territory "obviously we should all be together," and two days later he pledged "armed support" even for an attack upon Thailand, although this would require "a few days," the time, presumably, he would need to persuade Congress to act, perhaps to declare war.

Roosevelt sent a *pro forma* appeal for a 90-day truce to the Emperor on the night of December 6, while Americans deciphered most of Japan's rebuttal of their Ten Point Note. The President feared that "this means war," but insisted that a democracy could not strike first. Japan's final point—a break in relations—arrived next morning, and occasioned a final, futile war warning to Hawaii. Japanese diplomats were unable to deliver their formal text to Hull until shortly after two o'clock on Sunday afternoon, December 7, 1941, by which time the Americans had learned of Japan's ultimate response: an attack at dawn upon the fleet at Pearl Harbor that was the first wave of a massive assault stretching from the Hawaiian Islands through the Philippines, China, and Malaya.

On December 8th Roosevelt asked Congress to declare war on Japan, but not on Germany, despite Stimson's urgings and the belief of the President's closest aides, as Harry Hopkins recorded, that "the enemy was Hitler." The Führer, however, quickly resolved the American dilemma. Perhaps he was moved by his beliefs that a great man must seize the fateful moment, and that "a great power like Germany declares war itself and does not wait for war to be declared on it." Conceivably he was persuaded by his views in the 1930s that America was politically and economically effete and racially corrupt—"half Judaized and the other half Negrified," he said—and thus militarily inconsequential. Maybe the dynamic of National Socialism and Hitler's lust for power led him to raise his sights toward the New World even as German armies were bogging down in the winter's snow outside of Moscow. Whatever his reasons, he told a cheering Reichstag on December 11, 1941, that Roosevelt, like Woodrow Wilson before him, was "mad," and incited by the "full diabolical meanness of Jewry" to make war on Germany. But now the Führer was responding to divine providence to lead Germany in this "historic struggle" that would determine the fate of the world for the next "thousand years." Mussolini's Italy immediately followed in Hitler's steps, and later that afternoon the United States declared war on Germany and Italy. East and West were now joined in the Second World War.

THE FAILURES OF APPEASEMENT AND AGGRESSION

Historians will continue to debate the origins of World War II. Some have said that the Treaty of Versailles ensured that Germany would seek retribution, others blamed Hitler for exploiting Europe's weaknesses or simply lusting for conquest. The British have been blamed for not playing their proper balancing role, either because they cravenly sought peace in their time without regard for other nations, or because they lacked the resources to do otherwise. The United States has been faulted first for shaping the post-1919 world order and then for reneging on it, while lately some have said that American capitalism was at war with German autarchy long before shots were fired.

Clearly, from March 1933 until perhaps as late as March 1940, Americans sought to appease Germany politically and economically. Not until the spring of 1940 did the Roosevelt Administration use "methods short of war" to aid nations resisting aggression, and only later did the New Dealers use every political and economic resource at their disposal to defeat the Nazi state that sought to conquer all of Europe. If the Roosevelt Administration erred, it was not in misperceiving what Germany had done between 1933 and 1941—or might seek to do ultimately—but in not assuming more responsibility and acting cooperatively with the British to stabilize the European order, and then in the President's engaging in disingenuous or deceitful uses of "hemispheric defense," "patrols," incidents in the Atlantic, and dubious German maps or documents. He would have served the nation's legitimate interests better by being more forthright about the threat he perceived to America's national interest and security, and risking the inevitable fight with "isolationists" or noninterventionists. Instead, he compromised democratic principles, cast doubt on his real goals, and set unfortunate precedents for later administrations.

Similarly, historians have debated whether Japan pursued a policy of deliberate aggression during the decade from 1931 to 1941 or was drawn incrementally into the quagmire of its China Incident. Few dispute, however, that Japanese leaders finally argued more over tactics than goals and were determined to establish their Empire— or Co-Prosperity Sphere—even at risk of war because otherwise, they believed, the nation would die for lack of material and spiritual resources. Here, too, it is clear that the Roosevelt Administration never threatened Japan's hold on Manchukuo, virtually abandoned American interests in China by 1937–1938, and thereafter provided only limited aid to the Kuomintang, whose failings were all too evident. Admittedly, the Americans talked frequently about China's sovereignty, which everyone had so often violated, and about the international and political and economic principles they approved, but seemingly without regard for the extent to which these principles clashed with Japan's reality in Asia. But the Americans never threatened war over China, and while they might have gained additional time in late 1941 by cutting off aid to China *and* providing Japan's war machine with all necessary critical resources, this "Pacific Munich" would have occasioned a bitter reaction at home and abroad and probably undermined the effort to foster British—and Russian—resistance to Germany.

The ultimate issue was not only that Germany and Japan posed an intolerable threat to the world order in 1941, but that both nations made war the instrument of their national policy, both sought to use their military "alliance"—"bluff, power or accomplishment," as Roosevelt said in 1937—to intimidate other nations, and both quickly chose aggression and conquest when diplomacy proved unavailing. Consequently, they created a state of "international lawlessness" and by force of their arms summoned the New World to redress the balance of power in two older worlds.

Finally, if there is a lesson to be learned from the 1930s, it is not that appeasement failed but that aggression did. For in fulfilling his commitment to a thousand-year Reich and in ostensibly battling communism in Europe, Hitler's legacy to his nation was to see it crushed by the two powers he most loathed—the United States and the Soviet Union—and then to leave his country permanently divided, one half in the camp of each of the two superpowers who confronted one another across a prostrate continent. Similarly, in fulfilling their commitment to empire and defeating communism in Asia, the Japanese destroyed whatever slim chance remained for the Kuomintang to reform itself and to deal with China's problems before Mao Tse-tung's Communists would come to power, while the Japanese would suffer the agony of defeat and atomic attack. In this sense, one might conclude that for both victors and vanquished the legacy of war was not merely geopolitical convolutions but the horrors unimagined at the outset that quickly become realities.

SUGGESTED READINGS

For general assessments of American foreign policy, see Robert A. Divine, *The Reluctant Belligerent: American Entry into World War II*,

2 ed., (New York, 1979), Arnold A. Offner, *The Origins of the Second World War: American Foreign Policy and World Politics, 1917–1941* (New York, 1975), and John E. Wiltz, *From Isolation to War, 1931–1941* (Arlington Heights, Ill., 1968). Early "revisionist" accounts include Charles A. Beard. *American Foreign Policy in the Making, 1932–1940* (New Haven, 1946), and *President Roosevelt and the Coming of the War* (New Haven, 1948), and Charles Callan Tansill, *Back-door to War: The Roosevelt Foreign Policy, 1933–1941* (Chicago, 1952), while Basil Rauch, *Roosevelt: From Munich to Pearl Harbor* (New York, 1950) is too flattering. Careful, traditional accounts include Donald F. Drummond, *The Passing of American Neutrality, 1937–1941* (Ann Arbor, Mich., 1955), and William L. Langer and S. Everett Gleason, *The Challenge to Isolation, 1937–1940* (New York, 1952) and *The Undeclared War, 1940–1941* (New York, 1953). Economic interpretations include Lloyd C. Gardner, *Economic Aspects of New Deal Diplomacy* (Madison, Wis., 1964) and William A. Williams, *The Tragedy of American Diplomacy*, rev. ed. (New York, 1972).

President Roosevelt's leadership and diplomacy is keenly judged in James MacGregor Burns, *Roosevelt: The Lion and the Fox* (New York, 1956) and *The Soldier of Freedom* (New York, 1970), Robert A. Divine, *Roosevelt and World War II* (Baltimore, 1969), and Robert A. Dallek, *Franklin D. Roosevelt and American Foreign Policy, 1932–1945* (New York, 1980). The American-German connection is analyzed in Arnold A. Offner, *American Appeasement: United States Foreign Policy and Germany, 1933–1938* (Cambridge, Mass., 1969) and "Appeasement Revisited: The United States, Great Britain, and Germany, 1933–1940," *Journal of American History* 64 (September 1977): 373–393; James V. Compton, *The Swastika and the Eagle: Hitler, the United States, and the Origins of World War II* (Boston, 1967), and Alton B. Frye, *Nazi Germany and the Western Hemisphere, 1933–1941* (New Haven, 1967).

American-Chinese relations are treated in Dorothy Borg, *The United States and the Far Eastern Crisis of 1933–1938* (Cambridge, Mass., 1968), Russell D. Buhite, *Nelson T. Johnson and American Policy Toward China, 1925–1941* (East Lansing, Mich., 1968), Warren I. Cohen, *America's Response to China: An Interpretive History* (New York, 1971), Michael Schaller, *The United States Crusade in China, 1938–1945* (New York, 1979), and Barbara Tuchman, *Stilwell and the American Experience in China, 1911–1945* (New York, 1971).

Relations with Japan are detailed in Dorothy Borg and Shumpei Okamoto, eds., *Pearl Harbor as History: Japanese-American Relations, 1931–1941* (New York, 1973), Herbert Feis, *The Road to Pearl Harbor:*

The Coming of the War Between the United States and Japan (Princeton, 1950), Waldo H. Heinrichs, Jr., *American Ambassador: Joseph C. Grew and the American Diplomatic Tradition* (Boston, 1966), Paul Schroeder, *The Axis Alliance and Japanese-American Relations, 1941* (Ithaca, N.Y., 1958), and Robert J. C. Butow, *The John Doe Associates: Backdoor Diplomacy for Peace, 1941* (Stanford, 1974), a close look at the Hull-Nomura talks. Roberta Wohlstetter, *Pearl Harbor: Warning and Decision* (Stanford, 1962) masterfully explicates this intelligence failure, while Ernest R. May and James C. Thomson, eds. *American-East Asian Relations: A Survey* (Cambridge, Mass., 1972) provides bibliographic and retrospective analyses.

The Achievement of the New Deal

William E. Leuchtenburg

The fiftieth anniversary of the New Deal, launched on March 4, 1933, comes at a time when it has been going altogether out of fashion. Writers on the left, convinced that the Roosevelt experiment was either worthless or pernicious, have assigned it to the dustbin of history. Commentators on the right, though far less conspicuous, see in the New Deal the origins of the centralized state they seek to dismantle. Indeed, the half-century of the age of Roosevelt is being commemorated in the presidency of Ronald Reagan, who, while never tiring of quoting FDR, insists that the New Deal derived from Italian fascism.

To be sure, the New Deal has always had its critics. In Roosevelt's own day Marxists said that the New Deal had not done anything for agriculture that an earthquake could not have done better at the same time that conservatives were saying the FDR was unprincipled. Hoover even called him "a chameleon on plaid." Most historians have long since accepted the fact that New Deal policies were sometimes inconsistent, that Roosevelt failed to grasp countercyclical fiscal theory, that recovery did not come until armaments orders fueled the economy, that the President was credited with certain reforms like insurance of bank deposits that he, in fact, opposed, that a number of New Deal programs, notably aid for the marginal farmer, were inadequately financed, and that some New Deal agencies discriminated against blacks.

During the 1960s historians not only dressed up these objections as though they were new revelations but carried their disappointment with contemporary liberalism to the point of arguing either that the New Deal was not just inadequate but actually malign or that the New Deal was so negligible as to constitute a mean-ingless episode. This estimate derived in large part from disaffection with the welfare state, which Herbert Marcuse in *One-Dimensional Man* characterized as "a state of unfreedom," and which, as one critic noted, some considered "the ultimate form of repressive super-ego." The New Deal was now perceived to be elitist, since it had neglected to consult the poor about what legislation they wanted, or to encourage the participation of ghetto-dwellers in deci-sion-making. Roosevelt's policies, historians maintained, redounded to the benefit of those who already had advantages — wealthier sta-ple farmers, organized workers, business corporations, the "de-serving poor" — while displacing sharecroppers and neglecting the powerless. An "antirevolutionary response to a situation that had revolutionary potentialities," the New Deal, it was said, missed op-portunities to nationalize the banks and restructure the social order. Even "providing assistance to the needy and . . . rescuing them from starvation" served conservative ends, historians complained, for these efforts "sapped organized radicalism of its waning strength and of its potential constituency among the unorganized and dis-contented." The Roosevelt Administration, it has been asserted, failed to achieve more than it did not as a result of the strength of conservative opposition but because of the intellectual deficiencies of the New Dealers and because Roosevelt deliberately sought to save "large-scale corporate capitalism." In *Towards a New Past*, the New Left historian Barton Bernstein summed up this point of view: "The New Deal failed to solve the problem of depression, it failed to raise the impoverished, it failed to redistribute income, it failed to extend equality and generally countenanced racial discrimination and segregation."

Although the characterization of Bernstein as "New Left" sug-gests that he represents a deviant persuasion, the New Left perspec-tive has, in fact, all but become the new orthodoxy, even though there is not yet any New Left survey of the domestic history of the United States in the 1930s. This emphasis has so permeated writing on the New Deal in the past generation that an instructor who wishes to assign the latest thought on the age of Roosevelt has a wide choice of articles and anthologies that document the errors of the New Deal but no assessment of recent vintage that explores its ac-complishments.

The fiftieth anniversary of the New Deal provides the occasion for a modest proposal—that we reintroduce some tension into the argument over the interpretation of the Roosevelt years. If historians are to develop a credible synthesis, it is important to regain a sense of the achievement of the New Deal. As it now stands, we have a dialectic that is all antithesis with no thesis. The so-called "debate" about the New Deal is not truly a debate, for even some of the historians who dispute the New Left assertions agree that one can only take a melancholy view of the period. The single question asked is whether the failure of the New Deal was the fault of the Roosevelt Administration or the result of the strength of conservative forces beyond the government's control; the fact of failure is taken as the basic postulate. As a first step toward a more considered evaluation, one has to remind one's self not only of what the New Deal did not do, but of what it achieved.

NEW DEAL CHANGES

Above all, one needs to recognize how markedly the New Deal altered the character of the State in America. Indeed, though for decades past European theorists had been talking about *der Staat*, there can hardly be said to have been a State in America in the full meaning of the term before the New Deal. If you had walked into an American town in 1932, you would have had a hard time detecting any sign of a federal presence, save perhaps for the post office and even many of today's post offices date from the 1930s. Washington rarely affected people's lives directly. There was no national old-age pension system, no federal unemployment compensation, no aid to dependent children, no federal housing, no regulation of the stock market, no withholding tax, no federal school lunch, no farm subsidy, no national minimum wage law, no welfare state. As late as Herbert Hoover's presidency, it was regarded as axiomatic that government activity should be minimal. In the pre-Roosevelt era, even organized labor and the National Conference of Social Workers opposed federal action on behalf of the unemployed. The New Deal sharply challenged these shibboleths. From 1933 to 1938, the government intervened in a myriad of ways from energizing the economy to fostering unionization.

In the First Hundred Days of 1933, the New Deal reversed the familiar assumptions in an electrifying manner. André Maurois has commented:

One cannot help calling to mind, as one writes the history of these three crowded months, the Biblical account of the Creation. The first day, the Brain Trust put an embargo on gold; the second day, it peopled the forests; the third day, it created three point two beer; the fourth day, it broke the bonds that tied the dollar to gold; the fifth day, it set the farmers free; the sixth day, it created General Johnson, and then, looking upon what it had made of America, it saw that it was good.

But it could not rest on the seventh day.

This vast expansion of government led inevitably to the concentration of much greater power in the presidency, whose authority was greatly augmented under FDR. Rexford Tugwell has written of Roosevelt: "No monarch, . . . unless it may have been Elizabeth or her magnificent Tudor father, or maybe Alexander or Augustus Caesar, can have given quite that sense of serene presiding, of gathering up into himself, of really representing, a whole people." The President became, in Sidney Hyman's words, "the chief economic engineer," to whom Congress naturally turned for the setting of economic policy. Roosevelt stimulated interest in public affairs by his fireside chats and freewheeling press conferences, shifted the balance between the White House and Capitol Hill by assuming the role of Chief Legislator, and eluded the routinized traditional departments by creating emergency agencies. In 1939 he established the Executive Office of the President, giving the Chief Executive a central staff office for the first time. "The verdict of history," wrote Clinton Rossiter, "will surely be that he left the Presidency a more splendid instrument of democracy than he found it."

To staff the national agencies, Roosevelt turned to a new class of people: the university-trained experts. Before FDR, professors had not had an important role in the national government, save briefly in World War I, but when Roosevelt ran for president in 1932, he recruited advisers, most of them from Columbia University, who supplied him with ideas and helped write his speeches. During the First Hundred Days, large numbers of professors, encouraged by FDR's reliance on the Brain Trust, flocked to Washington to draft New Deal legislation and to administer New Deal agencies. The radical literary critic Edmund Wilson wrote, "Everywhere in the streets and offices you run into old acquaintances: the editors and writers of the liberal press, the 'progressive' young instructors from the colleges, the intelligent foundation workers, the practical idealists of settlement houses." He added: "The bright boys of the Eastern universities, instead of being obliged to choose, as they were twenty years ago, between business, the bond-selling game and the field of foreign missions, can come on and get jobs in Washington."

The capital had hitherto thought of government workers largely as civil service employees awaiting the rise in grade that would permit them to buy a house in Chevy Chase and it scarcely knew what to make of the invasion of eager newcomers. Everybody wanted to know the professors, reported one magazine: "Office-seekers dog their footsteps. Hostesses vie to land them as guest of honor. Professors are the fad." "On a routine administration matter you go to a Cabinet member," observed a reporter, "but on matters of policy and the higher statesmanship you consult the professoriat." "All Washington is going to school to the professors," he noted. "Debutantes hang on their exposition of the quantitative theory of money, the law of diminishing returns, and the intricacies of foreign exchange. Bookstores are selling their books like hot cakes. Their works are not available at the Library of Congress, the volumes having been withdrawn by the Senators and Congressmen."

Some may doubt today whether it is always an unmitigated good to have "the best and the brightest" in seats of power, but in the 1930s this infusion of talent gave an élan to the national government that had been sorely missing in the past. The *New Republic* commented: "We have in Washington not a soggy and insensitive mass of dough, as in some previous administrations, but a nervous, alert and hard-working group who are doing their level best to effectuate a program." Friends of Roosevelt's, like Felix Frankfurter, sent to Washington a cadre of brilliant young lawyers—men like David Lilienthal and Jerome Frank—who, immensely confident of their ability, generated new ideas, tested novel methods, and conveyed an infectious enthusiasm for the possibilities of government.

This corps of administrators made it possible for Roosevelt to carry out a major change in the role of the federal government. Although the New Deal always operated within a capitalist matrix and the government sought to enhance profitmaking, Roosevelt and his lieutenants rejected the traditional view that government was the handmaiden of business or that government and business were coequal sovereigns. As a consequence, they adopted measures to discipline corporations, to require a sharing of authority with government and unions, and to hold businessmen accountable. In the early days of the National Recovery Administration, the novelist Sherwood Anderson wrote:

> I went to several code hearings. No one has quite got their significance. Here for the first time you see these men of business, little ones and big ones , . . . coming up on the platform to give an accounting. It does seem the death knell of the old idea that a man owning a factory, office or store has a right to run it in his own way.
>
> There is at least an effort to relate it now to the whole thing, man's relations with his fellow men etc. Of course it is crude and there will be no end to crookedness, objections, etc. but I do think an entire new principle in American life is being established.

Through a series of edicts and statutes, the administration invaded the realm of the banker by establishing control over the nation's money supply. The government clamped an embargo on gold, took the United States off the gold standard, and nullified the requirement for the payment of gold in private contracts. In 1935 a resentful Supreme Court sustained this authority, although a dissenting justice said that this was Nero at his worst. The Glass-Steagall Banking Act (1933) stripped commercial banks of the privilege of engaging in investment banking, and established federal insurance of bank deposits, an innovation which the leading monetary historians have called "the structural change most conducive to monetary stability since bank notes were taxed out of existence immediately after the Civil War." The Banking Act of 1935 gave the United States what other industrial nations had long had, but America lacked—central banking. This series of changes transformed the relationship between the government and the financial community from what it had been when Grover Cleveland had gone, hat in hand, to beseech J. P. Morgan for help. As Charles Beard observed: "Having lost their gold coins and bullion to the Federal Government and having filled their vaults with federal bonds and other paper, bankers have become in a large measure mere agents of the Government in Washington. No longer do these powerful interests stand, so to speak, 'outside the Government' and in a position to control or dictate to it."

A number of other enactments helped transfer authority from Wall Street to Washington. The Securities Act of 1933 established government supervision of the issue of securities, and made company directors civilly and criminally liable for misinformation on the statements they were required to file with each new issue. The Securities and Exchange Act of 1934 initiated federal supervision of the stock exchanges, which to this day operate under the lens of the Securities and Exchange Commission (SEC). The Holding Company Act of 1935 levelled some of the utility pyramids, dissolving all utility holding companies that were more than twice removed from their operating companies, and increased the regulatory powers of the SEC over public utilities. Robert Sobel has concluded that the 1934 law marked "a shift of economic power from the lower part of Manhattan, where it had been for over a century, to Washington." To be sure, financiers continued to make important policy choices, but they never again operated in the uninhibited universe of the Great Bull Market. By the spring of 1934, one writer was already reporting:

> Financial news no longer originates in Wall Street. . . . News of a financial nature in Wall Street now is merely an echo of events which take place in Washington. . . . The pace of the ticker is determined now in Washington not in company boardrooms or in brokerage offices. . . . In Wall Street it is no longer asked what some big trader is doing, what some important banker thinks, what opinion some eminent lawyer holds about some pressing question of the day. The query in Wall Street has become: "What's the news from Washington?"

The age of Roosevelt focused attention on Washington, too, by initiatives in fields that had been regarded as exclusively within the private orbit, notably in housing. The Home Owners' Loan Corporation, created in 1933, saved tens of thousands of homes from foreclosure by refinancing mortgages. In 1934 the Federal Housing Administration (FHA) began its program of insuring loans for the construction and renovation of private homes, and over the next generation more than 10 million FHA-financed units were built. Before the New Deal, the national government had never engaged in public housing, except for the World War I emergency, but agencies like the Public Works Administration now broke precedent. The Tennessee Valley Authority laid out the model town of Norris, the Federal Emergency Relief Administration (FERA) experimented with subsistence homesteads, and the Resettlement Administration created greenbelt communities, entirely new towns girdled by green countryside. When in 1937 the Wagner-Steagall Act created the U.S. Housing Authority, it assured public housing a permanent place in American life.

A NEW DEAL FOR THE COMMON MAN

The New Deal profoundly altered industrial relations by throwing the weight of government behind efforts to unionize workers. At the outset of the Great Depression, the American labor movement was "an anachronism in the world," for only a tiny minority of factory workers were unionized. Employers hired and fired and imposed punishments at will, used thugs as strikebreakers and private police, stockpiled industrial munitions, and ran company towns as feudal fiefs. In an astonishingly short period in the Roosevelt years a very different pattern emerged. Under the umbrella of Section 7(a) of the National Industrial Recovery Act of 1933 and of the far-reaching Wagner Act of 1935, union organizers gained millions of recruits in such open-shop strongholds as steel, automobiles, and textiles. Employees won wage rises, reductions in hours, greater job security, freedom from the tyranny of company guards, and protection against arbitrary punishment. Thanks to the National Recovery Administration and the Guffey acts, coal miners achieved the outlawing of compulsory company houses and stores. Steel workers, who in 1920 labored twelve-hour shifts seven days a week at the blast furnaces, were to become so powerful that in the postwar era they would win not merely paid vacations but sabbatical leaves. A British analyst has concluded: "From one of the most restrictive among industrially advanced nations, the labour code of the United States (insofar as it could be said to exist before 1933) was rapidly transformed into one of the most liberal," and these reforms, he adds, "were not the harvest of long-sustained agitation by trade unions, but were forced upon a partly sceptical labor movement by a government which led or carried it into maturity."

Years later, when David E. Lilienthal, the director of the Tennessee Valley Authority, was being driven to the airport to fly to Roosevelt's funeral, the TVA driver said to him:

> I won't forget what he did for me. . . . I spent the best years of my life working at the Appalachian Mills . . . and they didn't even treat us

like humans. If you didn't do like they said, they always told you there was someone else to take your job. I had my mother and my sister to take care of. Sixteen cents an hour was what we got; a fellow can't live on that, and you had to get production even to get that, this Bedaux system; some fellows only got twelve cents. If you asked to get off on a Sunday, the foreman would say, "All right you stay away Sunday, but when you come back Monday someone else will have your job." No, sir, I won't forget what he done for us.

Helen Lynd has observed that the history of the United States is that of England fifty years later, and a half century after the welfare state had come to Western Europe, the New Deal brought it to America. The NRA wiped out sweatshops, and removed some 150,000 child laborers from factories. The Walsh-Healey Act of 1936 and the Fair Labor Standards Act of 1938 established the principle of a federally imposed minimal level of working conditions, and added further sanctions against child labor. If the New Deal did not do enough for the "one-third of a nation" to whom Roosevelt called attention, it at least made a beginning, through agencies like the Farm Security Administration, toward helping sharecroppers, tenant farmers, and migrants like John Steinbeck's Joads. Most important, it originated a new system of social rights to replace the dependence on private charity. The Social Security Act of 1935 created America's first national system of old-age pensions and initiated a federal-state program of unemployment insurance. It also authorized grants for the blind, for the incapacitated, and for dependent children, a feature that would have unimaginable long-range consequences.

The veteran social worker Grace Abbott, in explaining why, as a lifelong Republican, she was voting for Roosevelt in 1936, said that greater progress had been made in security for children "during the past three years than the previous thirty years." She added: "The support of the Child Labor Amendment by the President and his cabinet, the raising of Child Labor standards under the N.R.A., the inclusion of the sugar beet children in the benefits of the Costigan Sugar Act and the President's own pet project — the C.C.C. Camps — now so largely filled by young men and boys are also concrete evidence that the President considers the welfare of children of national importance."

Roosevelt himself affirmed the newly assumed attitudes in Washington in his annual message to Congress in 1938 when he declared: "Government has a final responsibility for the well-being of its citizenship. If private co-operative endeavor fails to provide work for willing hands and relief for the unfortunate, those suffering hardship from no fault of their own have a right to call upon the Government for aid; and a government worthy of its name must make fitting response."

A NEW DEAL FOR THE UNEMPLOYED

Nothing revealed this approach so well as the New Deal's attention to the plight of the millions of unemployed. During the ten years between 1929 and 1939, one scholar has written, "more progress was made in public welfare and relief than in the three hundred years after this country was first settled." A series of alphabet agencies — the FERA, the CWA, the WPA — provided government work for the jobless, while the National Youth Administration (NYA) employed college students in museums, libraries, and laboratories, enabled high school students to remain in school, and set up a program of apprentice training. In Texas, the twenty-seven-year-old NYA director Lyndon Johnson put penniless young men like John Connally to work building roadside parks, and in North Carolina, the NYA employed, at 35 cents an hour, a Duke University law student, Richard Nixon.

In an address in Los Angeles in 1936, the head of FDR's relief operations, Harry Hopkins, conveyed the attitude of the New Deal toward those who were down and out:

> I am getting sick and tired of these people on the W.P.A. and local relief rolls being called chiselers and cheats. . . . These people . . . are just like the rest of us. They don't drink any more than us, they don't lie any more, they're no lazier than the rest of us — they're pretty much a cross section of the American people. . . . I have never believed that with our capitalistic system people have to be poor. I think it is an outrage that we should permit hundreds and hundreds of thousands of people to be ill clad, to live in miserable homes, not to have enough to eat; not to be able to send their children to school for the only reason that they are poor. I don't believe ever again in America we are going to permit the things to happen that have happened in the past to people. We are never going back . . . to the days of putting the old people in the alms houses, when a decent dignified pen-

sion at home will keep them there. We are coming to the day when we are going to have decent houses for the poor, when there is genuine and real security for everybody. I have gone all over the moral hurdles that people are poor because they are bad. I don't believe it. A system of government on that basis is fallacious.

Under the leadership of men like Hopkins, "Santa Claus incomparable and privy-builder without peer," projects of relief agencies and of the Public Works Administration (PWA) changed the face of the land. The PWA built thoroughfares like the Skyline Drive in Virginia and the Overseas Highway from Miami to Key West, constructed the Medical Center in Jersey City, burrowed Chicago's new subway, and gave Natchez, Mississippi, a new bridge, and Denver a modern water-supply system. Few New Yorkers today realize the long reach of the New Deal. If they cross the Triborough Bridge, they are driving on a bridge the PWA built. If they fly into La Guardia Airport, they are landing at an airfield laid out by the WPA. If they get caught in a traffic jam on the FDR Drive, they are using yet another artery built by the WPA. Even the animal cages in the Central Park Zoo were reconstructed by WPA workers. In New York City, the WPA built or renovated hundreds of school buildings; gave Orchard Beach a bathhouse, a mall, and a lagoon; landscaped Bryant Park and the campus of Hunter College in the Bronx; conducted examinations for venereal disease, filled teeth, operated pollen count stations, and performed puppet shows for disturbed children; it built dioramas for the Brooklyn Museum; ran street dances in Harlem and an open-air night club in Central Park; and, by combing neglected archives, turned up forgotten documents like the court proceedings in the Aaron Burr libel case and the marriage license issued to Captain Kidd. In New York City alone the WPA employed more people than the entire War Department.

Though much of the makework inevitably concentrated on operations like road building, the Roosevelt government proved ingenious in devising other activities. Years later, John Steinbeck recalled:

When W.P.A. came, we were delighted, because it offered work. . . . I was given the project of taking a census of all the dogs on the Monterey Peninsula, their breeds, weight and characters. I did it very thoroughly and, since I knew my reports were not likely to get the to the hands of the mighty, I wrote some pretty searching character studies of poodles, and beagles and hounds. If such records were kept, somewhere in Washington, there will be a complete dog record of the Monterey Peninsula in the early Thirties.

The New Deal showed unusual sensitivity toward jobless white-collar workers, notably those in aesthetic fields. The Public Works of Art Project gave an opportunity to muralists eager for a chance to work in the style of Rivera, Orozco, and Siqueiros. The Federal Art Project fostered the careers of painters like Stuart Davis, Raphael Soyer, Yasuo Kuniyoshi, and Jackson Pollock. Out of the same project came a network of community art centers and the notable *Index of American Design*. A generation later the sculptor Louise Nevelson, summed up what it meant:

> When I came back from Germany where I studied with Hans Hoffman. . . . I got on the WPA. Now that gave me a certain kind of freedom and I think that our great artists like Rothko, de Kooning, Franz Kline, all these people that have promise today and are creative, had that moment of peace . . . to continue with their work. So, I feel that that was a great benefit, a great contribution to our creative people and very important in the history of art. And not only in the visual arts but in the theater, and the folk arts, there wasn't a thing that they didn't touch on. . . . At that period, people in our country didn't have jobs and the head of government was able so intelligently to use mankind and manpower. I think it's a high-light of our American history.

The Federal Writers' Project provided support for scores of talented novelists and poets, editors and literary critics, men like Ralph Ellison and Nelson Algren, John Cheever and Saul Bellow. These writers turned out an exceptional set of state guides, with such features as Conrad Aiken's carefully delineated portrayal of Deerfield, Massachusetts, and special volumes like *These Are Our Lives*, a graphic portfolio of life histories in North Carolina, and *Panorama*, in which Vincent McHugh depicts "the infinite pueblo of the Bronx." Project workers transcribed chain-gang blues songs, recovered folklore that would otherwise have been lost, and collected the narratives of elderly former slaves, an invaluable archive later published in *Lay My Burden Down*. When the magazine *Story* conducted a contest for the best contribution by a Project employee, the prize was won by an unpublished 29-year-old black who had been working on the essay on the Negro for the Illinois guide. With the prize money for his stories, subsequently published as *Uncle*

Tom's Children, Richard Wright gained the time to complete his remarkable first novel, *Native Son*.

Some thought it an ill omen that the Federal Theatre Project's first production was Shakespeare's *Comedy of Errors*, but that agency not only gave employment to actors and stage technicians but offered many communities their first glimpse of live drama. The "boy wonder" Orson Welles directed and acted in the Federal Theatre, which also discovered such unknowns as Joseph Cotten. Its Dance Group revealed the virtuosity of Katherine Dunham, Doris Humphrey, and Charles Weidman. The Federal Theatre sponsored the first U.S. presentation of T. S. Eliot's *Murder in the Cathedral*, and its Detroit unit staged the original professional production of Arthur Miller's first play.

If the creation of America's first state theatre was an unusual departure, the New Deal's ventures in documentary films seemed no less surprising. With Resettlement Administration funds, Pare Lorentz produced *The Plow That Broke the Plains* in 1936 and the classic *The River* in 1937. He engaged cameramen like Paul Strand, who had won acclaim for his movie on a fisherman's strike in Mexico; invited the young composer Virgil Thomson, who had just scored Gertrude Stein's *Four Saints in Three Acts*, to compose the background music; and employed Thomas Chalmers, who had sung at the Metropolitan Opera in the era of Caruso, to read the narration. Lorentz's films were eyeopeners. American government documentaries before the New Deal had been limited to short subjects on topics like the love life of the honeybee. *The River*, which won first prize in Venice at the International Exposition of Cinematographic Art in 1938, proved that there was an audience in the United States for well-wrought documentaries. By 1940 it had drawn more than 10 million people, while *The Plow That Broke the Plains*, said one critic, made "the rape of millions of acres . . . more moving than the downfall of a Hollywood blonde."

Lorentz's films suggest the concern of the New Deal for the American land. Roosevelt, it has been said, had a "proprietary interest in the nation's estate," and this helps account for the fact that the 1930s accomplished for soil conservation and river valley development what the era of Theodore Roosevelt had done for the forests. The Tennessee Valley Authority, which drew admirers from all over the world, put the national government in the business of generating electric power, controlled floods, terraced hillsides, and gave new hope to the people of the valley. In the Pacific Northwest the PWA constructed mammoth dams, Grand Coulee and Bonneville. Roosevelt's "tree army," the Civilian Conservation Corps, planted millions of trees, cleared forest trails, laid out picnic sites and camp-grounds, and aided the Forest Service in the vast undertaking of es-tablishing a shelterbelt — a windbreak of trees and shrubs: green ash and Chinese elm, apricot and blackberry, buffalo berry and Osage orange from the Canadian border to the Texas panhandle. Govern-ment agencies came to the aid of drought-stricken farmers in the Dust Bowl, and the Soil Conservation Service, another New Deal creation, instructed growers in methods of cultivation to save the land. As Alistair Cooke later said, the favorite of the New Dealers was the farmer with the will to "take up contour plowing late in life."

These services to farmers represented only a small part of the gov-ernment's program, for in the New Deal years, the business of agricul-ture was revolutionized. Roosevelt came to power at a time of mount-ing desperation for American farmers. Each month in 1932 another 20,000 farmers had lost their land because of inability to meet their debts in a period of collapsing prices. On a single day in May 1932, one-fourth of the state of Mississippi went under the sheriff's hammer. The Farm Credit Administration of 1933 came to the aid of the beleaguered farmer, and within eighteen months, it had refinanced one-fifth of all farm mortgages in the United States. In the Roosevelt years, too, the Rural Electrification Administration literally brought rural America out of darkness. At the beginning of the Roosevelt era, only one farm in nine had electricity; at the end, only one in nine did not have it. But more important than any of these developments was the progression of enactments starting with the first AAA (the Agricultural Adjustment Act) of 1933, which began the process of granting large-scale subsidies to growers. As William Faulkner later said, "Our economy is not agricultural any longer. Our economy is the federal government. We no longer farm in Mississippi cotton fields. We farm now in Washington corridors and Congressional committee rooms."

GOVERNMENT OF AND FOR
MORE OF THE PEOPLE

At the same time that its realm was being expanded under the New Deal, the national government changed the composition of its personnel and of its beneficiaries. Before 1933, the government had paid heed primarily to a single group—white Anglo-Saxon Protestant males. The Roosevelt Administration, however, recruited from a more ethnically diverse group, and the prominence of Catholics and Jews among the President's advisers is suggested by the scintillating team of the Second Hundred Days, Corcoran and Cohen. The Federal Writers' Project turned out books on Italians and Albanians, and the Federal Theatre staged productions in Yiddish and wrote a history of the Chinese stage in Los Angeles. In the 1930s women played a more prominent role in government than they ever had before, as the result of such appointments as that of Frances Perkins as the first female cabinet member, while the influence of Eleanor Roosevelt was pervasive.

Before Eleanor Roosevelt, First Ladies had been content to preside over the social functions of the White House. But by 1940 Mrs. Roosevelt had travelled more than 250,000 miles, written 1 million words, and became the leading advocate within the administration for the underprivileged, especially blacks and unemployed youth. No one knew where she would turn up next. In the most famous cartoon of the decade, a begrimed coal miner in the bowels of the earth cries out in astonishment to a fellow miner, "For gosh sakes, here comes Mrs. Roosevelt." Admiral Byrd, it was said, always set up two places for dinner at the South Pole "in case Eleanor should drop in." She was renowned for her informality. When the King and Queen of England visited America, she served them hot dogs and beer, and when during World War II, she travelled to Australia and New Zealand, she greeted her Maori guide by rubbing noses. No one captured the goals of the New Deal better than Eleanor Roosevelt. "As I have said all along," she remarked, "you have got to have the kind of country in which people's daily chance convinces them that democracy is a good thing."

Although in some respects the New Deal's performance with regard to blacks added to the sorry record of racial discrimination in America, important gains were also registered in the 1930s. Blacks, who had often been excluded from relief in the past, now received a share of WPA jobs considerably greater than their proportion of the population. Blacks moved into federal housing projects; federal funds went to schools and hospitals in black neighborhoods; and New Deal agencies like the Farm Security Administration (FSA) enabled 50,000 Negro tenant farmers and sharecroppers to become proprietors. "Indeed," one historian has written, "there is a high correlation between the location of extensive FSA operations in the 1930s and the rapidity of political modernization in black communities in the South in the 1960s." Roosevelt appointed a number of blacks, including William Hastie, Mary McLeod Bethune, and Robert Weaver, to high posts in the government. Negroes in the South who were disfranchised in white primaries voted in AAA crop referenda and in National Labor Relations Board plant elections, and a step was taken toward restoring their constitutional rights when Attorney General Frank Murphy set up a Civil Liberties Unit in the Department of Justice. The reign of Jim Crow in Washington offices, which had begun under Roosevelt's Democratic predecessor, Woodrow Wilson, was terminated by Secretary of the Interior Harold Ickes who desegregated cafeterias in his department. Ickes also had a role in the most dramatic episode of the times, for when the Daughters of the American Revolution (DAR) denied the use of their concert hall to the black contralto Marian Anderson, he made it possible for her to sing before thousands from the steps of Lincoln Memorial; and Mrs. Roosevelt joined in the rebuke to the DAR. Anderson's concert on Easter Sunday 1939 was heard by thousands at the Memorial, and three networks carried her voice to millions more. Blacks delivered their own verdict on the New Deal at the polling places. Committed to the party of Lincoln as late as 1932, when they voted overwhelmingly for Hoover, they shifted in large numbers to the party of FDR during Roosevelt's first term. This was a change of allegiance that many whites were also making in those years.

THE DURABLE LEGACY OF THE NEW DEAL

The Great Depression and the New Deal brought about a significant political realignment of the sort that occurs only rarely in America. The Depression wrenched many lifelong Republican voters from their moorings. In 1928, one couple christened their newborn son "Herbert Hoover Jones." Four years later they petitioned the court, "desiring to relieve the young man from the chagrin and mortification which he is suffering and will suffer," and asked that his name be changed to Franklin D. Roosevelt Jones. In 1932 FDR became the first Democrat to enter the White House with as much as 50 percent of the popular vote in eighty years — since Franklin K. Pierce in 1852. Roosevelt took advantage of this opportunity to mold "the FDR coalition," an alliance centered in the low-income districts of the great cities and, as recently as the 1980 election, the contours of the New Deal coalition could still be discerned. Indeed, over the past half-century, the once overpowering Republicans have won control of Congress only twice, for a total of four years. No less important was the shift in the character of the Democratic party from the conservative organization of John W. Davis and John J. Raskob to the country's main political instrumentality for reform. "One political result of the Roosevelt years," Robert Burke has observed, "was a basic change in the nature of the typical Congressional liberal." He was no longer a maverick, who made a fetish of orneriness, no longer one of the men Senator Moses called "the sons of the wild jackass," but "a party Democrat, labor-oriented, urban, and internationalist-minded."

Furthermore, the New Deal drastically altered the agenda of American politics. When Arthur Krock of the *New York Times* listed the main programmatic questions before the 1932 Democratic convention, he wrote: "What would be said about the repeal of prohibition that had split the Republicans? What would be said about tariffs?" By 1936, these concerns seemed altogether old fashioned, as campaigners discussed the Tennessee Valley Authority and industrial relations, slum clearance and aid to the jobless. That year, a Little Rock newspaper commented: "Such matters as tax and tariff laws have given way to universally human things, the living problems and opportunities of the average man and the average family."

The Roosevelt years changed the conception of the role of government not just in Washington but in the states, where a series of "Little New Deals" — under governors like Herbert Lehman in New York — added a thick sheaf of social legislation, and in the cities. In Boston, Charles Trout has observed, city council members in 1929 "devoted endless hours to street paving." After the coming of the New Deal, they were absorbed with NRA campaigns, public housing, and WPA allotments. "A year after the crash the council thought 5,000 dollars an excessive appropriation for the municipal employment bureau," but during the 1930s "the unemployed drained Boston's treasury of not less than 100,000,000 dollars in direct benefits, and the federal government spent even more."

In a cluster of pathbreaking decisions in 1937, the Supreme Court legitimized this vast exercise of authority by government at all levels. As late as 1936, the Supreme Court still denied the power of the United States government to regulate agriculture, even though crops were sold in a world market, or coal mining, a vital component of a national economy, and struck down a minimum wage law as beyond the authority of the state of New York. Roosevelt responded with a plan to "pack" the Court with as many as six additional Justices, and in short order the Court, in what has been called "the Constitutional Revolution of 1937," sounded retreat. Before 1937 the Supreme Court stood as a formidable barrier to social reform. Since 1937 not one piece of significant social legislation has been invalidated, and the Court has shifted its docket instead to civil rights and civil liberties.

What then did the New Deal do? It gave far greater amplitude to the national state, expanded the authority of the presidency, recruited university-trained administrators, won control of the money supply, established central banking, imposed regulation on Wall Street, rescued the debt-ridden farmer and homeowner, built model communities, financed the Federal Housing Administration, made federal housing a permanent feature, fostered unionization of the factories, reduced child labor, ended the tyranny of company towns, wiped out many sweatshops, mandated minimal working standards, enabled tenants to buy their own farms, built camps for migrants, introduced the welfare state with old-age pensions, unemployment insurance, and aid for dependent children, provided jobs for millions of unemployed, created a special program for the jobless young and for students, covered the American landscape with new edifices, subsidized painters and novelists, composers and ballet dancers, founded America's first state theater, created documentary films, gave birth to the impressive Tennessee Valley Authority, generated electrical power, sent the Civilian Conservation Corps boys into the forests, initiated the Soil Conservation Service, transformed the economy of agriculture, lighted up rural America, gave women greater recognition, made a start toward breaking the pattern of racial discrimination and segregation, put together a liberal party coalition, changed the agenda of American politics, and brought about a Constitutional Revolution.

But even this summary does not account for the full range of its activities. The New Deal offered the American Indian new opportunities for self-government and established the Indian Arts and Crafts Board, sponsored vaudeville troupes and circuses, taught counterpoint and *solfeggio*, was responsible for the founding of the Buffalo Philarmonic, the Oklahoma Symphony, and the Utah State Symphony, served hot lunches to school children and set up hundreds of nursery schools, sent bookmobiles into isolated communities, and where there were no roads, had books carried in by packhorses. And only a truly merciful and farsighted government would have taken such special pains to find jobs for unemployed historians.

The New Deal accomplished all of this at a critical time, when many were insisting that fascism was the wave of the future and denying that democracy could be effective. For those throughout the world who heard such jeremiads with foreboding, the American experience was enormously inspiriting. A decade after the end of the age of Roosevelt, Sir Isaiah Berlin wrote:

> When I say that some men occupy one's imagination for many years, this is literally true of Mr. Roosevelt and the young men of my own generation in England, and probably in many parts of Europe, and indeed the entire world. If one was young in the thirties, and lived in a democracy, then, whatever one's politics, if one had human feelings at all, the faintest spark of social idealism, or any love of life whatever, one must have felt very much as young men in Continental Europe probably felt after the defeat of Napoleon during the years of the Restoration: that all was dark and quiet, a great reaction was abroad, and little stirred, and nothing resisted.

In these "dark and leaden thirties," Professor Berlin continued, "the only light in the darkness that was left was the administration of Mr. Roosevelt and the New Deal in the United States. At a time of weakness and mounting despair in the democratic world Mr. Roosevelt radiated confidence and strength. . . . Even to-day, upon him alone, of all the statesmen of the thirties, no cloud rested neither on him nor on the New Deal, which to European eyes still looks a bright chapter in the history of mankind."

For the past generation, America has lived off the legacy of the New Deal. Successive administrations extended the provisions of statutes like the Social Security Act, adopted New Deal attitudes toward intervention in the economy to cope with recessions, and put New Deal ideas to modern purposes, as when the Civilian Conservation Corps served as the basis for both the Peace Corps and the VISTA program of the War on Poverty. Harry Truman performed under the shadow of FDR, Lyndon Johnson consciously patterned his administration on Roosevelt's, Jimmy Carter launched his first presidential campaign at Warm Springs, and Ronald Reagan has manifested an almost obsessive need to summon FDR to his side. Carl Degler has observed:

> Conventionally the end of the New Deal is dated with the enactment of the Wages and Hours Act of 1938. But in a fundamental sense the New Deal did not end then at all. Americans still live in the era of the New Deal, for its achievements are now the base mark below which no conservative government may go and from which all new reform now starts. . . . The reform efforts of the Democratic Truman, Kennedy, and Johnson administrations have been little more than fulfillments of the New Deal.

The British historian David K. Adams has pointed out that the philosophy of the New Frontier has "conscious overtones of the New Deal" and indeed that John Kennedy's "New Frontier" address of 1960 was "almost a paraphrase" of an FDR speech of 1935. Theodore White has commented that both John and Robert Kennedy shared sentences from a Roosevelt address that reporters called the "Dante sequence." When at a loss for words, each was wont to quote a favorite passage from Franklin Roosevelt: "Governments can err, Presidents do make mistakes, but the immortal Dante tells us that Divine Justice weighs the sins of the cold-blooded and the sins of the warm-hearted on a different scale. Better the occasional faults of a government living in the spirit of charity, than the consistent omissions of a government frozen in the ice of its own indifference."

By restoring to the debate over the significance of the New Deal acknowledgment of its achievements, we may hope to produce a more judicious estimate of where it succeeded and where it failed. For it unquestionably did fail in a number of respects. There were experiments of the 1930s which miscarried, opportunities that were fumbled, groups who were neglected, and power that was arrogantly used. Over the whole performance lies the dark cloud of the persistence of hard times. The shortcomings of the New Deal are formidable, and they must be recognized. But I am not persuaded that the New Deal experience was negligible. Indeed, it is hard to think of another period in the whole history of the republic that was so fruitful or of a crisis that was met with as much imagination.

SUGGESTED READINGS

The most extensive treatment of the New Deal may be found in Arthur M. Schlesinger's "The Age of Roosevelt," which embraces *The Crisis of the Old Order* (Boston, 1957), *The Coming of the New Deal* (Boston, 1959), and *The Politics of Upheaval* (Boston, 1960). William E. Leuchtenburg's *Franklin D. Roosevelt and the New Deal: 1932–1940* (New York, 1963) is a one-volume account. Leuchtenburg has also edited *Franklin D. Roosevelt: A Profile* (New York, 1967) and *The New Deal: A Documentary History* (Columbia, S.C., 1968). The time span of the fourth volume of Frank Freidel's ongoing biography of FDR is suggested by the title, *Franklin D. Roosevelt: Launching the New Deal* (Boston, 1973). James MacGregor Burns covers the New Deal in the first of his two volumes on FDR, *Roosevelt: The Lion and the Fox* (New York, 1956). For the New Left perspective, see Barton J. Bernstein, "The New Deal: The Conservative Achievements of Liberal Reform," in Bernstein, ed., *Towards a New Past* (New York, 1968) and Howard Zinn, ed., *New Deal Thought* (Indianapolis, 1966). Controversy about the New Deal is explored in Clark A. Chambers, "F.D.R., Pragmatist-Idealist: An Essay in Historiography," *Pacific Northwest Quarterly* 52 (April 1961): 50–55; Richard Kirkendall, "The New Deal as Watershed: The Recent Literature," *Journal of American History* 54 (March 1968): 839–852; Jerold Auerbach, "New Deal, Old Deal, or Raw Deal: Some Thoughts on New Left Historiography," *Journal of Southern History* 35 (February 1969): 18–30; and Otis L. Graham, Jr., ed., *The New Deal: The Critical Issues* (Boston, 1971). The most recent examination of the subject may be found in the two volumes edited by John Braeman, Robert H. Bremner, and David Brody, *The New Deal*: vol. 1, *The National Level*; vol. 2, *State and Local Levels* (Columbus, Ohio, 1975).

Index

About the Authors

ROBERT H. BREMNER is Professor of History Emeritus at Ohio State University. He attended Baldwin-Wallace College and received his Ph.D. from Ohio State University in 1943. A specialist in the history of social welfare, he has been a Fellow of the Social Science Research Council, the Huntington Library, the National Endowment for the Humanities, and the Charles Warren Center at Harvard University. His major publications include *From the Depths: The Discovery of Poverty in the United States* (1956), *American Philanthropy* (1960), and *The Public Good* (1980). In addition, he has edited *Change and Continuity in Modern America, Essays on History and Literature, Children and Youth in America,* and *The New Deal.*

RICHARD S. KIRKENDALL is Henry A. Wallace Professor of History at Iowa State University. He was educated at Gonzaga University and received his Ph.D. from the University of Wisconsin in 1958. He has also taught at Wesleyan College and the University of Missouri, Columbia, and was appointed Executive Secretary of the Organization of American Historians and Professor of History at Indiana University in 1973. He is the author of *Social Scientists and Farm Politics in the Age of Roosevelt* (1966), *The Global Power: The United States Since 1941* (1973), and *The United States, 1929–1945: Years of Crisis and Change* (1974); he has also edited *The Truman Period as a Research Field* and *The New Deal: The Historical Debate.*

R. ALAN LAWSON was educated at Brown University and the University of Wisconsin, and received his Ph.D. from the University of Michigan in 1966. His doctoral dissertation won the Allan Nevins Prize for the best work in the field of American history; it was published in 1971 as *The Failure of Independent Liberalism, 1930–1941.* He has taught at the University of California, Irvine, and at Smith College and is now a professor in the Department of History at Boston College. A specialist in American studies and intellectual history, Lawson has just completed a major study of the culture of the New Deal.

WILLIAM E. LEUCHTENBURG is William Rand Kenan, Jr., Professor of History at the University of North Carolina, Chapel Hill. He attended Cornell University and received his M.A. and

Ph.D. from Columbia University. He has taught at Smith College, Harvard University, New York University, and, for more than thirty years, at Columbia University, where he was De Witt Clinton Professor. He has also served as Harmsworth Professor at Oxford University, as President of the Society of American Historians, and as a Senior Fellow of the National Endowment for the Humanities. Among the numerous works he has written or edited on the Roosevelt era are the highly acclaimed *Franklin D. Roosevelt and the New Deal, 1932–1940,* which won both the Bancroft Prize and the Parkman Prize of the Society of American Historians; *The New Deal and Global War* (1964); *Franklin D. Roosevelt: A Profile* (1967); *The New Deal: A Documentary History* (1968), and *In the Shadow of FDR* (1983).

THOMAS K. McCRAW has taught at the University of Texas at Austin, and, since 1976, at the Harvard University Graduate School of Business Administration. He was educated at the University of Mississippi and the University of Wisconsin, where he was awarded the William P. Lyons Master's Essay Award and received his Ph.D. in 1970. His special interest is government-business relations and twentieth-century business history, and his major publications include *Morgan vs. Lilienthal: The Feud Within the TVA* (1970), and *TVA and the Power Fight, 1933–1939* (1971).

ARNOLD A. OFFNER attended Columbia University and received his M.A. and Ph.D. in diplomatic history from Indiana University. He has taught at Syracuse University and is now Professor of History at Boston University, where he was awarded the Metcalf Award for Excellence in Teaching. His *American Appeasement: United States Foreign Policy and Germany, 1933–1938* won the Phi Alpha Theta Book Award for the best first book in 1969; he also received the Phi Alpha Theta George P. Hammond Essay Award for his article on the historian and diplomat William E. Dodd. His other publications include *America and the Origins of World War II* (1971), and *The Origins of the Second World War: American Foreign Policy and World Politics, 1917–1941* (1975); he is currently working on a study of Harry S. Truman and the transformation of American foreign policy.

HARVARD SITKOFF is a graduate of Queens College of the City University of New York and of Columbia University, where he studied with William Leuchtenburg and received his Ph.D. in 1975. Before joining the Department of History at the University of New Hampshire in 1976, he taught at Queens College and Washington University. He has held fellowships from the National Endowment for the Humanities, the Robert Starobin Memorial, and the Charles Warren Center at Harvard University. He received the Fletcher M. Green Award of the Southern Historical Association for his essay on Harry Truman and the election of 1948 and the Columbia University biennial Allan Nevins Award for his doctoral dissertation, published in 1978 as *A New Deal for Blacks*. The author of numerous articles in the field of contemporary American politics and race relations, he has also written *The Struggle for Black Equality* (1981) and is currently completing a book on civil rights during the Second World War.

CHARLES H. TROUT is Provost and Dean of the Faculty at Colgate University. He is a graduate of Amherst College and received his doctorate in 1972 from Columbia University, where he too worked with William Leuchtenburg. He has also taught at Phillips Exeter Academy and Mt. Holyoke College and is a former editor-in-chief of *The New England Social Studies Bulletin*. He is the author of *Boston, The Great Depression, and the New Deal* (1977); his many articles on welfare, women, and urban affairs have appeared in such publications as *The Nation, Current History*, and *Feminist Studies*. He is presently writing a biography of Boston mayor and Massachusetts governor James Michael Curley.

SUSAN WARE attended Wellesley College and received her doctorate in 1978 from Harvard University. She has been a Radcliffe Research Scholar and has taught at the University of New Hampshire, Tufts University, and Harvard University, where she has been a Fellow at the Charles Warren Center. She is the author of *Beyond Suffrage: Women in the New Deal* (1981), and *Holding Their Own: American Women in the 1930s* (1983), and is now preparing a biography of the New Deal politician and feminist Molly Dewson.

A NOTE ON THE TYPE

The text of this book was set on the Editwriter 7500 in a typeface called Elante, a version of Electra. Electra is a Linotype face designed by W. A. Dwiggins (1880—1956). It cannot be classified as either modern or old-style. Electra is not based on any historical model, nor does it echo a particular period or style. It avoids the extreme contrast between thick and thin elements that marks most modern faces and attempts to give a feeling of fluidity, power, and speed.

Printed and bound by Banta Company, Harrisonburg, Virginia.

Please remember that this is a library book,
and that it belongs only temporarily to each
person who uses it. Be considerate. Do
not write in this, or any, library book.

DATE DUE

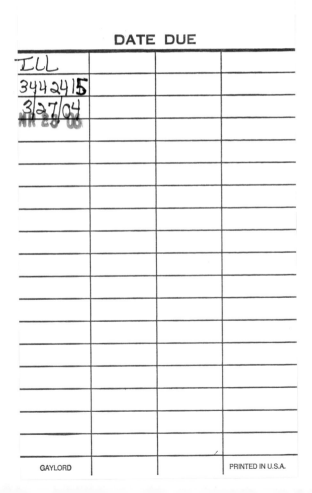

ILL			
34424Ι5			
3/27/04			
GAYLORD			PRINTED IN U.S.A.